Meridians feminism, race, transnationalism

VOLUME 20 · NUMBER 2 · OCTOBER 2021

Ginetta E. B. Candelario

Who's Terrorizing Who?

"I cannot undo what education did to you," she said, "how it makes people unaware why they are oppressed, of the causes in history, in the past, in the present."

"So transnationalism is to work and to fight and to struggle for justice, freedom— transnationally."
—Nawal El Saadawi

This issue coincides with the twentieth anniversary of the United States' initiation of the "war on terror" launched in the aftermath of the events of September 11, 2001. On that day, al-Qaeda operatives destroyed the World Trade Center in lower Manhattan by flying two hijacked planes into the twin towers; a third hijacked plane hit the first floor of the Pentagon's west wall; and a fourth plane crashed in a field in Shanksville, Pennsylvania when passengers successfully thwarted the hijackers. Ironically, that September 11 marked the thirtieth anniversary of the CIA-engineered military overthrow of Chilean President Salvador Allende in 1971. Although at the time "the extent of U.S. covert action against Allende's Popular Unity government was . . . a well-documented subject of public discussion," this blatant violation of Chilean sovereignty was not only justified by Secretary of State Henry Kissinger as "in the best interest of the people of Chile," but summarily forgotten by a US public long taught to consider Chile as "beneath" the United States, if they consider it all (Schoultz 1998: 361). Educating the public not only into willful disregard for, but condescending racialization of the victims of US settler-colonial and imperialist political

MERIDIANS · feminism, race, transnationalism   20:2 October 2021
DOI: 10.1215/15366936-9547841 © 2021 Smith College

violence as inherently inferior and subordinated has obtained throughout the country's history.

Perhaps it is not surprising, then, that

> Even before the first of the Trade Center's towers had collapsed, the 'news' media, as yet possessed of no hint as to who may have carried out the attacks, much less why they might have done so, were already and repeatedly proclaiming the whole thing 'unprovoked' and 'senseless.' Within a week, the assailants having meanwhile been presumably identified, *Newsweek* had recast the initial assertions of its colleagues in the form of a query bespeaking the aura of wide-eyed innocence in which the country was by then, as always, seeking to cloak itself. 'Why,' the magazine's cover whined from every newsstand, 'do they hate us so much?' (Churchill 2003: 5).

In other words, with a few notable exceptions such as Representative Barbara Lee (2001), instead of considering the geopolitical and historical contexts for the attacks, the media, elected officials, and the general public alike deployed the well-established White supremacist logic that insists against all facticity on US (read: White) political innocence and Middle Eastern (read: Muslim) irrational barbarism. After all, was the country not founded precisely on the premise of Anglo-Americans' God-given supremacy and their inherent entitlement to dominion over all the land, resources, and laboring BIPOC bodies that they claimed as part of their manifest destiny? Not surprisingly, therefore, when that history is called to account, whether through political violence, peaceful protest, culture work, or critical scholarship, White supremacist outrage ensues. As James Baldwin succinctly put it, "They are unable to conceive that their version of reality, which they want me to accept, is an insult to my history and a parody of theirs and an intolerable violation of myself" (Baldwin 1969).

To be clear, I am *not* arguing that the al-Qaeda attacks on US targets were in any way justified; rather, I am decrying the long-standing refusal in the United States to be held accountable for the country's "imperial arrogance and criminality" (Churchill 2003); the steadfast unwillingness to engage in a political process of truth, reconciliation and reparations (Coates 2014); the trenchant rejection of the historical truth and social fact of White supremacist violence as the recent right-wing attacks on *The 1619 Project* (Messer-Kruse 2020) and Critical Race Theory exemplify (Gluckman 2021);

and the decades-long racialization of Islamophobic violence, ideology, rhetoric, and policies (Razack 2008).

Thus, this guest-edited special issue of *Meridians* focused on "Transnational Feminist Responses to Anti-Muslim Racism" purposefully coincides with the twentieth anniversary of 9/11 and is intended to counter the hegemonic Islamophobic framings that have resurged. By now well established globally, Islamophobia is not simply ethnocentrism nor discrimination based on religion, nor is it typically negative political characterization of "the enemy." Instead, as the guest editors Zeynep Korkman and Sherene Halida Razack argue, Islamophobia is better understood as Anti-Muslim racism that is simultaneously global and local, and a type of racism that accordingly demands transnational feminist solidarities in response.

In light of that, I dedicate this issue to Egyptian feminist, activist, physician, psychiatrist, educator, and writer Nawal El Saadawi (October 27, 1931–March 21, 2021), who was a member of the *Meridians* Founding Advisory Board and who passed away earlier this year. I agree with El Saadawi that undoing what hegemonic "education" has done to people in the United States is the work of the people themselves as she explained in the 2018 interview excerpted above, and that our work at *Meridians* is to carry forward the transnational "struggle for justice, freedom."[1] Also in that spirit of searching for solidarities, both visible and subterranean but thriving, we present to you the winner of the 2021 Elizabeth Alexander Creative Writing Award, Gwendolyn Maya Wallace's "To Forage." About "To Forage," the Creative Writing Advisory Board said:

> The narrator of "To Forage" is an old soul inhabiting the body of a young, black woman: a forager of mushrooms, memories and stories that when woven together promise a "self" who is culturally grounded and spiritually whole. She is a gatherer: of the mother wit of her grandmother in South Carolina; the church women whose pastel suits and kitten heels tell you who they know themselves to be; the mother wit that carries the sounds and values of home no matter where she happens to live. She may be an old soul, but she is also incontestably of this moment: a girl-child of the city whose fascination with the growth cycles of plants is part scientific, part philosophical, and entirely the worldview of a black girl whose life is "unfolding" in call-and-response with her ancestors. She foraged for mushrooms, ancestors, and memories and for the power to conjure a world into existence (Andrea Harris, pers. comm., February 22, 2021).

Finally, appropriately wrapped around these features is our beautiful cover art, "When the World Sleeps" by the Palestinian artist Malak Mattar, who explains that "this piece was created from a space of trying to find tranquility through painting and sleeping . . . hoping to achieve peace." Like Wallace, Mattar reminds us that connecting with the peace deep within is made more difficult by the distorted "waking reality" we live in. Achieving any kind of peace requires imagining its possibility, painting it, writing it, and foraging for its traces wherever we may find ourselves. In the midst of all the deadly confluences we are currently living through simultaneously, that feels especially important to remember.

Notes

1 The text quoted in the epigraph comes from Crowcroft 2018 and *Meridians* Editorial Collective 2000: 15.

Works Cited

Baldwin, James. 1969. "The Price May Be Too High." *New York Times*, February 2.

Coates, Ta-Nehisi. 2014. "The Case for Reparations." *Atlantic*, June. www.theatlantic .com/magazine/archive/2014/06/the-case-for-reparations/361631/.

Churchill, Ward. 2003. *On the Justice of Roosting Chickens: Reflections on the Consequences of U.S. Imperial Arrogance and Criminality*. Chico, CA: AK Press.

Crowcroft, Orlando. 2018. "Nawal El Saadawi on Religion, Revolution, and Rage." *Newsweek*, June 22.

Gluckman, Nell. 2021. "Idaho Lawmakers Think Critical Race Theory Can 'Exacerbate and Inflame Divisions.' So They Passed a Law against It." *Chronicle of Higher Education*, April 29. www.chronicle.com/article/idaho-lawmakers-think-critical -race-theory-can-exacerbate-an d-inflame-divisions-so-they-passed-a-law- against-it.

Lee, Barbara. 2001. "Statement in Opposition to H.J. Res. 64." *American Rhetoric Online Speech Bank*, September 14. www.americanrhetoric.com/speeches /barbaraleeagainstinvasion.htm.

Meridians Editorial Collective. 2000. "Ama Ata Aidoo, Edna Acosta-Belén, Amrita Basu, Maryse Condé, Nell Painter, and Nawal El Saadawi Speak on Feminism, Race, and Transnationalism." *Meridians: Feminism, Race, Transnationalism* 1, no. 1: 1–28.

Messer-Kruse, Timothy. 2020. "What the 1619 Project Really Means." *Chronicle of Higher Education*, March 5. www.chronicle.com/article/what-the-1619-project -really-means/.

Razack, Sherene. 2008. *Casting Out: The Eviction of Muslims from Western Law and Politics*. Toronto: University of Toronto Press.

Schoultz, Lars. 1998. *Beneath the United States: A History of U.S. Policy toward Latin America*. Cambridge, MA: Harvard University Press.

Gwendolyn Maya Wallace

· ·

To Forage

I.

I go grocery shopping at 2:30 p.m. on Sundays. Well-acquainted with Black church services, I know the ease with which a 12:15 p.m. benediction can be pushed closer to 2:00 p.m. I arrive at my local Stop & Shop just in time to witness a procession of large hats and pastel cardigans, accompanied by the smells of lavender perfume and burnt hair. Slipping into this crowd ensures that my shopping trip will be saturated with the warmth that only older Black women can provide. *Baby, do you have the time? Can you grab that sugar on the top shelf for me, darling? Now that's a pretty dress, honey.* I respond in turn. *Of course I can, ma'am; That lipstick looks gorgeous on your skin; That skirt is absolutely stunning.* I slide the grocery list out of my pocket and smile at these small acts of cultivating each other, this closeness of strangers that will sustain me for the rest of the week. Churchwomen embrace friends next to gallons of milk, switch hats as they gossip at the seafood counter, and ask for the names of nail polish colors in the checkout line. I imagine roots creeping across the tile floors that connect me to every Black woman I see, flowers blooming from their ornate church hats.

o o o

A small patch of mushrooms, each adorned with a white cap, surprised me last Sunday on my way to Stop & Shop. I was certain that they had not been there the day before, arranged so comfortably between the garbage can and iron fence outside my apartment building. Always thinking of ways

MERIDIANS · feminism, race, transnationalism   20:2 October 2021
DOI: 10.1215/15366936-9547852 © 2021 Gwendolyn Maya Wallace

to prepare medicines with our nonhuman kin, I spent that night watching time-lapse videos of fungal growth and woke up early the next morning to begin reading Merlin Sheldrake's *Entangled Life: How Fungi Make Our Worlds, Change Our Minds, and Shape Our Futures.*

What amazes me most is how often fungi lives catch us unaware. The mushrooms I saw were simply the fruiting bodies of a vast and trans-formative underground network that could have been unfolding for months under my feet. Dozens of miles of mycelium, their threadlike structures, can wind their way through a couple cubic inches of dirt, invisible to the human eye. And yet, the tips of the mycelium can all communicate with each other in a constant call-and-response.

Fungi experiment with new ways to relate to their environment, reor-ganizing membranes, breaking down our dead, and distributing nutrients in the soil among plants. The intricate poetics of rebellion expand around us, laying waste to the distinction between group and individual. Fungi follow no leader, abide no fences.

o o o

One of my earliest memories is of raking my fingers through the dirt in Elgin, South Carolina. Grammy, my paternal grandmother, walked around her garden dressed in a straw gardening hat and linen pants, humming. Dozens of pots filled with cut leaves and branches dotted the backyard. Somehow, for reasons I didn't understand, Grammy could convince them to grow into plants all of their own. Even though she only watered the gar-den once or twice a day, every couple of hours Grammy would stand on the back porch with her hands on her hips and gaze fondly at her green com-panions. Sometimes Grammy would scoop me onto her hip and walk me through the lush backyard as we ate her homemade gingersnaps. "Isn't this just beautiful?" she'd say, as we marched past purple hydrangeas and tall tomato plants. Occasionally she'd bend down so I could smell a fragrant rose or squeeze a cucumber that was almost ready to be harvested. I crunched on my cookie and decided that Grammy was the most powerful person I knew for two reasons: every plant loved her, and she could scold my dad.

When I was nine, my family drove Grammy down to her childhood home in Monck's Corner, South Carolina. Grammy walked up to the white house she'd grown up in with her two sisters and touched the chipped paint, glowing in the sun. She circled her old home, telling stories about her childhood as she knelt down to pick weeds. I sat on a red patch of dirt with a stick I found and poked at the ground. Thirty minutes later, Grammy strode over to me and offered a fig she had just plucked off the tree. I scratched a mosquito bite on my arm and shook my head. "Suit yourself," she said, sinking her teeth into the juicy flesh. "You're missing out." The sweet scent of fresh fig filled the air.

Grammy moved to an assisted-living facility in Virginia five years ago. When my late grandfather's dementia started to progress, the family thought it would be better for her to be closer to her daughter in Richmond. Grammy was moved to an apartment with no backyard and no plants, and now lives two states from home with no husband and four children who rarely visit. I hear that she tells anyone who will listen how much she misses South Carolina.

But it's a gift, I think, to have a body that knows so viscerally where home is. I do not have a single limb that feels any connection to the Connecticut town where I was born and raised, so I settle for Stop & Shop. The last time I visited South Carolina was over ten years ago, but I sometimes entertain the possibility of a future where I sit in the red dirt of Monck's Corner and something in my stomach tells me I'm exactly where I need to be.

When I spoke with Grammy on the phone last month, she told me that her winter project will be knitting baby blankets for all ten of her grandchildren, as a future gift for the great-grandchildren she might never get to see. "I want you all to have something to pass down," she whispered.

II.

"Your outfit is so beautiful," I say to the woman next to me. She rolls a Honeycrisp apple in her palm and glances down at her lavender three-piece skirt set and matching kitten heels, admiring the outfit herself. "Why, thank you, baby," she coos. With a trembling hand, she adjusts the purple chiffon on her hat.

I grab the bunch of bananas nearest me and toss them into my tote bag, still watching the woman in lavender nod at the apple in her hand and lay it in her cart. I want to ask for the rest of the ingredients in the apple pie I imagine she's making. I should ask if her hands know how to create candied yams, collard greens, or poison to add to a white man's stew. I think about whose words come to her in dreams and if they would help me, too. It is possible I just want to thank her for the secret exchanges of herbs, the quilts sewn late into the night, and the dances around cramped kitchens. I want her to know I am trying to make her proud.

○ ○ ○

As a child, I was amazed by the way communities of mushrooms would emerge after a summer thunderstorm. I'd run out of my house as soon as the rain ceased, wearing my yellow rain boots, looking for mushrooms to trample. Laughter would burst from my mouth as mushrooms released clouds of spores en masse after each of my jumps. Little did I know that life filled the space left by my destruction. Mushrooms ignore the line between life and death, growing from dead plants and animals to make room for more.

Black women test existences capable of entirely new possibilities in the interstices, on plantations, in fire and brimstone. Is Black womanhood not also an emergent and anarchic form of life? Who knows more about existing as both graveyard and nursery, creating possibilities beyond the borders of language and rationality, birthing our mothers and learning from our children? Who else can weave underground networks, passing canned vegetables, knowing winks, and moments of freedom as fungi pass carbon between plants? Black women, too, construct beauty in the midst of decay, nourishing microplanets as blood flows through the streets.

○ ○ ○

Ma, my maternal grandmother, volunteers at the senior center every Saturday despite being ninety-one years old. When I see her for the holidays, the only question I ask is if she plans on going that week. I'm always met with the click of Ma's tongue against the few teeth she has left and the sharp reply, "God willing and the creek don't rise." Everyone in the room rolls their eyes. I laugh only because I haven't perfected the art of ungovernability.

My mother (child number nine of twelve) used to tell me stories about how Ma put her and her siblings to work as winter approached. The kids shelled peas, shucked corn, and threw crab apples at each other on the porch. Kicked out of the house in the early morning, the children were instructed not to come back inside until the streetlights turned on that evening. Inside the house, Ma blanched green beans, made peach cobbler, and melted wax to seal the jars that she would fill with peas.

At family gatherings, Ma is usually situated quietly on a couch in the corner, hunched over in a way that makes it look as though she might slip through the cushions. Her ten living children, seventeen grandchildren, and ten great-grandchildren swirl around her. She stands up only to use the bathroom or serve the food that she spent days preparing, shuffling around with Country Crock butter containers filled with candied sweet potatoes, rice, and mashed turnips. Even in her tiny home, we all manage to part as she carries the aluminum tray full of sliced ham across the room. The sweet smell of pineapple meets our noses at the same time as the salt of the pork, causing even the strongest among us to salivate. We wait to eat until Ma brings the yeast rolls out of the oven. Crisp on the outside and soft on the inside, they are the star attraction of the meal. When I was fourteen, Ma came over to my house to teach me how to make the precious rolls. Her measurements ranged from "a pinch" to "a good bit," and I was too nervous to ask any questions, so the recipe might just die with her.

Every time I see Ma, she looks smaller, more deflated. It seems impossible that this is the same woman who I heard once sewed my mom's thumb back together with dental floss after a childhood sledding accident. (I don't know what magic Ma did, but my mom's thumb doesn't even have a scar. I've looked.) Last Christmas, there were no yeast rolls on the table. Uncle Willie had to carry the ham out of the oven. I've always known that Ma won't live forever, but I believed it then.

At my best, I admire Ma's skill and ingenuity. At my worst, I pity her. I'm ashamed that I sometimes wonder if she feels as though she wasted her life by giving birth to and raising twelve children. But each day I grow more certain that the worlds we need are created by passing down recipes, gathering family around a table, or knowing more than one use for dental floss.

III.

"Pardon?" I say. A Black woman, wearing an emerald green dress with glasses, jewelry, and nails to match, smiles up at me.

"I said, 'You remind me of my grandniece, sweetheart.' "

Some nights, I can't stop thinking about that woman's grandniece. I should've asked what about me reminds her of her grandniece. I wonder what the girl smells like in the summer, how she holds her hands when she braids the hair on the back of her head, whether we'd recognize each other. As what, I'm not sure.

∘ ∘ ∘

I believe fungi disturb us most because they survive where we tell them they can't. Fungi have been found living inside rocks, at the edge of the geothermal areas of Yellowstone Park, and among the ice in Antarctica. After the Chernobyl disaster, fungi appeared, somehow able to use the radiation as an energy source. They can be trained to survive on cigarette butts. The same mushrooms that burst beneath my rain boots could also break through concrete if they needed to.

Despite everything that tries to kill them, fungi invent new ways to live free, forever plunging their hyphae deeper into the cracks.

○ ○ ○

Like many children, I believed that the only thing my mom had ever dreamed of was me. Well aware that the world had no intention of treating me tenderly, my mother filled my childhood with light. We'd drive to the appliance store down the street on weekends, where my mother would haul refrigerator boxes from the dumpster and into the back of our car. Once we got home, she'd set the boxes up in our living room with bags of markers so I could spend the rest of the afternoon decorating my houses and museums and skyscrapers and boats. I called out to her every time I needed a door or window cut and my mother would leap over with box cutters, asking "Circle, triangle, or square?"

When I grew too large to call cardboard boxes my home, my mother found other ways to make sure I never thought of living as anything less than an art. When I developed insomnia in elementary school, she would wrap me up in a knit blanket and tell me stories featuring the adventures of the rabbits and groundhogs and red-tailed hawks in our backyard. On winter mornings in middle school, she would wake me up with a mug of hot chocolate and clothes straight out of the dryer. "Rise and shine, my friend,' she said, throwing open the curtains of my room. When our house burned down my first year of boarding school on the day before her fiftieth birthday, she told me, "Who else gets the opportunity to start their life all over again?"

She calls me almost every day to tell me about her grand plans for the future. "I want to write a book," "I'm thinking about going back to school for film," "Listen, if I had a dog poop cleaning business, I'd call it 'Scoopy Doo.' Wouldn't that be hilarious?" "Let's take a road trip," she says, "You and me. We could go anywhere we want, just drive and never look back."

IV.

I let a woman dressed head-to-toe in light pink check out before me. Once a spot opens up at the self-checkout station, I shuffle between the rows of church women packing up their groceries and begin scanning the items in my bag. I pay and then take one last breath before walking out of the store.

I recall why my favorite part of church was leaving. Aisle by aisle, the congregation would flow toward the doors of the church, where elders were waiting to lay hands on every person. On both sides, Black churchwomen kissed cheeks, grasped hands, and gently patted backs. They held me close, leaving red lipstick and the scent of shea butter on my cheeks, tickling my neck with chiffon flowers. Each woman uttered "Bless you," as in, "I'm yours and you're mine." As in, "I made this place for you."

I haven't gone to church of my own volition in years. There was nothing more alienating than watching the people around me experience God as I felt nothing at all. But I left every service feeling the same love on my skin I feel now between the automatic doors.

∘ ∘ ∘

The fungal relationship I find myself most fascinated by is mycorrhiza, the partnership between fungi and trees. Threads of fungi wrap around the roots of trees, facilitating the exchange of phosphorous and nitrogen, as well as connecting them to other trees in a forest. Scientists have discovered that trees use this fungal network to communicate with one each other, sending water and other nutrients back and forth. They have been observed sending minerals to the stumps of trees that were cut down centuries ago, unwilling to desert their dead. When drought, disease, or insects begin to damage one tree, it will send chemical alarm signals through the fungi to the roots of others. Younger trees who don't get enough sunlight to photosynthesize are fed sugar by the taller trees around them. In Suzanne Simard's 2016 TED Talk entitled "How Trees Talk to Each Other," she calls the oldest trees with the most mycorrhizal connections in a forest "mother trees."

Saplings that are removed from this fungal entanglement often die.

∘ ∘ ∘

After a week of nightmares eight months ago, I decided to make my first ancestral altar in my childhood home. I smoothed a white cloth over a small wooden shelf in the corner of my bedroom. Trusting the lessons my body held, I let it tell me what items I needed to move toward as I grew. Led gently around my space, a small collection began to unfold on the altar: a gold bracelet my late grandfather gave Grammy for their anniversary, a pair of earrings carved from bone that I bargained for in Ghana, my tiger eye necklace, a handful of coriander seeds. I retrieved a small white candle from my closet. Last, I filled up a glass with cold water and placed it in the middle of the altar.

I dipped my ring finger into the cup and pressed the cool water into the center of my forehead. As droplets made a river out of the bridge of my nose, I reminded myself that while my life will last for a few unforgiving moments, my story and the stories of my foremothers run together as one. I have already been anointed by a long line of women who could smell the rain coming. I lit the candle and folded into a kneeling position in front of my altar, watching the flame dance. My chest received my deep breaths until my heartbeat accompanied the rhythms of sun-soaked hands shaping yeast rolls, knotted hair blooming into braids, palms slathering salves on mahogany chests, fingers coaxing seedlings out of the ground. I have been told that living is memory work. *Hello,* I said. *I love you. Thank you for holding me.* We exchanged memories and futures that words cannot hold.

I blew out the flame and noticed fingerlike threads of smoke creeping over and through the curves of my body, swaddling me in prayers. May I never forget whose I am. May I always find my way back to a body adorned, inseparable, enduring.

....

Gwendolyn Maya Wallace was born and raised in Danbury, Connecticut, and recently graduated with a degree in the history of science and medicine from Yale University. She currently works as a fellow at the International Museum of African-American History in Charleston, South Carolina. Along with her creative nonfiction, she is also the author of two forthcoming picture books. Her art practices and research are based in Black feminisms, community archiving, and ecomemory work. She can usually be found gardening, exploring used bookstores, or listening to the radical impulses of young children.

Zeynep K. Korkman, Sherene Halida Razack

. . . .

Transnational Feminist Approaches to Anti-Muslim Racism

This special issue brings together feminist scholars to theorize anti-Muslim racism. It specifically attends to an understanding of anti-Muslim racism as transnational, proliferating, and linked to other racisms and projects of rule. Three key questions are addressed: How do we understand global circuits of power as they travel and shape local contexts in which anti-Muslim racism operates, including contexts in which Muslims are the majority? How is global anti-Muslim racism a gendered phenomenon? What is a revolutionary politics in which resistant forms of Muslimness imagine another world? With its emphasis on the transnational, the special issue assembles scholars whose work on the regional contexts of Turkey, India, Pakistan, Bangladesh, Iran, the Middle East, Europe, Canada, and the United States, among other nations, reveals the global circuits along which anti-Muslim racism travels. Their explorations of how the global and the local are intertwined pay special attention to how discourses of anti-Muslim racism install white, Western subjects as superior and the heteronormative white family as the basis of political life. This is a racism that morphs as it travels transnationally and attaches itself to supremacist, colonial, and imperial projects everywhere. The special issue offers an explicit feminist analysis, paying attention to how racial discourses are gendered and sexualized and how those who are the targets of anti-Muslim racism articulate their gendered dreams of an alternative lifeworld in the face of their marginalization.

MERIDIANS · feminism, race, transnationalism   20:2   October 2021
DOI: 10.1215/15366936-9547863 © 2021 Smith College

Islam has long been the antonym to Europe, the Other of modernity. As Minoo Moallem explores in this issue, the colonial construct of Islam maintains the idea of Islam as a premodern, primitive, and fetishistic religion in which women are oppressed and compelled to veil. Installing Europe as modern and Islam as premodern, the idea that Muslims are an uncivilized people provides a path for the ascendancy of whiteness, a racial structure that relies on gender to establish its component parts. An institutionalized anti-Muslim racism has been developing for some time in the West building on earlier racial formations and Orientalisms but escalating in the post-9/11 period into authorized torture, extrajudicial killings, and a legally authorized eviction from political community apparent in such diverse legal projects as the Muslim travel ban in the United States and the banning of full-face veils (see Razack 2008; forthcoming). Muslims have been targeted by white supremacist shooters in Quebec City, Canada and Christchurch, New Zealand. Spectacular violence joins a more mundane everyday harassment and persecution including the disciplining and surveillance of anyone visibly associated with Muslim cultural practices. Each conflict is recast as a Muslim problem. For instance, the treatment of migrants, entailing a willful blindness to the deaths of migrants seeking to cross the Mediterranean into Europe, is often underwritten by a well-organized Right that insists that many refugees are "terrorists" and that people from Muslim cultures do not belong in Europe. Outside the West, the persecution of the Rohingya in Myanmar, Muslims in India, the Uyghurs in China, and Palestinians in Israel/Palestine all suggest a globally circulating discourse of anti-Muslim racism that provides a new intensity to long-standing local conflicts, infusing them with new life and contributing to international indifference over the fate of targeted Muslim communities. Genocides of Muslim populations are proliferating. This special issue generates a feminist dialogue on these pressing contemporary issues with an eye for transnational mis/translations and the potential for resistance.

The idea that anti-Muslim racism exists and operates in contexts where it forms a part of long-standing conflicts is often resisted. If, in the past few decades, Muslims have become the universal enemy, there is still a popular understanding that Muslims are a religious group and not a racial one. When recognized only as a faith community or a minority, Muslims are not considered to be racially targeted. Relatedly, when anti-Muslim racism is understood as prejudice or hate and uncoupled from projects of rule, we do not easily see its role in undermining the sovereignty of Muslim communities, nations, and regions. Anti-Muslim racism, or (more popularly) Islamophobia, has been called an imaginary racism. Yet racism remains central to how violence is authorized against Muslims. The violence that Muslim communities endure, ranging from evictions from political community to bombs, is legitimized as violence that is necessary to preserve Western civilization from the threat posed by a people considered barbaric and premodern.

In this special issue we begin with the contention that the figure of the Muslim in the West consolidates white supremacy and protects white property interests. We note that Muslim life is subjected to extraordinary violence, a violence that is key to how dominant groups in several parts of the world occupy Muslim lands and destroy Muslim communities. Anti-Muslim racism forges a global whiteness as it moves, installing a civilizational divide between Muslims, conjured as barbaric, misogynist, premodern Others who require force and Europeans, imagined as a people especially given to rationality and possessing a deep commitment to democracy and gender equality that must be protected. As it travels, anti-Muslim racism hitches a ride on local conflicts, enabling violence to be directed at Muslim communities with impunity in the name, for instance, of combatting "global terrorism." Muslims come to be cast as Europe's atavistic Others when they contest the supremacy of the West and resist racial and imperial governance. They become targets of violence when their lands are desired. Whether refugees at the border, citizens holding the state to its promise of liberal inclusion, or populations who stand in the way of empire, Muslims are imagined as threats who must be met with force.

The protection of white interests that is achieved through the figure of the Muslim in the West is a global phenomenon. Utilizing the idea of the Muslim as global "terrorist" and premodern Other to evict Muslims from political community, nations of the Global North and the Global South traffic in anti-Muslim racism. As Natasha Bahkt maps in this issue, attempts have been made to ban Muslim women's clothing, and specifically the niqab or full face covering in nine European countries as well as in several African and Asian nations. Revealing the interconnections between gendered anti-Muslim legal projects across the globe, it is striking that bans are articulated as the protection of women's equality even as they punish women who wear the niqab by imposing fines or imprisonment, limiting women's ability to work and travel, and subjecting them to a host of restrictions that seriously impair women's capacities to lead their lives. The legal regulation of Muslim communities not only connects diverse regions but travels at lightning speed. The transnational virtual circuits along which anti-Muslim racism travels from meme to podcast and through metadata and algorithmic circuits, Amira Jarmarkani shows, capture Muslims as "terrorists" and misogynists. The circuits are powered by money, hoaxes, and misinformation, generating Muslims as a population to be surveilled and disciplined, and equally, whites as a group whose interests must be protected through force.

Translations/Mistranslations

Insisting on the global quality of contemporary anti-Muslim racism demands a thorough attention to historical and geographical specificity and nuance to ward off the potential hazards of importing this analytic unproblematically (Korkman 2019). Attending to the transnational circulation of anti-Muslim racism discourses and policies requires abandoning any assumption that we already know or can predict prior to research and analyses how those forces might operate in different contexts. To begin with, Muslims and Muslim women are not stable constructs to be taken for granted but are produced as social subjects by competing political projects in various and dynamic ways. The infrastructures of violence targeting them similarly come in many moving forms and incarnations as they take shape in relation to globally proliferating anti-Muslim racisms.

This issue invites a heightened attention to the many translations and mistranslations of anti-Muslim racism, as it travels not only as a racist discourse and infrastructure but also as an analytical and political category by which we understand and resist violence and discrimination against Muslims around the world. A full recognition of the global circuits discussed here requires relativizing and provincializing our conceptual toolbox. It demands abandoning the imperially tinted expectation that things over there or back then translate readily into the prevailing languages of Euro-American feminist academia, so to speak. This move might include decentralizing Western imperial projects to make room for other, minor ones and carefully tracing their interconnections. The dominant US-based time/space of anti-Muslim racism, intensified after 9/11, operates alongside of and through other projects of domination with different genealogies.

The need to attend to local histories is especially acute for transnational feminist politics and analyses in times of a persistent reductionism concerning Islam and Muslim women, not only in right-wing, white supremacist, Christian conservative discourses but also in progressive and even feminist ones. How can we account for globally circulating forms of white supremacy and anti-Muslim racism with full attention to historicity and locality? How can we understand anti-Muslim racism as global without deeming all Muslim subjects singularly and uniformly shaped by one, overbearing structure of oppression? How do we instead approach Muslim peoples in their active and dynamic constitution in relation to a multitude of globally imbricated and locally embedded processes? Taking these questions seriously in this issue, we make room for Muslims as multiply constituted and not as any one thing. Neither simply targets of racism nor pious or non-pious subjects reacting to it, we emphasize Muslims as complex and dynamically constituted social and political subjects.

Islam can be an absent presence in Muslim feminist discourses. Included in this issue, Tom Joseph Abi Samra's translations from the 1950s issues of the Egyptian women's journal *Bint Al-Neel* highlight the voice of the journal's editor Doria Shafik, whose political activism in this period included storming the parliament to demand women's political rights. Shafik's editorials indicate how she articulated her feminist demands in dialogue with modernist, Orientalist, nationalist, and anticommunist sensibilities of her time. In these pieces where Shafik addressed non-elite Egyptian women in Arabic, Islam was absent from discourse except in Shafik's "excusing" of the men of religion who critiqued her, on account of their old age. In doing so, Shafik effectively dismissed religion as a relic of the past and Islam as the religion of archaic patriarchs, echoing the very civilizational tropes that fuel anti-Muslim racism today. In the book based on her doctoral thesis and published in French, however, Shafik took a closer interest in Islam, translating at length from Islamic reformists to argue, and demonstrate for her francophone audiences, that Islam did not prescribe Muslim women to veil, a practice she viewed as archaic and oppressive. Shafik may have subscribed to the hegemonic view that Islam is singularly misogynist or articulated women's freedom in secular modernist terms that carry implicit traces of Islam as the antonym of Europe. As Samra makes clear, Shafik spoke to many audiences in different mediums and languages. This archival fragment is a testament to the complexities of translation, temporally, literally, and figuratively.

Essays by Elora Shehabuddin, Amina Jamal, and Tatiana Rabinovich further situate the diverse construction of Muslim women as social and political subjects in their specific locales and histories. Shehabuddin brings into view Pakistani and especially Bengali women who negotiated the transitional spaces opened up by US Cold War–era imperialist ambitions to foster feminist alliances. In this historical context, Muslim women were not singularly apprehended as oppressed and in need of saving, nor did they see themselves exclusively within an Islamic frame. Jamal highlights pious Pakistani women for whom secularism is not a white, European concept, as Euro-American critical scholarship including transnational feminist scholarship might have it, but a potent political idiom by which to articulate their feminist demands for gender equality and their critiques of oppressive politics that masquerade as Islamic. Rabinovich brings into view veiled Muslim women in Russia who are disparagingly called "Black" and who resist their racialization in a context where Muslims are cast as civilizational others and "terrorists" by insisting that they are whiter looking than their assailants. At the same time, Muslim women in Russia draw on narratives of religious and cultural histories of strength, cultivating an ethics of perseverance to resist racism.

The essays in this special issue show that as we focus on the slippages and collapsing together of religion and race and follow the deployment of the category of Muslim and its ongoing racialization, we interrogate key terms such as *whiteness* and *Blackness*. These categories are flexibly inhabited and strategically negotiated by actors on the ground. They are also supplemented by other terms of analysis such as *secularism* and *modernization* (Jamal), *Cold War* and *Third World* (Shehabuddin), or *state socialism* and *neo-imperialism* (Rabinovich). That Muslims are othered and racialized along religious lines is not a timeless fact, as Shehabuddin shows, but the product of particular conjunctures. The period Shehabuddin highlights provides a much-needed reminder that Muslim women are not always already constructed as passive Oriental or religiously hyper-oppressed figures under Western eyes, nor are their feminism and self-consciousness timelessly preoccupied by responding to such constructions. As Jamal also shows, Muslims themselves do not always singularly prioritize Islam and Muslim identity in articulating their political and moral commitments. They situate themselves and are perceived at varying distances and proximities to religion, not readily reducible to the overbearing signifier of Muslimness. As Rabinovich argues, mistakenly familiar racial epithets like

Blackness can operate in unfamiliar ways (compared to the US racial formation), articulating racial otherness within civilizational hierarchies, class, nationality, ethnicity, gender, and last but not least, religion. Similarly, Rabinovich continues, familiar vocabularies of antiracist resistance like anti-imperialism can be deployed as a discursive tool of neo-imperialism, for example in the hands of the Russian government. These translations and mistranslations happen in ways that are radically irreducible but are in dynamic and constitutive relation to the transnational circuits of anti-Muslim racism.

Resistance

The contributors to this issue offer us a great deal to think about concerning what a revolutionary politics and resistance look like. Evelyn Azeeza Alsultany explores the limitations and possibilities of categorizing anti-Muslim racial violence as hate crimes. While it is clear that denial of anti-Muslim hate crimes is a denial of anti-Muslim racism, Alsultany observes that state recognition of hate crimes cannot bring justice. Hate crimes frame violence as an emotional response. The category *hate crime* individualizes and is understood as reactionary and unconnected to the structures of white supremacy in which the lives of People of Color are not valued and where they are seen as threats. Given that the state regulates and disciplines Muslims through law, any inclusive gesture is bound to be fraught. It brings Muslims into the game of Good Muslim/Bad Muslim, where legal protection is offered only to those who can present themselves for liberal inclusion as "respectable" Muslims, that is, as Muslims with state-approved Islamic connections, as opposed to those deemed "terrorist" and too religious. The question of what is to be gained by the hate crime designation is thus an important one, as is consideration of a radical alternative. Zulfikar Ali Bhutto joins Alsultany in the dialogue about a revolutionary politics, asking that we imagine the next intifada as a Muslim (and not only Palestinian) uprising against occupation. What does a revolutionary leader look like who is homo/trans welcoming? Exploring the aesthetic practices of Muslim artists including his own work, Bhutto finds inspiration in a "flamboyant, faggy, and high femme revolutionary leader." We should think of Muslim resistance as "a guerrilla movement on an international scale," Bhutto advises, and the revolutionary as a warrior drag queen who takes us to a Queer Muslim futurism. The queer Muslim future is not imagined in the linear/straight time of modernity and heteronormativity, but is conjured in the here and now as an alternative to the racialized and gendered normativities that set Muslim as queer and LBGTIQ as non-Muslim. Resonating with Queer Muslim Futurism, which draws richly upon Islamic imaginaries to unsettle anti-Muslim racism in its gendered and sexualized incarnations, Usama Alshaibi's film *Profane* features Muna, a Muslim Arab-American dominatrix who is haunted by the jinn. Taneem Husain analyzes Muna's divergences from the dominant representations of Muslim people, and emphasizes Muna's insistence on articulating her "perverse" Islamic practice and identity alongside her nonnormative sexuality. Husain concludes that the film proactively takes issue with the attempted stabilization of a Good Muslim/Bad Muslim dichotomy brokered in terms of sexual normativity, and that it undermines the centrality of gender to the mundane operations as well as the destabilizations of anti-Muslim racism.

As the articles in this issue attest, we cannot resist anti-Muslim racisms, imperialisms, wars, and occupations while relying on a universal and stable notion of gender. Gender itself comes into operation through race, and race through gender, each hierarchical and extractive formation relying on the boundaries that each system places on the limits of the human. Feminist and queer analyses of anti-Muslim racism offered in this issue thus reemphasize the centrality of gender and sexuality to formations of racial domination as well as to our capacities to build solidarities that forge, or even imagine, alternatives.

Conclusion

This issue is one step in a dialogue to foster transnational feminist translations that insist we learn from each other, sustaining feminist solidarities across the treacherous waters we are obliged to navigate. Both anti-Muslim racism and our analytical and political tools to address it travel transnationally and articulate in unexpected ways with local struggles for justice as well as domination, posing pitfalls for antiracist transnational feminists. A case in point is the authoritarian Islamist government of Turkey that has appropriated globally resonant progressive critiques of anti-Muslim racism. Turkey, under the government of Recep Tayyip Erdoğan, proclaims itself antiracist and draws on the North American vocabulary of the civil rights, Black power, and Black Lives Matter movements to mark its constituency as Black (aka Muslim) Turks. The appropriation of a discourse of antiracism garners legitimacy and lends support to Turkey's own neo-imperialist domination in the region and to the racist, misogynist, and homophobic oppression within the country. Without due attention to specificity and historicity, and without ongoing, mutual conversation with locally embedded feminists, US-based antiracist feminists risk finding themselves buying into such pseudoprogressive rhetoric. These pitfalls emerge as the result of a reductionist equation of *Muslim* with *oppressed* and a simplistic assumption that Muslims are a unitary group of people who exist primarily in relation to their oppression under anti-Muslim racism, and hence deserve solidarity regardless of political affiliation or gendered, national, ethnic, class, or other positionality. Clearly, such reductionism can leave feminists with unlikely bedfellows whose gender and sexual politics are far from aligned with feminist values (Korkman 2019). Nevertheless, the transnational terrain of anti-Muslim racism demands solidarities across regions. We thus call for vigilance as feminists pursue international solidarities. As this issue illustrates, we insist on learning and unlearning together as we contend with the many translations and mistranslations our dialogues will inevitably generate.

Zeynep K. Korkman is assistant professor of Gender Studies at the University of California, Los Angeles. Her research interests include transnational feminisms; affect, labor, and intimacy; and religion, secularism, and the public sphere in Turkey and the larger Middle East. Her book manuscript, "Gendered Fortunes," under contract with Duke University Press, focuses on the gendered economy of divinations in contemporary Turkey. Drawing upon ethnographic research and cultural analysis, the book explores how and why secular Muslim gender and sexual minorities of Turkey seek their gendered fortunes in divination in a country shaped by a secularist past and an Islamist present, a renewed gender conservatism, and economic neoliberalization. Korkman's work has appeared in *Gender and Society*, *Journal of Middle East Women's Studies*, *European Journal of Cultural Studies*, and *Journal of Ottoman and Turkish Studies*.

Sherene Halida Razack is Distinguished Professor and the Penny Kanner Endowed Chair in Women's Studies in the Department of Gender Studies, University of California, Los Angeles. Her research and teaching focus on racial violence. She is the founder of the virtual research and teaching network Racial Violence Hub (Racialviolencehub.com). Her publications illustrate the thematic areas and anticolonial, antiracist feminist scholarship she pursues. Her recent books include *Nothing Has to Make Sense: Upholding White Supremacy through Anti-Muslim Racism* (forthcoming) and *Dying from Improvement: Inquests and Inquiries into Indigenous Deaths in Custody* (2015).

Works Cited

Korkman, Zeynep K. 2019. "(Mis)Translations of Anti-Muslim Racism Discourse and the Repercussions for Transnational Feminist Solidarities." Unpublished paper presented at the conference "Feminist Approaches to Understanding Global Anti-Muslim Racism," University of California, Los Angeles, December 6.

Razack, Sherene Halida. 2008. *Casting Out: The Eviction of Muslims from Western Law and Politics*. Toronto: University of Toronto Press.

Razack, Sherene Halida. Forthcoming. *Nothing Has to Make Sense: Upholding White Supremacy through Anti-Muslim Racism*. Minneapolis: University of Minnesota Press.

Minoo Moallem

. . . .

Race, Gender, and Religion:
Islamophobia and Beyond

Abstract: This article focuses on anti-Muslim racism as a discourse that collapses race and religion and cannot be reduced to phobia. It is instead
about a racial project of accumulation based on European superiority and
how cultural racism upholds the European civilizational project. The author
argues that Islamophobia should be traced back to colonial modernity, its
regimes of othering, and its perception of Islam as Mohammedanism that
conceals its nature as a fetishistic, primitive, barbaric, patriarchal, and irrational set of beliefs. To illustrate anti-Muslim racism, the author elaborates
briefly on three interconnected ideas: the construction of Islam as a unified
religious and cultural mindset, its fetishistic character, and its enigmatic
image of the woman to reflect on how Islam is presented as the antonym of
Western civilization.

Islamophobia and anti-Muslim racism as discourse is not new and cannot
be reduced to a phobia.[1] It is instead about a racial project of accumulation
based on the idea of European superiority. Islamophobia and anti-Muslim
racism should be traced back to colonial modernity, its regimes of othering
through racialism and racism, and its perception of Islam as a unified
religious doctrine that conceals its nature as a fetishistic, primitive, barbaric, patriarchal, and irrational set of beliefs. The colonialist construction
of Islam, along with other Indigenous religious practices—as an essen-
tialized force that limits the cultural capacity of its adherents—was historically crucial to the formation of Whiteness, civilizational superiority, and
the hegemony of Christianity in Euro-American literature.[2] The rampant

MERIDIANS · feminism, race, transnationalism   20:2 October 2021
DOI: 10.1215/15366936-9547874 © 2021 Smith College

reference to Europeans as civilized races versus uncivilized people, savages, and barbarians distinguished between not only cultures but also religious practices.[3] In the case of Islam, what remains less developed is the more neutral racialist discourse on religion since colonial modernity.[4] Thus, it is important to interrogate how Islam is constructed as the antonym of Western civilization and how cultural racism upholds the European civilizational project.

In this essay, I focus on racism against Muslims, elaborating on what was called *Mohammedanism*.[5] Colonialists, both French and British, constructed Mohammedanism as a set of homogeneous religious practices characterized by several interconnected ideas. That included its construction as a unified religious and cultural mindset, justifying its civilizational inferiority, its fetishistic character, and its enigmatic image of women. By focusing on a few examples in each case, I hope to offer an intertextual reading of race, gender, and religion and the construction of what was referred to as the "Muslim race" in colonial and postcolonial contexts. I show how the collapse of these discourses not only provided space for colonial and imperial forces to justify their colonization of North Africa and the Middle East but also have been constitutive of contemporary discourse on Islamophobia within and beyond academic circles in a postcolonial era.[6]

I am interested in interrogating somehow innocent or mostly neutrally articulated notions of primitivism, fetishism, mindset, tradition, and the spirit of the nation rather than blatantly racist ideologies. In other words, a colonialist desire to defeat supposedly inferior religious and cultural traditions that rises not merely from a fear of strangers, but also from the perception that those "inferior" traditions will degrade or replace "superior" Western civilization. So, in my view, it is critical to bring the notion of Islamophobia into conversation with the discourse of race, and specifically of cultural racism, discursively, figuratively, and materially. To do so, I build upon Aníbal Quijano's notion of "coloniality of knowledge." Quijano argues that one of the fundamental axes of power of global capitalism and its Eurocentric rationality is the idea of race. The Eurocentric perspective of knowledge used the idea of race to naturalize colonial relations between Europeans and non-Europeans (Quijano 2000: 533–34). Sherene Razack (2008) further illustrates the connection of power and knowledge by bringing contemporary debates on race and the discourse of the "war on terror" into conversation with history, politics, and law. She makes a strong case for the relations between race thinking as a structure of thought in its institutional and legal implementations vis-à-vis Muslims in the context of 9/11, where the denial of human rights of those constructed as the "other" to European people, led to the atrocities of Abu Ghraib and Guantanamo and the deferral of rights for racialized groups under the rubric of national security. I want to provide new evidence from discursive knowledge production fields concerning the encounter of colonial modernity with Islam and Muslims. It is essential to interrogate the epistemic hegemony of Euro-American discourse on what was referred to as the "Muslim race" and "Mohammedanism" to open up space for what Michel Foucault (1980: 83) calls "subjugated knowledge."

The discourse of Islamophobia in its intertextual relation with xenophobia, as it is defined through the fear of the foreigners populating a country, is not sufficient to explain its material and symbolic aspects, especially as a form of cultural and commodity racism.[7] The concept of Islamophobia does rely on the older idea of xenophobia, the fear of strangers. The reference to "phobia" grasps the affective and emotional relationship with the other, including attraction, hatred, desire, and disavowal.

However, Islamophobia as a concept cannot be separated from the history of race, racialism, and racism; of consumerism and questions of labor, including the institution of slavery; and of indentured labor, its formation under colonial and imperial rule, and its continuation in a postcolonial era. To bring the concept of Islamophobia into conversation with the discourse of race and anti-Muslim racism, I would like to elaborate on three interconnected ideas briefly: (1) The concept of Mohammedanism, the idea of religion and culture as intrinsic to social groups, and references to mindsets that reduce cultural and religious traditions to homogenized entities and situate them within the myth of progress; (2) the attribution of fetishism and primitivism to describe religious otherness; (3) the figure of the veiled woman as central to such constructions of Muslim otherness.

Mohammedanism and Civilizational Thinking

Anti-Islam and Muslim racism emerged after Muslims and Jews were expelled from Spain.[8] However, a significant shift came in the eighteenth century with the rise of scientific racism, which constructs race as genetically programmed and biologically determined, leading to some races' supposed inferiority, especially Blacks. Some European racialist scholars, including anthropologists in the nineteenth and twentieth centuries, followed suit by constructing the concept of "Mohammedanism" to depict cultural inferiority intrinsic to Islam and Muslims.[9] This radical shift from what was external to what became internal to cultural differences was crucial in the formation of what I have elsewhere called "civilizational thinking," in which concepts of cultural racism, gender, and consumption become entangled.

The shift from culture's naturalness to culture as intrinsic to various groups took place through a few interconnected discourses. Modern ideas of nature versus culture were primarily developed in the nineteenth and twentieth centuries and referred to "natural marking" as an intrinsic system and an inherent cause of a group occupying social relationships vis-à-vis sex, race, and class. The natural marking in colonial modernity differs from premodern marking. According to the feminist sociologist Colette Guillaumin (1995), a pioneer in the study of the articulation of race, gender, and sexuality in France, the modern idea of race and the idea of a natural group are imaginary formulations guaranteed by legal systems and theoretically ascribed to scientific facts (146–47). In her view, the old marking system was perceived as imposed upon bodies as a consequence of social relationships. However, the natural mark is not presumed to be a mark but the very origin of these relationships (Guillaumin 1995: 142). Therefore, endogenous determinism, or innate capacities determining social facts, are part and parcel of the scientific idea of natural groups (Guillaumin 1972).

The idea of the naturalness of cultures in colonial modernity set the scene for applying the myth of progress. The naturalness of culture is combined with another concept: the idea of the mindset and modern naturalist ideology proclaiming that the status of a human group "est programè de l'intériur de la matière vivante," or, is internally programmed, in Guillaumin's terms (1978: 10) and, I will add, is programmed from within the group culture. This idea continues to persist in more recent writing depicting Islam, including the work of neo-Orientalists such as Samuel Huntington in his reference to the clash of civilizations (2011). Spatial notions informed the idea of a unified mindset being programmed from within a closed cultural system and transcending spatial differences. The idea of a primitive mentality put forth by the French philosopher Lucien Lévy-Bruhl (1857–1939) is one example of such a theorization of culture and civilization. According to Lévy-Bruhl (1963: 19), the primitive mentality is radically different from the civilized one because primitive people cannot distinguish between the natural and supernatural worlds. In *Les fonctions mentales dans les sociétés Inférieures,* published in 1910, he considers the primitive mind as prelogical and mystical ("La mentalité primitive est à la fois mystique et prélogique," 458).[10] The assignment of the Prophet Muhammad as the "god" of Islam—which goes against Muslims' belief that he was the messenger of God—constructed "Jesus as the sinless and Muhammad as the sinful" (Noble 1893: 36). Furthermore, according to Sir John Malcolm (1827: 189), "No Mohammedan country can ever be great, or far advanced in art, science, and literature, for their religion is the great barrier that keeps them back and binds their mind in a shroud of mental darkness." Mohammedanism was blamed for causing backwardness and the degeneration of those civilizations, including of Persians who had adopted Islam.[11]

A more nuanced and sophisticated version of this dichotomy can be found in Cartesian philosophers' writing and in later discourse among anthropologists and sociologists in the twentieth century. The work of Rafael Patai on *The Arab Mind* (1973) is a good example. In his pioneer work, *Orientalism,* Edward Said questioned Patai's book, showing the linkage between the Orientalist texts and the context of empire. As noted by Nadia Abu El-Haj (2005: 541):

> He [Said] sought to understand how, in the context of specific historical encounters between Europe and the Arab Middle East, representing otherness—demarcating the difference between East and West, between Christianity and Islam—generated imperial power in the West and helped to elaborate the patterns of thought and culture that made that imperial endeavor imaginable, sustainable, and, quite centrally, (morally) "good."

Using a transnational and postcolonial theoretical framework, Ella Shohat and Robert Stam (2012, 1994) have elaborated extensively on the Eurocentric narrative of knowledge disseminated in the academic field, and in film and media, tracing the linkage between race and coloniality, including anti-Islamic ideas.

As documented by the investigative journalist Seymour Hersh (2004), it is no surprise that Rafael Patai's book has been used as the bible of neo-conservatives and was integrated into Guantanamo interrogation and torture techniques.[12] More recently, what is referred to as "Islamofascism"—which collapses Muslims with fascists and Islam with national socialism in

the United States and Europe—has been weaponized against any critique
of Islamophobia and anti-Muslim racism undermining the intertextual
connection of Islamophobia with anti-Semitism.[13]

The Myth of Progress

The naturalness of culture, combined with the myth of progress and development, was central to the construction of European modernity as rational,
progressive, and reflexive, leading the way for every other culture to follow
the route to civilization by abandoning their cultural traditions as fixed. In
that context, Europe was able to transform tradition, including religion
(Christianity), into secularism and rationalism. Other monotheistic religions such as Islam and Judaism were deemed inferior because of their lack
of spirituality. However, Islam, along with other so-called primitive religions including African or Latin American Indigenous spiritual practices,[14]
was considered fetishistic and idolatrous.[15] African Muhammadanism, as it
is referred to in the Christian missionary literature, arose when "Muhammad's mythology of angels and demons, of ghouls and jinns assimilated
itself with Negro beliefs in good and evil spirits" (Noble 1894: 75).

The mobilization of these notions of culture, civilization, and tradition
enabled cultural racism as a discourse, and put it into circulation through
the representational practices that constructed Islam and Muslims as the
other of modernity. For example, Patai (1973: 117) states that "in contrast to
the West, the Arab world still sees the universe running its predestined
course, determined by the will of Allah, who not only guides the world at
large, but also predestines the fate of each and every man individually." In
this context, while some religious practices became a site of evolutionary
progress, rational reflexivity, and development, others were perceived as
stuck in the anachronistic world of primitivism, barbarism, and fixed traditions. In other words, the enlightenment discourse, with its emphasis on
reason over religion, promoted civilizational thinking and created a hierarchy of cultures, from primitive and traditional to civilized and modern,
situating Muslims not only as religiously different but also as culturally
inferior. Civilization was referred to as a dividing line between cultures living in a state of childhood and unreason, and those able to use reason to
reflect upon the irrational. This evolutionary and biological model of
thinking referred to civilization as moving from irrational to rational,
primitive to modern, and barbaric to civilized. These ideas were circulated
through multiple discourses, including the discourse of development,

modernization, Westernization, and so on. They also created space for the national elite in various parts of the colonized or semi-colonized world to marginalize and depower local knowledges in the guise of rejecting backward traditions to join the route to progress and civilization.

The idea that a cultural or religious system can be intrinsic to a society has its roots in European race relations including anti-Black racism, older notions of anti-Semitism, and ideas of primitivism.[16] The development of the concept of Islam as homogeneous and related to racial and civilizational distinctions made possible the reference to the inferiority of the Muslim race within the context of nineteenth-century Europe. For example, according to Arthur de Gobineau (1865: 54), one of the major nineteenth-century scholars of Oriental religions who, along with Ernest Renan, was very influential in the formation of racialism and the propagation of French cultural racism, Islam is not compatible with the civilized worlds because of its sectarianism and "ses formules vagues et inconsistantes semblait inviter tout le monde à reconaître sans forcer personne à abandonner rien de ce qu'il pensait" (its inconsistent formulas inviting everyone to recognize it, without forcing anyone to give up anything they thought). Gobineau perceived miscegenation and mixing of races as causing civilizational degeneration and Islamism as incapable of understanding the nation system and what bonds societies together (1859: 472). Gobineau also considered Christianity as "a civilizing force as it makes a man better mannered" ([1854] 1915: 65). Ernest Renan (1883: 2–3), another theorist of race, declared in his famous paper titled "Islam and Science": "Anyone even somehow acquainted with our times clearly sees the present inferiority of the Islamic countries, the decadence of the states governed by Islam, the intellectual insignificance of the races that derive their culture and education from this religion alone."

As noted by Horkheimer and Adorno ([1944] 1987: 168), the idea of an "opposing race as the embodiment of the negative principal" is key to the process of racialization. Also, as I have noted elsewhere, such references to Islam provoked a reaction from Muslim scholars, intellectuals, and modernizers, either calling for "Westernization from head to toe," or claiming a form of Islamic revivalism and nationalism (Moallem 2005).[17]

The Idea of Primitive and Fetishistic Religions

The construction of what was called the primitive and fetishistic religions, or those religious beliefs and practices where the objects of worship are animals and inanimate things, was central to the myth of progress. It was also crucial to the formation of the separation of humans from objects. Both primitivism and fetishism were temporal concepts. While primitivism referred to when people were childlike[18] and pure savages, plunged in ignorance and barbarism (Morris and Leonard 2017: 47), fetishism represented the repetitious worship of a static object, a time repeatable without progress. In other words, the first notion constructed time in a linear and teleological way and put it in the service of colonial modernity. The second notion made time permanent and subordinated historical time to the time of the fetish, a circular time, a time without progress.

While it was hard to collapse a monotheistic religion such as Islam with fetishism (textual Islam being anti-idolatry itself), several aspects of Islam have become a site of fetishism and primitivism. Among others, the adoption of Islam by many communities in Africa and Haiti, and its mélange with spiritual practices such as voodoo were to provide evidence for the primitivism and fetishism of Islam.[19] What was referred to as the pre-Islamic idolatry of Egyptians and Meccans made Islam potentially prone to animism and fetishism. The magical, irrational, and fetishistic nature of things Oriental or "Musulmann" was material proof of Islamic animism and fetishism. As I have shown in my recent book on Persian carpets, Orientalia or things Oriental took Orientalism and primitivism to the realm of consumerism through fetishistic representational practices (Moallem 2018).

For example, in *The Cults of the Primitive Religions / Du culte des dieux fétiches*, published in 1750, Charles de Brosses (one of the most influential French scholars in the late eighteenth century) uses fetishism to refer to humanity's primordial cult practiced both by the so-called savages and by the ancient Egyptians. He calls attention to Orientals and what he calls "Mohamatens" as continuing to be fetishistic regardless of their monotheism. He writes:

> To begin this description of fetishism of Asia with a nation closest to Egypt, the Arabs' ancient divinity was nothing more than a square stone. There is hardly any reason to doubt that the famous and very ancient black stone in the temple of Mecca, which is revered by the Mohamatens despite the reasonable ideas they have of a single god, and about which they tell a tale related to Israel was once such a fetish. (Translated from French and qtd. in Morris and Leonard 2017: 77)

For de Brosses, all non-European Indigenous nations are idolatrous. He writes:

> The savage nations of Africa, Asia and America are all idolatrous. There has not been found a single exception to this rule. So that if one were to suppose a traveler transported to an unknown land where he finds educated and civilized nations, which is the most favorable case, nonetheless no one would dare to assume before verifying the facts, that the religion there truly is pure and intellectual as it is among us, whereas if the people were savage and barbarous, one could predict in advance that they would be idolatrous, without fear of being wrong. (qtd. in Morris and Leonard 2017: 107)

Fetishism requires "a visible object and the childlike capacity for 'make believe,' and the desire for a god that can be possessed," as noted by Alfred Haddon (1906: 94) in the case of West African religious practices. The fear of the inanimate world mixed up with the world of humans coincided with the rise of capitalism, the idea of humans separated from everything else and the impossibility of particular objects moving into the commodity exchange. As I have argued elsewhere (Moallem 2018), echoing William Pietz (1993),[20] with the formation of the academic disciplines of anthropology, art, psychoanalysis, sociology, and political economy in the nineteenth and twentieth centuries, this fear indexed the otherness within the bourgeois subject and liberal political economy. For example, for Freud, the possibility of a corporeal, affective, desiring engagement of a human subject with an inanimate object is a form of perversion; and for Marx, anxiety about how objects might come to embody the relations between humans and the inanimate worlds of commodities displaces the locus of value production in social labor-time. Both of these approaches overlap since they emphasize the separation of the human and nonhuman and the superiority of the category of humans over the worlds of objects and commodities (Pietz 1993).

Anne McClintock (1996: 187–88) has pointed out that fetishism enabled Europeans to do two things: (1) they could draw the unfamiliar and unaccountable cultures of the world into a systematic universe of value; and (2) within this universe, they could represent the foreign as deviant and errant. In this way, the discourse of fetishism enabled scholars to invent new borders between the time of modernity and the fetishism of colonized peoples.

The fetishism of Islam may be the most persistent in the consumption of things Oriental, or what I elsewhere call "Orientalia" (Moallem 2018). I have argued that Orientalia refers to commodities belonging to the colonial discourse described as Muhammadan, Musulman, Oriental, and Persian, as both masking and displaying the fetishism and primitivism of Islam and Muslim cultures similar to African fetishistic and animistic religious practices. Colonialism has indeed considered commodities with supernatural powers an extension of the mysterious and irrational Oriental life as contrasted with modernity's scientific rationality. The expansion of international commerce and the availability of Orientalia turned the Orient (in the colonial mind) into commodities and Islam into something of a fad, demonstrating a passing phase in religious "progress." As I have argued before, Orientalia has enabled a tangible and material Orient that can be touched, smelled, felt, and consumed (Moallem 2018). In this context, continuous consumption of things Oriental has become a site of redemption of the crisis of consumer capitalism. Also, the collapse of race and culture has enabled more investment in a textual Islam controlled by the Islamic male knowledge elite and has marginalized creolization and *métissage* of both Islamic practices and Muslims as heterogeneous communities of culture and history.[21]

The Woman Question

Another component of the juxtaposition of race and religion is the reference to the "woman question," the debate as to a woman's proper sphere and how much agency she should be permitted. When applying the woman question to Oriental cultures, the discourse is visually represented by the veil and veiling. This discourse emerged in the context of colonial modernity and referred to the woman question as crucial to the inferiority of certain religious and cultural practices. Indeed, the woman question became a measure of barbarism and civilization, establishing a boundary between the civilized and the primitive.

In other words, racialization through gender and sex created a gendered discourse both visually and discursively displaying the gap between Western and Oriental cultures. For example, as early as 1888, *Harper's Magazine* stated that "the difference between the Western and the Oriental civilizations is most plainly and decisively measured by the different position and estimate of women" (*Harper's Magazine* 1888). Ironically, the colonial discussion of Islam's failure to allow women to exercise agency invariably assumed that Muslim women could not already speak out against mistreatment, or even know that they were being mistreated.[22]

Of course, the woman question along with issues of sex are important parts of the construction of Islamic otherness. The discourse on sex vis-à-vis Africans, Arabs, and Muslims is also central to the gendering of Muslim otherness. Early writings on sex depicted Arabs and Muslims as paradoxically indulgent and perverse while vested with shame, honor, and repression, as part of "the Arab sexual mores and Arab child-rearing practices" as stated by Rafael Patai (1973: 105–12). In contrast, with the rise of homonationalism and pinkwashing, Arabs and Muslims are now being portrayed not only as repressive but also homophobic.[23]

Many colonial writings on Muslim women specifically commented on the position of women in Muslim societies. For example, a report called "How to Win Over Moslem Races" (1906), presented at the first missionary conference, emphasized Muslim ways of life as causing women's suffering. The report highlighted winning Muslims over "by showing them a new way of life." The report also includes a section written by Miss G. Y. Holliday, who states:

> The religion of Islam is the cause of special suffering to women. The Muslim woman suffers physically from her religion: she suffers mentally from the sense of degradation and inferiority ground into her by the veil and the curtain which never allow her for a moment to forget herself; she suffers from fear of her husband, her family and society, the fear of marriage, of divorce, and the fear of death; she suffers from ignorance and from her own follies. ("How to Win Over Moslem Races" 1906: 111–12)

In this context, the Muslim woman was used as a signifier drawing the boundary between civilization and barbarism. As Meyda Yeğenoğlu (1998: 56) has stated:

> The display of difference establishes a chain: the woman is the Orient, the Orient is the woman, the Orient like the woman exists veiled. If the Orient is feminine and if the feminine is Oriental, we can claim that the nature of femininity and the nature of Orient are figured as the same thing. In this case, the other culture is always the other sex.

In other words, the truth of culture can always be traced back to the woman question.[24]

Veiling as Racial Marking

Colette Guillaumin (1995: 142) argues that "l'idée de race est définie par un système socio-symbolique de marques mises sur des groups sociaux" ("the idea of race is defined by a socio-symbolic system of marks put on social groups"). Linking the notions of race, sex, and class with each other, she notes that the idea of a social group as the product of its specific nature is the synthesis of two systems: the economic relations based on new types of marking and "the archaeo-scientific deterministic system which sees in any object whatever a substance which secrets its own causes, which is itself its own cause."

Also, the formation of the modernizing nation-states in Muslim-majority countries has been part and parcel of subordinating Islam to the discourse of development and progress.[25] For example, in the case of Iran, I have elsewhere (Moallem 2005) shown how the formation of the Iranian nation-state relied on gendered notions of Islamic otherness. As I have argued extensively, Islamic otherness was based on the gendered racialization of Islam within a field of visibility that emphasized veiling as the ultimate site of the oppression and barbarism of Islam. Within the context of Iran, I made the point that veiling was both a site of gendered racialization in the global encounter of colonial modernity and Islam and a space for an affirmation of Muslim identity or a form of transnational ethnicity.

In my view, veiling functioned as a fetish, a trope, material evidence, as well as a signifier of Muslim barbarism and savagery. As a sign of backwardness, the veil and the veiling practice operated as a system of marking that throws all Muslims into one category.[26] Veiling, and what I call Muslim women's enigmatic image, enabled a dynamic network of gender and racial marking. This form of racial marking opened up Islam to the panoptic gaze of modernity, its technologies of vision including photography, and the idea of progress, while exposing Islam's fetishistic nature (Jay 2012; Behdad 2016). As noted by Malek Alloula (1986: 5), "History knows of no other society in which women have been photographed on such a large scale to be delivered to public view. Behind this image of Algerian women, probably reproduced in the millions, there is visible the broad outline of one of the figures of the colonial perception of the native."

The enigma of veiled Muslim women enabled a homogeneous iconography through the display of a racialized, gendered, and sexualized other. Islam as a fragmented religion, according to European theorists of race, was too disjointed,[27] so the signifier of "veiling" created a system of racial marking and a site of homogenization and unification of Islam and Muslims as the other of modernity, stuck in the world of tradition.[28]

The image or the enigma of the veiled Muslim woman carries the notion of race in the binary system of colonial modernity. *Race* in this context is defined as a cultural marking system and the veil as a symbol and tangible material object; a threshold separating the Orient and the Occident, religious and secular, traditional and modern, and barbaric and civilized. The veiled Muslim woman became a symbol of the "dark" and the hidden continent of femininity and represented a culturally intrinsic notion of religious barbarism. The veil functioned as a boundary object, an object dividing the savages from the civilized, a lower stage of civilization from a higher one. An evolutionary theory of clothing displaying different stages of civilization was crucial to this construction, especially with the rise of consumer capitalism. The feminine enigma since modernity has already equated to the construction of the other, a concept that is defined by a given norm. However, the veiled Muslim woman's enigma within the same dichotomous system also carries the notion of race in the binary system of colonial modernity.

The creation of a temporal sequence or a "system of before and after" that was open and visible to the gaze of colonial modernity put a series of actions into motion. As I have argued before, this system of marking could be changed through the process of modernization/Westernization, or one could turn it into a system where a network of actors could bring the time of the past to the time and space of modernity. In other words, veiling as a signifier has been critical in the practices of governmentality by the colonial states, the modernizing patriarchal local elite, and the Islamist reiteration of it as a site of Muslim identity. It continues to manage the crisis of modernity and governmentality. For example, the entanglement of such discourses and networks of social actors is displayed in the convergence of state-imposed veiling in Iran with women's challenge to a patriarchal state and the diasporic US- and European-funded campaign for the liberation of Iranian women.[29]

Conclusion

"For people of color have always theorized—but in forms quite different from the Western form of abstract logic. And I am inclined to say that our theorizing (and I intentionally use the verb rather than the noun) is often in narrative forms, in the stories we create, in riddles and proverbs, in the play with language, because dynamic rather than fixed ideas seem more to our liking."

—Barbara Christian, "Race for Theory"

In "Race for Theory," Barbara Christian challenges the marginalization of literature and scholarship that have been denigrated as political or exclusive to third world and Black women. She calls for reading that compels you to read differently, a passionate response to the writer to whom there is often no response. I use Christian's insight in the opposite direction to read differently the texts that claim neutrality yet have authorized and put into circulation racialist and civilizational rationales.

In this essay, I have argued that deconstructing Islamophobia and anti-Muslim racism is crucial in the age of globalization and transnationalism. However, interrogating colonial modernity's historical residue is fundamental to an understanding of what maintains investing and reinvesting value linking race and religion. The folding of race and religion through gender and sex and the symbolic and material culture of images and material objects, I argue, has enabled a system of marking that links fields of visibility with the production of racialized and gendered knowledge about Islam and Muslims. I showed that the intersection of the myth of progress and the idea of mindset, the fetishism of Islam, the myth of, and the figure of, veiled Muslim woman have all been crucial in founding a racialist and eventually racist discourse as the backbone of the racialization of Muslims. To challenge Islamophobia, one must deconstruct not only the geopolitics but also the body politics of coloniality, and its knowledge frames within global political society and specific nation-states.

Minoo Moallem is professor of gender and women's studies and director of media studies at the University of California, Berkeley. Trained as a sociologist, she writes on postcolonial and transnational feminist studies, Islamic nationalism and transnationalism, consumer cultures, Middle Eastern studies, and Iranian cultural politics and diasporas.

Notes

1   A critique of Islamophobia emerged in the era of 9/11, the war on terror, and the rise of blatant racism against Muslims in the United States, Canada, and Europe. There are, of course, many scholarly books and articles on Islamophobia, its industry, and its discourse in the United States. Several scholars including Junaid Rana (2007) and Evelyn Alsultany (2012) have already shed light on Islamophobia—or what Nathan Lean (2012) calls "the Islamophobia industry" —in the United States and Europe. A focus on Islamophobia in the context of the United States—more specifically, on what Khaled Beydoun (2018) refers to as "American Islamophobia," or Deepa Kumar (2012) calls "the US empire"—

has helped build an understanding of this phenomenon. Also, various issues of *Islamophobia Studies Journal* edited by Hatem Bazian since 2012 have contributed to an understanding of Islamophobia. However, the field is still wide open for analysis of race and religion concerning Islam and Muslims in colonial modernity, and Islam as the other of modernity.

2   According to Robert H. Milligan (1912: 8), "Civilization is but the secular side of Christianity." Also see Tylor 1892.

3   There are numerous early anthropological texts that take this distinction for granted. See, among others, Garson and Read 1892.

4   While Islamophobia and Whiteness are inseparable, the discourse is also circulated among diasporic populations from the Middle East. The discourse of race and religion is not new to immigrants from colonized or semi-colonized contexts since modern ideas of race were implicated through the project of nation-state building. As I have noted elsewhere in the Orientalist discourse on "Persia" or Persians, there is a reference to a pre-Islamic civilized Persia corrupted by Islam and Islamization. The modernizing Iranian elite reiterated this discourse to justify Westernization as a road to progress. Under Reza Shah's rule and his alliances with Nazism in Germany, the claim to the purity of the Aryan race became a component of nation-state building in Iran. The affirmation of Persia or Persians as a site of identification distinct from Iran and Iranians, and the traumatic experience of dislocation of some Iranian immigrants, have facilitated the reception of Islamophobic ideas among some members of the Iranian diasporic communities.

5   *Mohammedanism* has been spelled differently in the literature. Examples include *Muhamedanism*, *Mohammadinism*, and so on.

6   It should be noted that Islamophobia and anti-Muslim racism are generated by states, media, and commonsense ideologies in Europe and the United States. While the study of each one of these sites is crucial, I am interested in the academic discourses that feed Islamophobia in perhaps a more covert and nuanced way.

7   For a comprehensive analysis of commodity racism see McClintock 1996. Also, I have extensively elaborated on the commodity of racism in relation to "Orientalia" in my recent book on Persian carpets (Moallem 2018).

8   Among others, the feminist scholar Ella Shohat and the film scholar Robert Stam have made significant contributions to the understanding of the expulsion of Jews and Muslims from Spain and the rise of Eurocentrism (Shohat and Stam 2012, 1994). See also Mohanty 1984.

9   The depiction of prophet Muhammad in *Charlie Hebdo*'s 2015 cartoons, as well as the *Jyllands-Posten* portrayals of the prophet Muhammad, are examples of the continuation of European perceptions of Islam as "Muhammadanism." The stereotypical image of Arab men as ugly, violent, and irrational circulated in many Islamophobic and anti-Muslim racist films and media. The *Charlie Hebdo* and *Jyllands-Posten* cartoons are good examples of this phenomenon. The projection of such stereotypical images onto the prophet Muhammad reduces Islam

to Muhammad as a violent Arab man and reveals the continuation of a colonial depiction of Islam as "Muhammadanism" in a postcolonial era.

10 As I have argued elsewhere, these ideas have been used to justify imperial intervention. For example, according to Heiss (1997: 230), the Iranian prime minister, Mohammad Mossadeq, was characterized by Anglo-American officials as a "wily Oriental" whose approach to oil was "almost mystical," and the Iranian people were considered incapable of choosing and following their leaders (Moallem 2005: 40).

11 I should mention that these ideas are still circulating in many Muslim countries. For example, in Iran *Akhound*, or Molla, a pejorative reference to Muslim clergymen as the incarnation of irrationality and stupidity, has undermined the cultural, political, and popular appeal of the religious political elite.

12 Edward Said (1978: 308–9) was one of the first scholars who questioned Patai's book in *Orientalism*. Seymour M. Hersh (2004) revealed that Patai's book became the bible of the neocons as well as the US military post 9/11. It influenced their views on Arab behavior and the sexualization of torture by conveying two notions: "One, that Arabs only understand force, and two, that the biggest weakness of Arabs is shame and humiliation."

13 By separating anti-Semitism and Islamophobia, pro-Israelis and other right-wing groups have used Islamofascism to censure a critique of the Israeli settler colonial state.

14 For example, Arthur de Gobineau ([1854] 1915: 28) writes: "I cannot imagine anything more fanatical than a society like that of Aztecs which rested on a religious foundation continued watered by the blood of human sacrifice."

15 Ironically, textual Islam in its origin myth considers itself against idolatry of pre-Islamic female goddesses. For more information, see Al Sabbah 1986.

16 While the discourse of anti-Semitism vis-à-vis Jewish communities both in Europe and in the United States is still alive, targeting Jewish communities to fuel various forms of xenophobia as well as Islamophobia, a number of scholars have argued that the discussion of Jewish Whiteness in the United States along with the collaboration of Israelis' anti-Arab, Islamophobic, and Iranophobic discourses with the conservative and right-wing groups in the United States create a more paradoxical and complex situation. See, among others, Brodkin 1998.

17 As I have argued in "The Ethnicity of an Islamic Fundamentalism," published in 1992, the attribution of fundamentalism to Islam and Muslims in Euro-American contexts, and the discourses of identity claiming Islamic nationalism and transnationalism that emerged in a colonial and postcolonial era, have to do with what Stuart Hall refers to as the dominant ethnicity of the West, in relation to the otherness of the rest (1991). In this work, I show how a defensive ethnicity, or a form of "we-ness" in the Shia narratives emerged in opposition to the global and hegemonic power of what was referred to in the Iranian revolutionary discourse as the alliance between Zionism and imperialism. See Moallem 1992.

18 For example, Milligan (1912: 301) writes, "And the question is whether we shall send to Africa our civilization, with all its burden of new demands and moral

responsibilities, without disclosing to its primitive and childlike people that which alone supports our material civilization and enables us to bear its moral weight—that which is deepest and best in our thought and life."

19 According to Beynon 1938, the "Nation of Islam" was usually known as the "Voodoo Cult."

20 For an enlightening analysis and critique of Marx's notion of fetishism, see Pietz 1993: 119–51.

21 The Muslim knowledge elite has always claimed that Islam is the religion of reason and this has marginalized mystical or popular forms of Islam by investing more in clerical and textual Islam.

22 Marnia Lazreg (1994) shows the complexity of women's lives in colonized Algeria and challenges ideas about the unquestionable powerlessness of Algerian women.

23 For an analysis of homonationalism and pinkwashing see Puar 2017; Massad 2007; Mikdashi 2011; and other Middle Eastern scholars working at the intersection of queer studies and Islamophobia.

24 As noted by Inderpal Grewal (1996: 49), "The move to civilize 'Eastern' women functioned to make them less opaque, to strip them of their veils, and to remove them from harems where they lived lives hidden from the European male."

25 One could give the example of Iran, Turkey, Egypt, and many other locations in the Middle East and North Africa.

26 Feminist historian Joan Scott (2007) has substantially elaborated on the contemporary headscarf debates in France and the French colonial project of *mission civilisatrice*. Ratna Kapur (2002) interrogates the essentialist cultural and religious assumptions that form the discourse of gender equality both in India and in France casting Muslim women as other.

27 For example, Gobineau (1865: 21) writes, "As there is not any sizable group united by the bonds of a strictly accepted doctrine, there is not collective enthusiasm or well-defined, common hatred either."

28 As noted by Radha Hedge (2019), Muslim women wearing hijab have been marked as the embodiment of danger and terror and subjected to technologies of surveillance at the US borders.

29 An example is the veiling boycott campaign of Masih Alinejad, an exiled Iranian journalist and collaborator with the Trump administration and right-wing organizations to liberate Iranian women. The campaign suppresses various ways in which Iranian women have resisted state-imposed veiling along with other gender issues for years. It also undermines masses of women who used veiling as a site of agency, anti-imperialism, Islamic nationalism, and citizenship during the Iranian Revolution and afterward.

Works Cited

Abu El-Haj, Nadia. 2005. "Edward Said and the Political Present." *American Ethnologist* 32, no. 4: 538–55.

Alloula, Malek. 1986. *The Colonial Harem*. Minneapolis: University of Minnesota Press.

Al Sabbah, Fatna (Fatima Mernissi). 1986. *La femme dans l'inconscient musulman*. Paris: Albin Michel.

Alsultany, Evelyn. 2012. *Arabs and Muslims in the Media: Race and Representation after 9/11*. New York: New York University Press.

Behdad, Ali. 2016. *Camera Orientalis*. Chicago: University of Chicago Press.

Beydoun, Khaled A. 2018. *American Islamophobia: Understanding the Roots and Rise of Fear*. Berkeley: University of California Press.

Beynon, Ardmann Doane. 1938. "The Voodoo Cult among Negro Migrants in Detroit." *American Journal of Sociology* 43, no. 6: 894–907.

Brodkin, Karen. 1998. *How Jews Became White Folks and What That Says about Race in America*. New Brunswick, NJ: Rutgers University Press.

Christian, Barbara. 1988. "Race for Theory." *Feminist Studies* 14, no. 1: 67–79.

Foucault, Michel. 1980. "Two Lectures." In *Power/Knowledge: Selected Interviews and Other Writings 1972–1977*, by Michel Foucault, edited by Colin Gordon, 78–108. New York: Pantheon Books.

Garson, John George, and Charles Hercules Read. 1892. *Notes and Queries on Anthropology*. London: Anthropological Institute.

Grewal, Inderpal. 1996. *Home and Harem: Nation, Gender, Empire, and the Cultures of Travel*. Durham, NC: Duke University Press.

Gobineau, Arthur cmte de. (1854) 1915. *The Inequality of Human Races*. London: William Heineman.

Gobineau, Arthur cmte de. 1859. *Trois ans en Asie (de 1855 à 1858)*. Paris: L. Hachette et cie.

Gobineau, Arthur cmte de. 1865. *Les religions et les philosophies dans l'Asie centrale*. Paris: Librairie Académique.

Guillaumin, Colette. 1972. *L'idéologie raciste: Genèse et langage actuel*. Paris-La Haye: Mouton.

Guillaumin, Colette. 1978. "Pratique du pouvoir et idée de nature 2: Le discours de la Nature." *Questions féministes*, no. 3: 5–28.

Guillaumin, Colette. 1995. *Racism, Sexism, Power, and Ideology*. New York: Routledge.

Hall, Stuart. 1991. "The Local and the Global: Globalization and Ethnicity." In *Culture, Globalization and the World System*, edited by Anthony King, 19–40. Binghamton: State University of New York.

Haddon, Alfred C. 1906. *Magic and Fetishism*. London: Archibald Contable.

Harper's Magazine. 1888. Vol. 786, no. 55.

Hedge, Radha. S. 2019. "Itinerant Data: Unveiling Gendered Scrutiny at the Border." *Television and New Media*, July 4.

Hersh, Seymour M. 2004. "The Gray Zone: How a Secret Pentagon Program Came to Abu Ghraib." *New Yorker*, May 17.

Horkheimer, Max, and Theodor Adorno. (1944) 1987. *Dialectic of Enlightenment*. New York: Continuum.

Huntington, Samuel P. 2011. *The Clash of Civilzations and the Remaking of the World Order*. New York: Simon and Schuster.

"How to Win Over Moslem Races." 1906. Report for the First Missionary Conference on behalf of the Mohammaden World. London: Fleming H. Revell Company.

Jay, Martin. 2012. *Cultural Semantics: Keywords of Our Time.* Amherst: University of Massachusetts Press.

Kapur, Ratna. 2002. "Un-veiling Women's Rights in the 'War on Terrorism.'" *Duke Journal of Law and Policy* 9: 211–25.

Kapur, Ratna. 2012. "Un-veiling Equality: Disciplining the 'Other' Woman through Human Rights Discourse." In *Islamic Law and International Human Rights Law: Searching for Common Ground*, edited by Mark Ellis, Anver Emon, and Benjamin Glahn, 10–18. New York: Oxford University Press.

Kumar, Deepa. 2012. *Islamophobia and the Politics of Empire.* Chicago: Haymarket Books.

Lazreg, Marnia. 1994. *The Eloquence of Silence.* New York: Routledge.

Lean, Nathan. 2012. *The Islamophobia Industry: How the Right Manufactures Fear of Muslims.* London: Pluto Press.

Lévy-Bruhl, Lucien. 1910. *Les fonctions mentales dans les sociétés inférieures.* Paris: Fèlix Alcan.

Lévy-Bruhl, Lucien. 1927. *L'âme primitive, collection des travaux de l'Année sociologique.* Paris: Alcan.

Malcolm, Sir John. 1827. *Sketches of Persia: From the Journals of a Traveler in the East.* Vol. I. London: John Murray.

Massad, Joseph. 2007. *Desiring Arabs.* Chicago: University of Chicago Press.

McClintock, Anne. 1996. *Imperial Leather: Race, Gender, and Sexuality in the Colonial Contest.* New York: Routledge.

Mikdashi, Maya. 2011. "Gay Rights as Human Rights: Pinkwashing Homonationalism." *Jadaliyya*, December 16. www.jadaliyya.com/pages/index/3560/gay-rights-as-human-rights_pinkwashing-homonationalism.

Milligan, Robert H. 1912. *The Fetish Folks of West Africa.* London: Fleming H. Revell.

Moallem, Minoo. 1992. "The Ethnicity of an Islamic Fundamentalism: The Case of Iran." *South Asia Bulletin* 12, no. 2: 25–34.

Moallem, Minoo. 2005. *Between Warrior Brother and Veiled Sister.* Berkeley and Los Angeles: University of California Press.

Moallem, Minoo. 2018. *Persian Carpets: The Nation as a Transnational Commodity.* New York: Routledge.

Mohanty, Chandra Talpade. 1984. "Under Western Eyes: Feminist Scholarship and Colonial Discourses." *boundary 2* 13, no. 1: 333–58.

Morris, Rosalind C., and Daniel H. Leonard. 2017. *The Return of Fetishism.* Chicago: University of Chicago Press.

Noble, Frederic Perry. 1893. *The Redemption of Africa: A Story of Civilization.* Vol. 1. New York: Young People's Missionary Movement.

Noble, Frederic Perry. 1894. Secretary of the Chicago Congress on Africa, Columbian Exposition. Chicago, New York, and Toronto: The Fleming H. Revell Co.

Patai, Raphael. 1973. *The Arab Mind.* New York: Hatherleigh Press.

Pietz, William. 1993. "Fetishism and Materialism: The Limits of Theory in Marx." In *Fetishism as Cultural Discourse*, edited by Emily Apter and William Pietz, 119–51. Ithaca, NY: Cornell University Press.

Puar, Jasbir. 2017. *Terrorist Assemblages: Homonationalism in Queer Times*. Durham, NC: Duke University Press.

Rana, Junaid. 2007. "The Story of Islamophobia." *Souls* 9, no. 2: 148–61.

Razack, Sherene. 2008. *Casting Out: The Eviction of Muslims from Western Law and Politics*. Toronto: University of Toronto Press.

Renan, Ernest. 1883. "Islam and Science." *Journal des débats*, May 18.

Said, Edward. 1979. *Orientalism*. New York: Vintage Books.

Said, Edward. 1997. *Covering Islam: How the Media and the Experts Determine How We See the Rest of the World*. New York: Vintage Books.

Scott, Joan Wallach. 2007. *The Politics of the Veil*. Princeton, NJ: Princeton University Press.

Shohat, Ella, and Robert Stam. 1994. *Unthinking Eurocentrism: Multiculturalism and the Media*. New York: Routledge.

Shohat, Ella, and Robert Stam. 2012. *Race in Translation: Culture Wars around the Postcolonial Atlantic*. New York: New York University Press.

Tylor, Edward Burnett. 1892. "Religion, Fetishes, etc." In Garson and Read 1892: 130–40.

Quijano, Anibal. 2000. "Coloniality of Power, Eurocentrism, and Latin America." *Nepantla: Views from South* 1, no. 3: 533–80.

Yeğenoğlu, Meyda. 1998. *Colonial Fantasies: Towards a Feminist Reading of Orientalism*. Cambridge: Cambridge University Press.

Natasha Bakht

Transnational Anti-Muslim Racism:
Routes in Law

Abstract: Bans or attempts to ban the niqab have traveled global circuits, with disastrous consequences for Muslim women who wear the face veil. These women have evoked a repugnance that insists on erasing them from public spaces. An analysis of niqab bans reveals that: (1) a transnational proliferation of racist methods of regulating Muslim women's dress occurs through law; (2) they have been initiated by politicians to protect majoritarian values; (3) justifications for bans are based on specious logic; and (4) some are defended using gender equality on the erroneous assumption that women are universally coerced into wearing this garment despite empirical research noting that women wear the niqab as an expression of faith. The treatment of niqab-wearing women requires close attention to the transnational routes of legalized anti-Muslim racism.

Bans or attempts to ban the niqab have traveled global circuits, leaving in their wake disastrous consequences for Muslim women who wear the face veil. Though these women are a minority in terms of their numbers, they have evoked in politicians and in the public, urged by politicians, a repugnance that insists on erasing them from public spaces. The repugnance they inspire requires that we pay close attention to the transnational routes of legalized anti-Muslim racism. An analysis of niqab bans reveals that: (1) a transnational proliferation of racist methods of regulating Muslim women's dress occurs through law; (2) they have been initiated by politicians to protect majoritarian values; (3) justifications for bans are based on specious logic; and (4) some are defended using gender equality on the

MERIDIANS · feminism, race, transnationalism 20:2 October 2021
DOI: 10.1215/15366936-9547885 © 2021 Smith College

erroneous assumption that women are universally coerced into wearing this garment despite empirical research in several countries noting that women wear the niqab as an expression of faith.

France was the first country in 2010 to prohibit face veils in public spaces, relying on, among other justifications, the novel perspective that face coverings hamper social relations and make living together impossible.[1] France's national prohibition on face veils was followed by ten other countries: Belgium, Bulgaria, Austria, Denmark, the Netherlands, Luxembourg, Switzerland, Chad, Congo-Brazzaville, and Sri Lanka (Bakht 2020: 116–22). Regional bans of the niqab or bans affecting certain sectors such as the receipt of public services or voting have been enacted in Canada, Spain, Italy, Germany, Syria, Cameroon, Tunisia, Algeria, Niger, China, and India (Bakht 2020: 116–22; Oltermann 2021; Reuters 2021). Prohibitions of face veils have been debated, proposed, or had failed attempts at enactment in the United Kingdom, Egypt, Indonesia, Estonia, Finland, Hungary, Slovenia, Latvia, and Lithuania (Bakht, 2020: 122). Grillo and Shah (2012: 12) have aptly stated that the way criminalization of face veiling has moved from country to country makes it seem like a form of political swine flu.

These multiple and widespread attempts to regulate Muslim women's dress are both sobering and supportive of the idea that discriminatory and racist laws and practices in one country lend backing to similar strategies in other countries. Parallel discourses from different regions of the world reveal the interconnectedness of gendered anti-Muslim rhetoric and the ways in which niqab-wearing women's demonization is both shored up and made local. For example, the province of Quebec has drawn on the French foundational principle of secularism,[2] claiming it a common Quebec value,[3] as one reason justifying the prohibition of niqabs.[4] Setting aside the relatively new emergence of secularism as supposedly universal, this also demonstrates the very particular racial logic that is borrowed from France's interpretation of the principle.

In each country, calls for niqab bans emerged because political elites formed an agenda to protect majoritarian culture against a potential menace: niqab-wearing women. Politicians transformed niqab wearing from a nonexistent issue to a spectacular threat to the nation. Politicians have insisted that niqab-wearing women do not belong to the nation-state, despite vociferous declarations by the women themselves that they very much belong to the nation (Bakht 2020: 124). Niqab-wearing women are construed as a threat to the shared values and practices of nationhood because it is assumed that they are connected to Islamic terrorism or "Islamist" ideals. In Belgium, despite a national crisis that divided the francophone and Flemish elite and paralyzed federal politics in 2011, politicians were able to coalesce in large numbers around the idea of banning face veils (Brems et al. 2014). Anti-Muslim racism emerged as the symbolic ground upon which national unity became articulated. The 2018 Dutch national niqab ban was similarly and explicitly referred to by one senator as "the first step to de-Islamize the Netherlands" (Associated Press 2018). The narrative of national belonging has been used by politicians globally to demarcate the conditions under which Muslim women may inhabit the public sphere.

Niqab bans are grounded in a powerful illogic that need not cohere on any level (Razack 2018). Simply articulating that the niqab is contrary to majoritarian values is enough. No further explanation is required to secure agreement and stimulate action from multiple countries with differing relationships to Muslim communities. It also makes no difference that niqab bans can produce absurd results: in the context of the current global health pandemic, one can be fined for *not* covering one's face and women who wear the niqab will also be fined *for* covering their faces (Silverstein 2020). Sherene Razack (forthcoming) has argued that "in seeking to exercise sovereignty over Muslim women, bans are a key part of maintaining a global color line in which white nations establish supremacy through the regulation of Muslim populations, and non-white nations position themselves within a global white supremacy that targets Muslims."

The narratives that circulate within, between, and among these countries justifying niqab bans are surprisingly similar and specious in their rationality. Niqab bans are defended on the basis that seeing the face is required for reasons of communication, identification, and security.[5] In fact, the COVID-19 health pandemic has revealed how disingenuous these justifications are. Face coverings, which are now government mandated in many public spaces, have not prevented effective communication; it is very possible for societies to function with many people covering parts of their faces, while still interacting, communicating, and performing their regular functions. When it has been necessary to identify people such as in hospitals in order to receive certain treatments, staff have simply relied on identification documents (Stansbury 2020). Security arguments are similarly irrational because needing to see someone's face at all times does not increase the safety of society. As the Human Rights Committee noted with respect to France's ban of niqabs, general bans on face coverings for security purposes are too sweeping in their means and not proportional to the objective in question.[6] The insistence that seeing the face at all times is necessary is actually about the subjective feelings of insecurity or unease of the majority toward a minority practice that causes no harm (Bakht 2020: 26, 48, 50).

Simultaneous to the aforementioned rationales that construct niqab-wearing women as a threat to society, is the apparent concern that these women are forced into this attire. Niqab bans are thus purported to further gender equality.[7] In six of the liberal democracies where interview-based research has been conducted with niqab-wearing women, most have stated they made the personal choice to wear the niqab after prolonged periods of thought or study because of a desire to lead a faith-based life (Brems 2014; Clarke 2013; Bakht 2020: 18–20). While decisions about clothing are almost always made in relational contexts that undoubtedly constrain and influence behavior, the regulation of Muslim women's clothing explicitly questions their capacity to make agentic choices in ways that other people's decisions are not scrutinized (Campbell 2013: 2–3). For several niqab-wearing women in Canada, the decision to wear the niqab meant acting in defiance of their loved ones or having to convince family members that it was an appropriate choice (Bakht 2020: 23).

The gender equality justification for niqab bans is also entirely insincere because a true concern for these women would not impose the devastating consequences of such prohibitions. Niqab bans limit women's ability to work; travel; testify in courtrooms; and access healthcare, education, and other public services.[8] Such bans potentially criminalize harmless activity with fines and imprisonment and subject niqab-wearing women to violence on the streets.[9] The gendered consequences of niqab bans are far-reaching and thwart the very prerequisites needed to ensure women's equality.

Niqab bans have moved from one country to the next, adopting similar strategies and rhetoric that become localized expressions of anti-Muslim racism. The narratives that circulate within, between, and among these countries reinforce false, illogical, yet effective ideas about niqab-wearing women as untrustworthy and abhorrent. The sheer number of niqab bans debated, proposed, and enacted across diverse jurisdictions demonstrates the extent of global anti-Muslim racism. Repugnance and aggression toward niqab-wearing women become part of a shared vocabulary or repository of civilizational superiority that operates irrespective of the specificity of each national context, forming a circulating anti-Muslim affect.[9] Anti-Muslim racism has found a reliable and conducive transnational route in law.

. . . .

Natasha Bakht is professor of law at the University of Ottawa and the Shirley Greenberg Chair for Women and the Legal Profession. Her work explores the intersection between religious freedom and women's equality. She recently published *In Your Face: Law, Justice and Niqab-Wearing Women in Canada* (2020).

Notes

1   SAS v. France, No. 43835/11 (2014) ECHR 1, para. 122.
2   France relied on secularism to justify banning headscarves in schools. It could not, however, use a similar rationale for its much wider ban on niqabs in public spaces, as secularism is a concept that applies to public institutions. It could not be used to restrict the practices of individuals at large. Whether secularism or *laïcité* is in fact a founding principle of the French Republic is debatable. See Denli 2004: 422.
3   It has been argued that the government's reliance on secularism is "newly asserted as a common value of the Québec people" (Jahangeer 2020: 121).
4   Bill 21, an Act respecting the laicity of the State, 1st Sess., 42nd Leg., Québec, 2019.
5   See, for example, Canada: Bill 62, An Act to foster adherence to State religious neutrality and, in particular, to provide a framework for requests for accommodations on religious grounds in certain bodies, SQ 2017, c 19; France: Loi no. 2010-1192 du 11 octobre 2010, JO, October 11, 2010, 18344; Belgium: Loi du 1er juin 2011 visant à interdire le port de tout vêtement cachant totalement ou de manière principale le visage, June 1, 2011; Netherlands: Instelling van een gedeeltelijk verbod op het dragen van gezichtsbedekkende kleding in het onderwijs, het openbaar vervoer, overheidsgebouwen en de zorg (Wet gedeeltelijk verbod gezichtsbedekkende kleding), April 26, 2018, 34349; Bulgaria: Krasimirov 2016; Denmark: *Guardian* Staff and Agencies 2018; Austria: *Deutsche Welle* 2017.
6   Human Rights Committee, Miriana Hebbadj v. France, CCPR/C/123/D/2807/ 2016 (October 17, 2018); Human Rights Committee, Sonia Yaker v. France, CCPR/C/123/D/2747/2016 (December 7, 2018).
7   See, for example, Bill 21, preamble; Bill 62, s 10(2); SAS v. France, para. 119.
8   See Bill 21; Loi no. 2010-1192; Police v. Razamjoo, (2005) DCR 408 (DCNZ); R v. NS, 2012 SCC 72; The Queen v. D(R) (September 16, 2013), Crown Court at Blackfriars, unreported decision, www.judiciary.uk/judgments/thequeenvd; Bakht 2020: 132–37.
9   See Bakht 2020; Loi du 1er juin 2011 visant à interdire le port de tout vêtement cachant totalement ou de manière principale le visage, June 1, 2011; Mason-Bish and Zempi 2019; Razack, forthcoming.

Works Cited

Associated Press. 2018. "Dutch Parliament Approves Limited Ban on Burqa, Niqab." *New York Daily News*, June 27. www.nydailynews.com/news/world/ny-news-dutch -parliament-ban-burqa-20180627-story.html.

Bakht, Natasha. 2020. *In Your Face: Law, Justice and Niqab-Wearing Women in Canada*. Toronto: Irwin Law.

Brems, Eva, ed. 2014. *The Experiences of Face Veil Wearers in Europe and the Law*. Cambridge: Cambridge University Press.

Brems, Eva, Yaiza Janssens, Kim Lecoyer, Saïla Ouald Chaib, Victoria Vandersteen, Jogchum Vrielink. 2014. "The Belgian 'Burqa Ban' Confronted with Insider Realities." In Brems 2014: 77–114.

Campbell, Angela. 2013. *Sister Wives, Surrogates, and Sex Workers: Outlaws by Choice?* Surrey, UK: Ashgate.

Clarke, Lynda. 2013. "Women in Niqab Speak: A Study of the Niqab in Canada." Canadian Council of Muslim Women. ccmw.com/wp-content/uploads/2013/10 /WEB_EN_WiNiqab_FINAL.pdf.

Denli, Özlem. 2004. "Between Laicist State Ideology and Modern Public Religion: The Head-Cover Controversy in Contemporary Turkey." In *Facilitating Freedom of Religion or Belief: A Deskbook*, edited by Tore Lindholm, Cole W. Durham, and Bahi Tahzib-Lie, 497–511. Leiden: Martinus Nijhoff/Brill Academic.

Deutsche Welle. 2017. "Austrian Full-Face Veil Ban Comes into Effect." October 1. www .dw.com/en/austrian-full-face-veil-ban-comes-into-effect/a-40765541.

Grillo, Ralph, and Prakash Shah. 2012. "Reasons to Ban? The Anti-burqa Movement in Western Europe." Working Paper 12-05, Max Planck Institute for the Study of Religious and Ethnic Diversity. core.ac.uk/download/pdf/30696227.pdf.

Guardian Staff and Agencies. 2018. "Denmark Passes Law Banning Burqa and Niqab." *Guardian*, May 31. www.theguardian.com/world/2018/may/31/denmark-passes-law -banning-burqa-and-niqab.

Jahangeer, Roshan Arah. 2020. "Anti-veiling and the Charter of Québec Values: 'Native Testimonials,' Erasure, and Violence against Montreal's Muslim Women." *Canadian Journal of Women and the Law* 32, no. 1: 114–39.

Krasimirov, Angel. 2016. "Bulgaria Bans Full-Face Veils in Public Places." *Reuters*, September 30. www.reuters.com/article/us-religion-burqa-bulgaria/bulgaria-bans -full-face-veils-in-public-places-idUSKCN1201FV.

Mason-Bish, Hannah, and Irene Zempi. 2019. "Misogyny, Racism, and Islamophobia: Street Harassment at the Intersections." *Feminist Criminology* 14: no 5: 540–59.

Oltermann, Philip. 2021. "Switzerland to Ban Wearing of Burqa and Niqab in Public Places." *Guardian*, March 7. www.theguardian.com/world/2021/mar/07 /switzerland-on-course-to-ban-wearing-of-burqa-and-niqab-in-public-places.

Razack, Sherene H. 2018. "A Site/Sight We Cannot Bear: The Racial/Spatial Politics of Banning the Muslim Woman's Niqab." *Canadian Journal of Women and the Law* 30, no. 1: 169–89.

Razack, Sherene H. Forthcoming. *Nothing Has to Make Sense: Anti-Muslim Racism, White Supremacy, and Law*. Minneapolis: University of Minnesota Press.

Reuters. 2021. "Sri Lanka to Ban Burqas and Shut Islamic Schools for 'National Security.'" CNN, March 5. www.cnn.com/2021/03/15/asia/sri-lanka-burqa-ban -intl-hnk/index.html.

Silverstein, Jason. 2020. "France Will Still Ban Islamic Face Coverings Even after Making Masks Mandatory." *CBS News*, May 12. www.cbsnews.com/news/france -burqa-ban-islamic-face-coverings-masks-mandatory/.

Stansbury, Tasha. 2020. "COVID-19 Exposes the Hypocrisy of Face Covering in Quebec." *Toronto Star*, April 21. www.thestar.com/opinion/contributors/2020/04/21 /covid-19-exposes-the-hypocrisy-of-face-covering-in-quebec.html.

Amira Jarmakani

....

Shari'a Barbie's Afterlives:
Apprehending Racialized and Sexualized Islam through Social Media

Abstract: This article investigates a sprawling archive of memes (about "Shakira law," "shari'a Barbie," and the "jihad squad,") and incorporates analysis of the original *Serial* podcast (about the case of Adnan Syed) to look at the role of metadata and dataveillance in criminalizing and apprehending Muslims. Given technological innovations, like autocorrect functions that "correct" conversations about the "racialization" of Muslims to the "radicalization" of Muslims (to give one example), algorithmic manipulations of data depend on sexualizing and racializing assemblages that tell a familiar story about the way Muslim lives are shaped by the discourses and representations through which they are figured and apprehended. The author explores the way that this archive of memes figures Muslims as a "measurable type"—whereby they are profiled into highly fraught categories, like "terrorist," through algorithmic interpretations of their online activity— therefore enabling what John Cheney-Lippold calls "soft biopolitics." Given the ability of this sort of data to materially shape a person's life, the author looks at the roles of metadata and big data in apprehending Muslims, Arabs, and SWANA-identified people through a biopolitical framing of population, where *apprehend* is understood in both senses of the word—in terms of understanding Muslims as well as criminalizing them.

Shakira Law: Accidental Apprehension

Toward the end of Barack Obama's second presidential term, a set of fairly widely circulating memes decrying the potential threat that "Shakira law"

MERIDIANS · feminism, race, transnationalism 20:2 October 2021
DOI: 10.1215/15366936-9547896 © 2021 Smith College

Figure 1. Meme portraying DJ Khaled as a representative of "ISIS" working with Obama to implement "Shakira law" in the United States.

would soon be implemented in the global north demonstrates some of the networked circuits through which anti-Muslim sentiments travel, their virality, and their metaphorical overlap with the notion of contagion. What seems to be the original meme is simply a photo of President Obama standing to the right of DJ Khaled; there are blue curtains and two American flags in the background. Overlaid on the photo is text that reads, "Here is a photo of Obama and the leader of ISIS. They are plotting to steal a third term AND IMPLEMENT SHAKIRA LAW IN AMERICA" (fig. 1). The meme clearly relies on the idea of DJ Khaled as a generic bearded-Muslim-terrorist in order to be read as the "leader of ISIS." Another Shakira law meme inexplicably depicts a donut with a cursive form of writing forming the literal icing on the donut, claiming that "free Islamic donuts" were being distributed to children in order to perpetuate "Shakira law in America" (fig. 2).[1]

Though likely a humorous parody of Islamophobic discourses about shari'a law, the messages in these memes were taken at face value in at least some of the contexts in which they circulated, and similar memes—like the donut example—have also circulated as solemn warnings about the dangers of shari'a law as a potential contagion in liberal-democratic societies.[2] Sensationalistic popular understandings of shari'a law associate it with intimate forms of gendered oppression, such as the practice of taking multiple wives, women being forced to cover (i.e., wear the hijab), and even female genital cutting. In other words, shari'a law is often understood to frame the female (Muslim) body as belonging to men. Shakira, herself invoking the opposite of these gendered and sexualized stereotypes—i.e., connoting sexual freedom and even lasciviousness—creates an

Figure 2. A spoof meme about "Islamic donuts" used for propaganda, which was evidently believable to some people.

informative tension and even dissonance about the flexibility of stereotypical associations that cohere in seemingly lighthearted cultural productions. In these memes, the phrase "Shakira law" demonstrates how Muslims are often apprehended through flexible racialized and sexualized associations that can nevertheless have rigid and material consequences.

What can memes and their circulation tell us about how notions of contagion shape the context of surveilling Muslims in the United States? Memes are often discussed in terms of their ability to go "viral," suggesting a link to contagion. In the case of memes that invoke Muslim subjectivities, they also depend on the socially embedded idea of "terrorism as contractible" (Cacho 2012: 100)—i.e., as a dangerous disease that needs to be contained. These contemporary associations build on the history and legacy of immigration exclusions, xenophobia, and racializations of Asian Americans, including Southwest Asia and North Africa (SWANA) diasporas (Shah 2001; Gualtieri 2020). In this essay, I build on these observations about the racist deployments of the metaphor of virality to look at how popular cultural productions—traveling through viral circuits—ultimately buttress an infrastructure geared toward apprehending, and essentially capturing, Muslims.

Given their economic composition, memes are able to synthesize particularly gendered, sexualized, and racialized modes of capture that materially impact US Muslims' lives, as well as the life of anyone perceived to be such. Thinking about what it means for such memes to "go viral," memes also enable a consideration of contagion as a motivating metaphor that literally frames US/Muslim life. Moving beyond the humorous or ridiculous sentiments expressed in Shakira law memes and tweets, this essay explores the circuits of memes, internet hoax stories, and podcasts in relation to the technological (as embedded in a heteronormative and racialized) infrastructure of big data. Considering the enormity of the amount of data coupled with the tools to manipulate and collate it (e.g., including algorithms and metadata as aspects of this techno-universe), I look at how Muslims are apprehended, by which I mean interpreted and criminalized in order to justify representational and literal capture. Though notions of contagion are clearly entrenched in the logic of representational circuits, this essay will also foreground the metaphor of radiation to think in particular about the infrastructures of violence (embedded in the technological infrastructures of big data) as perpetuating "the fundamental violence of American inclusion, exclusion, and extraction" (Masco 2021: 9). The metaphor of radiation helps us think further about how these technologies—e.g., predictive algorithms that cull and shape data in motivated ways—can present themselves through the conceit of scientific objectivity while actually presenting a permeating silent and deadly threat.

Glitches

While "Shakira" law seems to reference a clearly human mistake or slippage—whereby the word *shari'a* slips into the more familiar name of a popular singer—it mimics the kinds of slippages that are increasingly common throughout predictive technologies. Operating through algorithms, which are often presented as disinterested compu-mathematical formulas, the technological infrastructure of prediction can be deadly. Ruha Benjamin (2019: 11) describes algorithms as "a set of instructions, rules, and calculations designed to solve problems" while micha cárdenas (2018: 27–29) offers that "algorithms can be low tech. Their form is similar to a cooking recipe."[3] In these definitions, algorithms can potentially be abolitionist and world-making tools. Yet as these same scholars note, insofar as the dominant use of algorithms has been to wield "historical information to make a prediction about the future,"[4] it is hard to miss the insidious consequences of prediction inherent in them. Predictive algorithms have been deployed toward deadly racist ends, particularly in state systems of capture, like domestic and military prisons (Benjamin 2016, 2019; Cheney-Lippold 2017; Miller 2019; O'Neil 2016; Stop LAPD Spying Coalition 2018, 2020).

As the example of predictive technologies demonstrates, supposedly objective technologies are necessarily built upon a classification scheme that is deeply embedded in social institutions of sexism, racism, heteronormativity, and other systems of oppression. The example of the slip from shari'a to Shakira demonstrates the feedback loop between social categorizations and the way the technologies both reify and operationalize these classifications. One only has to look at a couple of examples brought to us by the "autocorrect" function built into most email and social networking platforms to see this sort of slippage at work more widely. For example, consider a tweet by Huda F @yesimhotinthis (2018) that reads, "My iPhone just autocorrected hijab to hijack."[5] This tweet parallels the Shakira example insofar as it transforms the Arabic word *hijab* into the term *hijack*, a verb literally and figuratively associated with Arabs-as-terrorists since (at least) the 1970s. Another is my (personal) experience of emailing colleagues about our shared research on the racialization of Muslims, only to find that the email program consistently—and aggressively, I might add, as it would re-correct even after I went back to fix it—refigured the phrase into the *radicalization* of Muslims, a term used often in the realm of security studies, which frames Muslims through the racist and Orientalist lens of extremism.[6] Junaid Rana (2016: 120) uses the rubric of "racial infrastructure" to describe how the "racialization of Muslims is a flexible process that incorporates the portability of a number of race concepts, such as Blackness, Indigeneity, colonialism, genocide, immigration, and religion, in a system that appears contradictory and nonsensical." In this essay, I build on Rana's formulation of "racial infrastructure" to explore the way such infrastructures, perpetuated by technological infrastructures, lead to the apprehension and capture of Muslim subjects.

Theorizing the heteropatriarchal racial infrastructure exemplified in the Shakira law slip demonstrates that it depends on a tripartite structure, where classification and categorization schemata are reinforced by the technological infrastructure of big data to collect, arrange, manage, and flexibly manipulate huge troves of categorized data, while both of these schemata are motivated and bolstered by racial capitalism. Thinking about the social power of classification, Geoffrey Bowker and Susan Star (1999: 3) note that "the material force of categories appears always and instantly." Adding to this a consideration of the tendency of algorithms to miscategorize through what John Cheney-Lippold (2017: 65) describes as "neocategorization," the power of these social and technological infrastructures to shape our realities comes into greater focus. Taken together, these structures and processes coalesce in the ability to capture, a phenomenon that I will theorize through the idea of being apprehended.

Ruha Benjamin's (2019: 80) *Race after Technology* invites us to think capaciously and creatively about "glitches" like those we find in the autocorrect examples above and, in particular, to think of them as generative and informative rather than a fleeting mistake: "Glitches are generally considered a fleeting interruption of an otherwise benign system, not an enduring and constitutive feature of social life. But what if we understand glitches instead to be a slippery place . . . between fleeting and durable, micro-interactions and macro-structures, individual hate and institutional indifference?" Below, I follow up on the suggestion to ask questions about how the flexible heteropatriarchal racism of glitches—and, in this case, autocorrects—is built into the infrastructure of technology.

Most companies decline to discuss their autocorrect software, and the one that did discuss the topic gave an indication as to why: "Surreptitiousness seems to be the operating philosophy here: 'You do your best not to be noticed,' says Scott Taylor, the vice president of mobile solutions at Nuance [the company that created T9]" (Manjoo 2010). On phones (at least in 2010, according to what I could find), the software works by comparing what you type against a built-in dictionary. This seemingly straightforward explanation begs several questions: Which dictionary does the phone use? How does the phone deal with context in terms of what to suggest? And finally, how/does the phone "machine learn"? In 2010, the indication was that phone autocorrect software was moving toward crowdsourcing, which is a more open model (like Google Suggest), in which case what you are typing on your phone would be open and available to the internet broadly. Though there are "substantial privacy concerns with this approach—you would essentially be sending everything you type to servers in the Web" and one article speculated in 2010 that "phone makers would likely incorporate them only on an opt-in basis, if at all" (Manjoo 2010), it wouldn't be unreasonable to assume that autocorrect software now generally operates at that level.

Nevertheless, we can assume the two main examples named above—racialization and hijab—were already subject to this sort of sourcing, since they didn't occur in phones but rather in more embedded systems: like web-based media or email. So that would imply that *radicalization* and *hijack* were commonly used in mass online media. But we would also have to figure in the context-bound feature of autocorrect systems. This machine learning, therefore, demonstrates a learned affiliation between Muslims and associated characteristics (e.g., what they wear—hijab), and *radicalization* or *hijacking*.

These examples go beyond marking a quantitative fact about the frequency with which such terms are used and point toward a recognition of the ways that Muslims are usually figured in online discourses, coupled with the fact that the terms *hijab* and *racialization* do not appear as legitimate words in computer dictionaries. They chart an existing set of discourses associated with the populations they reference, in combination with a process—indicated by the term *speculative thought*—of creating the set of possibilities for apprehending these populations (here, understanding Muslims, Arabs, and others from SWANA through a biopolitical framing of population). I use *apprehend* intentionally to draw on its double meaning: both "to arrest someone for a crime" and "to understand or perceive." In other words, it is connected both to creating knowledge and to framing criminality. In relation to framing Muslims, I would suggest that we can also add a third meaning of the root word *apprehend*, this time in relation to the noun *apprehension*. Criminalizing Muslims depends on a melding of the earlier two meanings ("understand" and "criminalize") as well as the unease or anxiety that serves as a justification for capturing data in the first place. Ultimately, I argue that these three meanings coalesce around the core activity of capture—apprehending Muslims depends on a heteropatriarchal racial infrastructure that supports the cultural circuits of memes and other ephemeral products that circulate. Their circulation, in turn, creates knowledge and builds fear, helping to fuel the criminalization and capture of Muslims.

To Apprehend, Take 1: "Innocent Knowledge"

Setting the scene for how these three meanings (understanding, fearing, and capturing) of *apprehend* coalesce to frame Muslim life as criminal, the first part of this essay explores the game-changing National Public Radio (NPR) podcast *Serial*. The podcast focused on the case of Adnan Syed, who was accused of killing his ex-girlfriend Hae Min Lee and convicted, in large part, using "evidence" based on Islamophobic assumptions. Both the case and its sensationalized re-telling through a series of podcasts and other media demonstrate that through arbitrations of liberal notions of universality, "Whiteness is made through the Muslim" and that "the law is where white supremacy and racial violence get legitimated" (Razack, forthcoming). Here, the circuits I explore are the podcasts that retrospectively piece together the case. While the more well-known *Serial* popularizes Syed's case, the follow-up podcast *Undisclosed* convincingly argues that Syed was apprehended—both criminalized and captured—based on anti-Muslim racism. In this case, then, the court is a site where the practice of apprehending Muslims through racist filters gets codified. Significantly, Syed's case is also possibly one of the first court cases ever to employ metadata as part of the prosecution's evidence. Given that metadata can be marshaled as scientific-objective data at the same time that they are inherently abstracted from the particular details and contexts they reference, they are a brilliant example of how the technological infrastructure of big data operates as a tool of capture and apprehension of Muslims through and with racist infrastructures.

In the first season of *Serial*, the motivations of alleged killer Adnan Syed are uncritically presented through the long-standing Orientalist idea that "Muslim rage" emerges from "feelings of resentment, jealousy, and impotency" (Sheehi 2011: 69). Even an academic essay exploring whether Syed was racialized falls sway to the romanticism of a Shakespearean frame and uncritically accepts the explanatory power of Syed's "besmirched" honor as a compelling motivation for murder (Corredera 2016: 36). While the podcast purports to explore every possible facet of the case against Adnan Syed, a Pakistani Muslim teen who was later convicted of murdering his ex-girlfriend, *Serial* never questions the discursive framework of the honor-shame nexus as a compelling motivation for murder. Despite the journalist Sarah Koenig's evident desire to exonerate Syed, she never questions the prosecutor's framing of Syed's alleged motivation—that he had sacrificed so much to be with his non-Muslim girlfriend that their breakup created an unbearable severing of his Muslim honor, and an anguish that drove him to murder.[7] That the explanatory frame for the alleged murder was not read nor even considered through the tediously common language of the "crime of passion," endlessly invoked in mainstream domestic violence cases, demonstrates how Syed's case figured him through the lens of Muslim ways of life—as collectively bound by honor and shame—and not through the lens of "our" (i.e., US) way of life, through which he would have had recourse to the individualized logic of the legal category of the crime of passion, which figures the murder as the regrettable action of an otherwise reasonable person overcome by a fleeting surge of emotion. In other words, the prosecution would have had to build a case about Syed as an individual who fits the profile of a domestic violence batterer rather than the broader religio-cultural "commonsense" racist argument about Islam.

Despite a plethora of online blogs and articles defending Sarah Koenig and *Serial* in general for its framing of the case, the narrative momentum of the podcast (known for shifting the landscape of podcasts from single, contained stories to a serialized episodic format that keeps people tuning in week after week) depends on anti-Muslim racist assumptions. Despite revealing the dearth of convictable evidence in Syed's case, Koenig maintains the possibility of Syed's culpability through two mechanisms. The first is an alleged eyewitness account on which the prosecution's case mostly relied (in the interest of space, I won't go into this here), and the second is the power of the Islamophobic narrative that casts Adnan as a jilted lover who murdered his ex-girlfriend because she coerced him to date outside of his religion and then broke up with him—the assumption being that since he had betrayed his religious/cultural context, her leaving him pushed him into a murderous state.

The sheer improbability of such an interpretation is completely undercut by the "Islamophobic industry" that has cropped up all around to provide countless documents attesting to the criminalizing and murderous practices supposedly lurking inside of Islam. Prosecuted in a time period before the advent of memes and podcasts (the early 2000s), the circuits of apprehension in Syed's case pass through what Colin Powell would come to describe as a "terror-industrial complex" and what James Risen describes as a "Homeland security-industrial complex" (Rana 2016: 113). In Syed's case, a report produced by the Enehey Group (1999) on behalf of the state's detectives offers the following analysis of Syed's case:

> Clearly Mr. Syed faced almost insurmountable odds to meet with this "infidel or devil" [his high school girlfriend] in secret. Ownership is not outside of his cultural belief system. After giving her a veil, literally covering her so that only he could have her, he set her apart from all others and for him alone. . . . Under Islamic law her murder was sanctioned. For many "ethnic" Pakistanis incidents like these are common-place and in Pakistan this would not have been a crime but probably a matter of honor.

That such a report would exist is not in itself surprising, but what does surprise Rabia Chaudry—a friend of Adnan Syed's family who brought his case to Koenig's attention—is the extent to which Koenig accepts the report as fact. For example, Koenig meets with Chaudry to ask if it is true that "if a Muslim man gives a woman a scarf, he owns her or it's like some form of ownership" (Chaudry 2016). Indeed, over the course of the podcast, Koenig demonstrates both this kind of direct racism as well as "racist love" (Chin and Chan 1972; Lott 1993). As one critical online article notes: "If Koenig is a flawed, unreliable narrator, we should add 'cultural tourist' to the list of flaws" (Kang 2014).

The aforementioned report clearly parallels the language of the so-called Muslim ban executive order (Trump 2017), which sought to exclude "those who engage in acts of bigotry or hatred (including 'honor' killings [and] other forms of violence against women)" and which relied on the logic of Islam as intrinsically violent toward women, framing Islam as inherently backward with respect to gender, sexuality, and women's rights. An additional detail—uncovered in a separate podcast, *Undisclosed*—further demonstrates how Syed's case was always already figured through a monster-terrorist-fag framework (Puar and Rai 2002). A key alibi witness for Syed, Bilal, who could testify that he was with Syed at the alleged time of the murder (Syed was practicing a speech he was scheduled to deliver the following night at his mosque) failed to show up to Syed's trial or respond to a subpoena. Following up on this detail, the *Undisclosed* podcast revealed that Bilal had been arrested by Baltimore County police on charges of sexual misconduct with a fourteen-year-old boy; they told him they would drop the charges if he left the country for a few years. Such direct interference in the types of evidence that could be presented suggests that Syed's case was determined by a racializing-sexualizing assemblage that figures Islam and Muslims through the hazy associations illustrated by the Shakira law meme, themselves shored up by the heteropatriarchal racial infrastructure of anti-Muslim racism. Racializing and sexualizing assemblages invoke and create incorporeal transformations—Gilles Deleuze and Félix Guattari's ([1980] 1987: 80) term for the process by which people and bodies can be materially impacted by the significations and "overcoding" that shape how others understand them. One example could be the figure of the "thug" (wearing a hoodie), which in the case of Trayvon Martin (to name only one high-profile case) led not only to his death but to the exoneration of his killer under stand-your-ground laws, since Martin's hoodie effectively incorporeally transformed him into an always already dangerous criminal.[8] Another example that particularly informs anti-Muslim racism is the category of the "terrorist," which creates a literal framework for capturing Muslims and/or Arabs and questioning them in search of "actionable intelligence." In these cases and others like them, the two meanings of *apprehend* slide into one another—a category for understanding and framing a group of people shifts into a category used to criminalize and literally capture and charge them. This melding, in fact, coalesces in the idea of framing a group of people. Playing out through "data assemblages," the heteropatriarchal racial infrastructure here shadows the technological infrastructures, which can incorporeally transform people's lives through manipulation of even purportedly innocuous metadata.

Circuits/Contagion v. Infrastructure/Radiation

As mentioned above, contagion is also built into the Shakira law meme; the fear specifically named is that shari'a law will spread in the United States, with the underlying idea that it would metastasize and eventually take over. As Sherene Razack (2008: 149) notes, the moral panics activated in relation to shari'a law—sometimes even in small towns, with no foreign-born or Muslim residents at all, that feel "compelled to announce [their] prohibition of the stoning of women" succumb to a fear-logic that the "Muslims are coming" (see also Naber 2008; Kundnani 2015). One trajectory of this fear-contagion logic leads to a painful irony of Syed's case: Syed was denied bail (a fact that the podcast *Undisclosed* credits with leading to his eventual conviction as it redirected resources that would have gone into his defense) based on the state's argument that he was a "flight risk." Despite all that Syed offered in exchange for bail (he agreed to waive extradition; his passport was expired but he offered to give it up anyway; his parents and others offered to put up their house for collateral as part of a forfeiture agreement; and he offered to submit to electronic monitoring under house arrest), the state deployed racist logic to argue that he should remain in jail. For example, the state responded that (1) Syed had a lot of resources that could help him escape; (2) because Muslims have similar names, it would be easy for him to get another passport; and (3) there is a record of jilted Pakistani men who have killed their lovers and escaped to Pakistan (which was untrue, but even if it were accurate, Syed is a US, not a Pakistani, citizen). The denial of bail to Syed demonstrates the tenacity of Islamophobic narratives (even before 9/11, of course), but it also reveals a particular framing of "terrorism as contractible" (Cacho 2012: 100).

We can draw several conclusions from this exploration of Adnan Syed's case as popularized through *Serial* and subsequently through several podcasts and even an HBO special series. As a case study, NPR's *Serial* is embedded in the liberal logics of the justice system and its redemptive possibilities despite its proven flaws. In this respect, it is an excellent example of the way that the will to knowledge—the meaning of *apprehend* that depends on the conceit of innocent knowledge—can operate in tandem with the impetus toward criminalization and capture. Because the case was argued in 1999, it demonstrates that the racialized/sexualized/ gendered stereotype of the "terrorist" was not inaugurated with 9/11, and, indeed, has been in development and operation since well before. Finally, the podcast framework itself references the metaphor of contagion, and provokes a consideration of how information goes "viral"—whether in the form of memes, storytelling mechanisms like podcasts, or metadata—and what its modes of infection are.

To Apprehend, Take 2: Metadata

So far, these observations about the Syed case, as framed by the kinds of sexualizing and racializing assemblages that we saw in the Shakira law meme, tell a familiar story about the way Muslim lives are shaped by the discourses and representations through which they are figured and apprehended. Yet another vector through which to analyze the Shakira meme is through its relationship to data assemblages (Kitchin 2014: 25) and "speculative thought." "Speculative thought, or 'soft thought,' is not a form of reasoning modeled after any form of human reasoning. It is a particular form of algorithmic cognition that is independent of human thought or intervention" (Dixon-Román 2016: 486). In the data sense, speculative thought therefore gestures to the way that machines and software can impact material realities. Kitchin notes that since the word *data* comes from the Latin root "to give," the word is actually a misnomer: "Technically, then, what we understand as data are actually *capta* (derived from the Latin *capere*, meaning 'to take'); those units of data that have been selected and harvested from the sum of all potential data" (Kitchin and Dodge 2011). As Johanna Drucker (2011) argues, "No 'data' pre-exist their parameterization. *Data are capta*, taken not given, constructed as an interpretation of the phenomenal world, not inherent in it." The concept of data assemblages, then, combines the harvesting—to denote both the selective taking and the uses to which they are put—of data with their ability to materially shape a person's life. Recalling Junaid Rana's description of the racialization of Muslims as flexible, it is important to contextualize the processes of

classifying and creating categories in relation to the process of collecting
and managing endlessly culled and stored data, and the machine-learned
ability to apply these data to existing categories, or create new ones, in
whatever way matches the desired narrative. There is perhaps no better
example of such a practice than the potential uses and deployments of
metadata, and the idea that Syed's case is potentially the first to use them in
a court is significant precisely because of the way that anti-Muslim bias was
hidden under the radar of this supposedly objective evidence.

Because, as Dixon-Román (2016: 483) argues, "Data are assemblages
that are more-than-human ontologies that consist of the forces of socio-
political relations," these captured data also actively interact with existing
racializing and sexualizing assemblages. The case of Adnan Syed likely
represents the first time that cell phone data was introduced as evidence in
a court case in the state of Maryland. Beyond its novelty, this interesting
fact becomes all the more so once we realize that the cell phone data
introduced in Syed's case actually represent possibly the first time that
metadata were introduced to literally frame a criminal. The state (prosecution) argued that Syed could be placed at the scene of the disposal and
burial of Lee's body through the use of evidence cataloging cell phone
"pings." It used cell phone records and expert witnesses to argue that
incoming calls to Syed's cell phone "pinged" the cell phone tower closest to
the burial site (a park on the outskirts of town) at the approximate time that
her body was placed there, according to the state's own time line. Serial
does not question this evidence and therefore mobilizes it to sustain and
animate the question of whether Adnan did kill Hae. As the Undisclosed
podcast uncovers, though, the assumptions about such metadata were
inherently false—even according to experts who could have been called
(but were never contacted) at the time. When cell phone towers are over-
loaded with a glut of incoming and outgoing calls, excess calls will auto-
matically be redirected to another, less occupied tower, so the record of
"pings" doesn't actually provide evidence of Syed's location. Nevertheless,
it functioned to serve as evidence of his location in the eyes of the jury that
convicted him. In this way, the Syed case foreshadows (or, indeed, establishes the precedent for) the capture of metadata in the current context—a
practice that President Obama would later attempt to downplay in his
comments following the Snowden revelations about the PRISM program,
when he said: "No one is listening to your telephone calls" (Feldmann
2013). Though PRISM allowed the NSA to collect bulk data from private

corporations like Google, Facebook, Apple, Yahoo, and Microsoft, Obama's comments imply that direct surveillance of the content of personal communication would be a breach of privacy laws, whereas capturing the bulk data form of those same communications (the metadata of the time and place during which a phone call or text is sent and received, along with its duration) is not a breach of privacy. In the case of Adnan Syed, as is the implication for subsequent and future cases, his cell phone metadata provided material evidence for his capture and incarceration, despite the fact that it could not actually link him to the crime. If Adnan Syed's case is the analog precursor to the kind of predictive analytics that currently operate in countless social media (and other) platforms, it is a chilling and foreboding case to say the least. Wielding the notion that data are actually capta—pieces of information that are taken—metadata can in fact be captured and harvested to serve the argument of the state.

Obama's dismissive comment that the state is not listening to our phone calls aims to invisibilize the technological infrastructure that serves to apprehend Muslims through racist patterns. Using metadata to apprehend and criminalize Muslims, algorithmic manipulations of data create what John Cheney-Lippold (2017: 47) calls "measurable types," which are "ultimately classifications, empirically observed and transcoded as data, that become discrete analytical models for use in profiling and/or knowledge abstraction." Developed and honed by private companies like Google, the concept of measurable types also demonstrates how private capital interests can partner with the state, shoring up the terror-industrial and homeland security complexes mentioned above. The (viral) circulation of (toxic) memes tells a familiar story about the way Muslim lives are shaped by the discourses and representations through which they are apprehended. When people are profiled into highly fraught categories, like "terrorist," through algorithmic interpretations of their online activity, they are subject to a big-data form of "soft biopolitics" (Cheney-Lippold 2017: 132–37).

To Apprehend, Take 3: Data Industrial-Complexes/ Infrastructure

The form of criminal apprehension demonstrated in Syed's case, now more popularly operating through cyber- or information technology, has roots in what Robert Scheer (2015: 103) calls the "military intelligence complex." It is an apt description given that the Pentagon's Defense Advanced Research Project Agency (DARPA), one of the key drivers of the weaponization of cyber/data, was created under the Eisenhower administration (Scheer 2015: 106). Referring to the role of private corporations and the dubious role of the profit imperative to perpetuate punishing institutions, like the military and prisons, the idea of the "military intelligence complex" also allows us to consider how our everyday and leisure uses of technology can be weaponized. Shoshana Zuboff argues in *The Age of Surveillance Capitalism* (2019: 182) that "both the world and our lives are pervasively rendered as information." Our lives-rendered-as-information are then transformed into a form of "behavioral surplus" (i.e., a catalog of behaviors, likes, and interests that can be monetized), which are then subject to extraction— through an "extraction architecture" (Zuboff 2019: 129)—by information-service companies that can sell our lives-rendered-as-information for profit.

With the "extraction architecture" already developed and in place, it is a relatively short path to the ability of the state to harness data toward capture, and even to think of data in relation to weapons of mass destruction (WMDs). As the example of convicting Syed based on metadata demonstrates, our "digital selves" (Cheney-Lippold 2017) can be weaponized, a move that we could also connect to the 2004 additions to the definition of "weapons of mass destruction." Taking advantage of the US invasion of Iraq in 2003, the *National Military Strategy of the United States*, issued in 2004, extended the phrase "WMDs" to "Weapons of Mass Destruction or Effect (WMD/E)," which was designed to include "more asymmetrical" weapons such as "cyberattacks" (*National Military Strategy of the United States* 2004). In this way, the internet, and information technology more generally, were codified as weapons in relation to military strategy.

Though momentum had been building for decades, the events of 9/11 paved the way for the decimation of privacy in the service of security, which in turn enabled private corporations like Google and Facebook to play a crucial role in the weaponization of data. One of the prime examples of this is a governmental program called "Total Information Awareness" proposed by the admiral John Poindexter in 2002.[9] This chilling and direct plan to create a "surveillance society," described by the American Civil Liberties Union (ACLU) as a "virtual dragnet," was defunded by Congress in 2003 (Diresta 2018; see also Scheer 2015: 107–13; Zuboff 2019: 116). Yet as Zuboff, Scheer, and others note, private sector companies like Google and Facebook were simultaneously busy developing technologies to gather, store, and mine capta for capital/ist purposes. As private companies, they were able to sidestep regulatory processes designed to guard against the sort of extraction their services render, and punitive state institutions have benefited from the secrecy with which they have been able to access and deploy such privately obtained data.

The weaponization of information is, of course, nothing new in the long, overlapping histories of policing and military warfare. In particular, we can locate these histories in relation to the keyword *intelligence* and its deployment in governmental institutions like the Federal Bureau of Investigation (FBI) and the Central Intelligence Agency (CIA) that frame their work through the rubrics of counterinsurgency. Significant here is the role that private companies play in the mining, capturing, and ultimately criminalizing of data, and the ability of governmental entities to hide behind the protections of private corporations to cull the data in the first place. Once they are culled, all that is needed is a security-based justification to commandeer them. That justification is easily fabricated and perpetuated through the prolific terror-industrial complex.

Going Viral—Circuits

Another means for *apprehending* in the criminalizing sense operates through the ("viral") spread of fear. Looking more closely at the role of private corporations in enabling and disseminating racism and white supremacy, here I explore the virality of memes and the ways they shape anti-Muslim racist rhetoric. Though mainstream companies like Facebook may claim to be merely a venue for the exchange of ideas, Jane Lytvynenko (2019) notes that Islamophobia makes these companies a lot of money: "Researchers say Facebook is the primary mainstream platform where extremists organize and anti-Muslim content is deliberately spread." They also reported that out of the top ten stories published on websites "publishing disinformation for profit . . . eight had the word 'Muslim' in the title." Indeed, there is a whole industry working to actively proliferate (if not produce, since those associations were long active well before these technologies) such racist associations.

Hoax-based stories that go viral about Muslims often have long afterlives. Consider, for example, a hoax about a made-up group called "Public Purity" that "posted flyers asking people to 'limit the presence of dogs in the public sphere' out of sensitivity to the area's 'large Muslim community'" (Daro 2018). The story that went viral operated on the false assumption that Muslims are offended by dogs, and fabricated outrage that such a

Figure 3. A meme portraying AOC saying to Ilhan Omar, "Now that you divorced your husband, does that mean you are no longer sister and brother?"

cultural-religious belief would curtail the public actions of non-Muslims and their dogs. Despite having been disproven in 2016, the hoax was still actively circulating in 2018. While we could certainly describe the circulation of this story in terms of its virality, the impact of its active afterlife also draws our attention to the metaphor of radioactivity. Like the depleted uranium used in US munitions because of its ability to penetrate armor and its relatively low radioactive status, which has nevertheless caused devastating long-term, chronic, and deadly health problems among the population in Iraq living with its remnants, pervasive and tenacious hoaxes about Muslims also have deleterious effects.

A similar thing could be said about the fabricated scandal that Ilhan Omar married her brother. Even in an online article by *Business Insider* ostensibly disproving the claim, it opens with the statement that "Omar has still not explained some puzzling discrepancies and inconsistencies in her marriage history" (Panetta 2019). These "inconsistencies," of course, can only be understood as such within a heteronormative frame of reference in relation to the institution of marriage and with sexualized Orientalist and Islamophobic stereotypes fueling the story (fig. 3). One of the several memes addressing the Omar hoax depicts Congress members Ilhan Omar and Alexandria Ocasio-Cortez sitting next to one another, with overlaid text putting the following words in AOC's mouth: "Now that you divorced your husband, does that mean you are no longer sister and brother?" As such memes go viral, despite being completely divorced from reality, they demonstrate both how lucrative anti-Muslim racism is and how easily such hoaxes can materially impact lives—in the case of the so-called jihad squad, this impact is evident in the number of death threats they receive. In her analysis of the way that Trump exacerbated such death threats—for example, by amplifying a meme suggesting that Ilhan Omar downplayed the gravity of 9/11—Zeinab Farokhi (2021: 21) describes such activity as "state-sponsored cyber Islamophobia" which results in "legitimizing and normalizing dehumanization and criminalization of the Muslim body, albeit in more subtle and invisible ways" in the digital realm (16).

Though we are used to thinking about these kinds of hoaxes and misinformation as "going viral," Wendy Hui Kyong Chun (2016: 3) points out that virality is perhaps an incomplete or faulty metaphor, particularly given the way it is prone to fear-based assumptions. She suggests that "information spreads not like a powerful, overwhelming virus, but rather like a long, updated thin chain. Information is not Ebola but instead the common cold." Brought into exaggerated relief during the current pandemic, as applied to the memes about Ilhan Omar and her brother, this suggestion implies that such memes are pervasive and persistent, consistently spreading and renewing the underlying Orientalist assumptions about Islam as immoral and hyperpatriarchal, and they can spread easily in unsensational ways. Indeed, the colloquial way of describing memes and other cultural products as going viral suggests that they are quite benign, and the economy that depends on their circulation also depends, to some extent, on this underlying assumption of benign intents and effects. This essay has sought to expose how the circuits of such memes shore up anti-Black, anti-Asian, and anti-Muslim infrastructures and how the anti-Muslim racism of memes like the Omar marriage hoax ultimately serves to shore up white supremacy (Razack, forthcoming).

Afterlives of Data

If the circuits of anti-Muslim memes and internet hoaxes can be understood as a permeating, long thin chain of toxic misinformation, the underlying heteropatriarchal racist infrastructure that sustains them can be theorized in terms of the metaphor of radiation. Here, I draw inspiration from Lars MacKenzie's article "The Afterlife of Data," which focuses on how trans people who obtain legal name changes can be "haunted by data." *Haunting* is appropriate, and I begin with haunting and the idea of afterlives here because of the backdrop of violence and death that impacts these communities.

Bridging back to the idea of "going viral," multiple online articles report that "Politicians have also used anti-Muslim rhetoric to bolster their popularity among voters, which then takes off on social media" (Lytvynenko 2019). And also, to Wendy Hui Kyong Chun's point about letting go of an attachment to the origins of these memes and hoaxes, a clear strategy is to release a sensationalized meme/tweet/story and simply apologize later, as the Illinois Republican County Chairman Association did after sharing the meme that inaugurated the term "the jihad squad" (Chiu 2019). Apologizing after the fact, of course, does not prevent the afterlives that the meme/image will have and, in this sense, it may be more useful to think about it in terms of a half-life of radiation. What essentially makes matter radioactive is its instability; radiation is the energy released in particles or rays from this highly unstable matter, a decay that is measured by the unit of a half-life.

Though the concept of a "half-life" implies that it is constantly trending toward stability, the process of decay inherent to a half-life means that radiation is consistently released. In other words, it also accounts for the decay built into the system, but the decay and the tendency toward decay are precisely the source of the potential illness. Yet it doesn't necessarily have a precise target or host, nor does it have to. It simply radiates—indeed, the metaphor here correlatively maps onto the substance.

My case study meme here is the Shari'a Barbie meme. Much like the Shakira law meme, it draws on sexualized, racialized, Orientalist, anti-Muslim stereotypes. The Shari'a Barbie meme started circulating in November 2017, when Mattel released a muhajabah Barbie, inspired by Olympic fencer Ibtihaj Muhammad. Various versions of the meme depict Barbie with black eyes and bruises, and in one case with a melted face presumably due to an acid attack. They also include text that reads, "Comes with jihab [sic], bruises, and quran" and "stoning accessories available for additional purchase" (fig. 4). Captions accompanying the circulation of Shari'a Barbie memes say things like, "I will not celebrate the subjugation of women being symbolized in a child's toy," demonstrating the popular equation of Islam with brutal gender violence and oppression. Yet though the meme originated in relation to the hijab-wearing Barbie, it was revived by Daniel P. Leonard, a school board member in Illinois in the summer of 2019 when he posted a tweet directed toward Rashida Tlaib. In response to a Fox News report about Tlaib calling for a hunger strike to shut down Immigration and Customs Enforcement (ICE), Leonard tweeted: "My life would be complete if she/they die" (Bella 2019). He also connected Tlaib to the revived Shari'a Barbie meme. In this literal death wish, Leonard's tweet demonstrates how the meme's half-life (in the radiation sense) and afterlife (in the sense of being revived in circulation) are permeated with and, in turn, continue to radiate, lethal anti-Muslim racism.

Tracing the paths, not to mention the interpretations, of ephemeral artifacts like the Shakira law and Shari'a Barbie memes is impossible, and

Figure 4. A racist meme response to the first Barbie in hijab. Part of Mattel's "Sheroes" series, the doll was designed after Olympic fencer Ibtihaj Muhammad.

yet that is precisely part of their power. The assemblages these memes synthesize and capture illuminate the sexualized and racialized assumptions attached to shari'a law and even Islam more generally, coalescing to perpetuate quotidian, but no less dangerous—and potentially deadly—forms of anti-Muslim racism. Thinking back to the "speculative thought" of autocorrect functions, particularly those that correct discussions of "racialized" Muslims to "radicalized" Muslims, one also has to wonder at the "data afterlives" (MacKenzie 2017) that such mistaken "corrections" will have.

Toward a Conclusion

In her book *Updating to Remain the Same*, Wendy Hui Kyong Chun (2016: 15) encourages us to move away from "dramatic chartings and maps of 'viral spread' toward questions of infrastructure and justice." Describing information spread as having an "undead" quality, she also suggests that we shift "away from an epistemology of outing, in which we are obsessed with 'discovering' 'Patient Zero,'as though knowing the first case could solve all subsequent problems."[10] In other words, we would do well to ask in what ways the metaphors of virus and contagion feed into the logics of anti-Asian (including SWANA) and anti-Muslim racism. Thinking about Christina Sharpe's (2016: 5) discussion of the "afterlives of slavery" as well as Lars MacKenzie's consideration of how the "afterlife of data" impacts trans subjectivity and material life can also invite us to shift toward different metaphors for understanding the deadly impact of data/intelligence/ weaponization in the service of institutional anti-Muslim racism, and foundational modes of anti-Blackness.

Building on the argument in the introduction of *An Imperialist Love Story* (Jarmakani 2015: 39) about the way the metaphor of radiation "reflects the structure of hegemony—the ways power can operate in seemingly

invisible, unsuspecting ways while simultaneously having powerful material effects," I suggest we think about the deployment of data through the
metaphor of radiation, and particularly in relation to the question of its
"undead" quality and its multiple "afterlives." The metaphor accounts for
the way the toxin can live on in silent and potentially deadly ways. Through
the idea of the "half-life" of radiation, it also accounts for the decay built
into the system, and the way in which the decay and the tendency toward
decay (radioactive half-life) are precisely the potential source of illness. Yet
it doesn't necessarily have a precise target or host. It simply radiates. What
essentially makes matter radioactive is instability. Far from an innocent
mistake or a disinterested capture, the unstable circulation of data,
whether through viral memes or silently culled metadata, plays a central
role in the perpetuation of gendered anti-Muslim racism.

· ·

Amira Jarmakani, she/her/hers, is professor of women's, gender, and sexuality studies and affiliated faculty with the Center for Islamic and Arabic Studies at San Diego
State University. She is the author of two books, *An Imperialist Love Story: Desert
Romances and the War on Terror* (2015) and *Imagining Arab Womanhood: The Cultural Mythology of Veils, Harems, and Belly Dancers in the U.S.* (2008), which won the National
Women's Studies Association Gloria E. Anzaldúa book prize. She is also a coeditor of
the forthcoming collection *Sajjilu Arab American: A Reader in SWANA Studies*. She is
past-president of the Arab American Studies Association and a series advisor for the
Critical Arab American Studies Series with Syracuse University Press.

Notes

1   Adding to the humor, Snopes and other sites revealed the writing to actually be
    a made-up language from *Lord of the Rings*. www.snopes.com/fact-check/lord
    -rings-donut/.

2   For more on the "Shakira law" meme, see Jarmakani 2020.

3   Similarly, in an antiracist Critical Code Studies discussion group, moderated by
    Mark Marino, Sarah Ciston, Zach Mann, and Jeremy Douglass, @Samya offers
    this explanation of an algorithm: how you conceptualize a process from start to
    end (and then describe that process to the computer), see Roy 2021.

4   The quote comes from the documentary *Coded Bias* (Kantayya 2020), which
    focuses on the analysis and advocacy of computer scientist Joy Buolamwini and
    features the work of Cathy O'Neil, Safiya Umoja Noble, and others who work on
    exposing the racial biases built into the infrastructure of artificial intelligence
    and facial recognition technologies.

5   Thanks to Layla Zbinden for bringing this to my attention.

6   One of the first times I remember this happening was in email communication
    with Andrea Miller in 2013. Another example of this sort of autocorrect slippage
    comes from my colleague Keith Feldman, who reports having the word

coloniality autocorrected to *collegiality*, a humorous slip when considering how universities have sought to temper faculty critiques of colonialism and settler colonialism (particularly in relation to Palestinian advocacy) through the discourse of "civility" (pers. comm., November 16, 2020). For more on the weaponization of "civility" in the academy, see Salaita 2015.

7   While Koenig (2014) does consider the possibility that anti-Muslim bias played a role in Adnan Syed's case, she presents it through the sweeping and unnuanced claim made by Syed's mother that he was convicted because he is Muslim. Not bothering to put this claim into context, Koenig therefore quickly and easily dismisses it.

8   For more on theorizations of the "thug" and the "hoodie," see Amar 2017 and Nguyen 2015.

9   Thanks to Lucas Power for first making me aware of TIA, and especially for formative and ongoing conversations about data, big and small.

10 Noting, in particular, how abysmally efforts to contain COVID-19 failed, even our experience with an actual viral pathogen during the COVID-19 global pandemic suggests the wisdom of such an approach, which emphasizes shifts in habit rather than locating and rooting out the "original" pathogen.

Works Cited

Amar, Paul. 2017. "Thug Love: Populism, Policing, and Resistance from Egypt and Brazil to Trump's America." Bruce E. Porteous lecture, San Diego State University, San Diego, CA, April 10.

Bella, Timothy. 2019. "A School Board Member's Facebook Post Suggested His 'Life Would Be Complete' if Rashida Tlaib Died." *Washington Post*, July 25. www.washingtonpost.com/nation/2019/07/25/daniel-leonard-rashida-tlaib-death-new-jersey-school-board/.

Benjamin, Ruha. 2016. "Catching Our Breath: Critical Race STS and the Carceral Imagination." *Engaging Science, Technology, and Society* 2: 145–56.

Benjamin, Ruha. 2019. *Race after Technology: Abolitionist Tools for the New Jim Code*. Cambridge, MA: Polity Press.

Bowker, Geoffrey C., and Susan Leigh Star. 1999. *Sorting Things Out: Classification and Its Consequences*. Cambridge, MA: MIT Press.

Cacho, Lisa Marie. 2012. *Social Death: Racialized Rightlessness and the Criminalization of the Unprotected*. New York: New York University Press.

cárdenas, micha. 2018. "The Android Goddess Declaration: After Man(ifestos)." In *Bodies of Information: Intersectional Feminism and Digital Humanities*, edited by Elizabeth Losh and Jacqueline Wernimont, 25–38. Minneapolis: University of Minnesota Press.

Chaudry, Rabia. 2016. "Islamophobia in the Trial of Adnan Syed: Rabia Chaudry on America's Anti-Muslim Industry." *Lit Hub*, August 24. lithub.com/islamophobia-in-the-trial-of-adnan-syed/.

Cheney-Lippold, John. 2017. *We Are Data: Algorithms and the Making of Our Digital Selves*. New York: New York University Press.

Chin, Frank, and Jeffery Paul Chan. 1972. "Racist Love." In *Seeing Through Shuck*, edited by Richard Kostelanetz, 65–79. New York: Ballantine Books.

Chiu, Allyson. 2019. "A Meme Called Four Democrats 'The Jihad Squad.' A State GOP Group Is Sorry for Sharing It." *Washington Post*, July 22. www.washingtonpost .com/nation/2019/07/22/meme-called-four-democrats-jihad-squad-state-gop -group-is-sorry-sharing-it/.

Chun, Wendy Hui Kyong. 2016. *Updating to Remain the Same: Habitual New Media*. Cambridge, MA: MIT Press.

Corredera, Vanessa. 2016. "'Not a Moor Exactly': Shakespeare, *Serial*, and Modern Constructions of Race." *Shakespeare Quarterly* 67, no. 1: 30–50.

Daro, Ishmael N. 2018. "How a Hoax about Muslims Wanting to Ban Dogs in Public Keeps Going Viral." *BuzzFeed News*, April 6. www.buzzfeednews.com/article /ishmaeldaro/hoax-muslims-ban-dogs-for-public-purity-manchester.

Deleuze, Gilles and Félix Guattari. (1980) 1987. *A Thousand Plateaus*. Translated by Brian Massumi. Minneapolis: University of Minnesota Press, 1987.

Diresta, Renee. 2018. "How the Tech Giants Created What Darpa Couldn't." *Wired*, May 29. www.wired.com/story/darpa-total-informatio-awareness/.

Dixon-Román, Ezekiel. 2016. "Algo-Ritmo: More-Than-Human Performative Acts and the Racializing Assemblages of Algorithmic Architectures." *Cultural Studies, Critical Methodologies* 16, no. 5: 482–90.

Drucker, Johanna. 2011. "Humanities Approaches to Graphical Display." *Digital Humanities Quarterly* 5, no. 1: paragraph 8. www.digitalhumanities.org/dhq/vol/5/1 /000091/000091.html.

Enehey Group. 1999. "Report on Islamic Thought and Culture with Emphasis on Pakistan: A Comparative Study Relevant to the Upcoming Trial of Adnan Syed." undisclosed-podcast.com/docs/6/Consultant%27s%20Report%20on%20Islamic %20Thought%20and%20Culture.pdf.

F., Huda (@yesimhotinthis). 2018. "My iPhone just corrected hijab to hijacked." Twitter, July 28, 8:01 p.m. twitter.com/yesimhotinthis/status/1023357836603080710.

Farokhi, Zeinab. 2021. "Cyber *Homo Sacer*: A Critical Analysis of Cyber Islamophobia in the Wake of the Muslim Ban." *Islamophobia Studies Journal* 6, no. 1 (Spring): 14–32.

Feldmann, Linda. 2013. "Obama on NSA Data-mining: 'Nobody is Listening to Your Telephone Calls.'" *Christian Science Monitor*, June 7. https://www.csmonitor.com /USA/Politics/DC-Decoder/2013/0607/Obama-on-NSA-data-mining-Nobody-is -listening-to-your-telephone-calls.

Gualtieri, Sarah M. A. 2020. *Arab Routes: Pathways to Syrian California*. Stanford, CA: Stanford University Press.

Jarmakani, Amira. 2015. *An Imperialist Love Story: Desert Romances and the War on Terror*. New York: New York University Press.

Jarmakani, Amira. 2020. "Shiny, Happy Imperialism: An Affective Exploration of Ways of Life in the War on Terror." In *Affect and Literature*, edited by Alex Houen, 373–89. Cambridge: Cambridge University Press.

Kang, Jay Caspian. 2014. "White Reporter Privilege." *Awl*, November. www.theawl .com/2014/11/white-reporter-privilege/.

Kantayya, Shalini, dir. 2020. *Coded Bias.* Coproduced by Sabine Hoffman. Released November 11. Brooklyn, NY: 7th Empire Media.

Kitchin, Rob. 2014. *The Data Revolution: Big Data, Open Data, Data Infrastructures and their Consequences.* Los Angeles, CA: Sage.

Kitchin, Rob, and Martin Dodge. 2011. *Code/Space: Software and Everyday Life.* Cambridge, MA: MIT Press.

Koenig, Sarah. 2014. "The Best Defense is a Good Defense." In *Serial,* podcast, December 4. serialpodcast.org/season-one/10/the-best-defense-is-a-good -defense.

Kundnani, Arun. 2015. *The Muslims Are Coming! Islamophobia, Extremism, and the Domestic War on Terror.* London: Verso.

Lott, Eric. 1993. *Love and Theft: Blackface Minstrelsy and the American Working Class.* Oxford: Oxford University Press.

Lytvynenko, Jane. 2019. "Anti-Muslim Hate Speech Is Absolutely Relentless on Social Media Even as Platforms Crack Down on Other Extremist Groups." *BuzzFeed News,* March 18. www.buzzfeednews.com/article/janelytvynenko/islamophobia -absolutely-relentless-social-media.

MacKenzie, Lars Z. 2017. "The Afterlife of Data: Identity, Surveillance, and Capitalism in Trans Credit Reporting." *Transgender Studies Quarterly* 4, no. 1: 45–60.

Manjoo, Farhad. 2010. "Yes, I'll Matty You." *Slate,* July 13. slate.com/technology/2010 /07/how-your-cell-phone-s-autocorrect-software-works-and-why-it-s-getting -better.html.

Masco, Joseph. 2021. *The Future of Fallout, and Other Episodes in Radioactive World-Making.* Durham, NC: Duke University Press.

Miller, Andrea. 2019. "Shadows of War, Traces of Policing: The Weaponization of Space and the Sensible in Preemption." In *Captivating Technology: Race, Carceral Technoscience, and Liberatory Imagination in Everyday Life,* edited by Ruha Benjamin, 86–106. Durham, NC: Duke University Press.

Nguyen, Mimi Thi. 2015. "Hoodie as Sign, Screen, Expectation, and Force." *Signs: Journal of Women in Culture and Society* 40, no. 4: 791–816.

Naber, Nadine. 2008. "'Look, Mohammed the Terrorist is Coming!': Cultural Racism, Nation-Based Racism, and the Intersectionality of Oppressions after 9/11." In *Race and Arab Americans before and after 9/11: From Invisible Citizens to Visible Subjects,* edited by Amaney Jamal and Nadine Naber, 276–304. Syracuse, NY: Syracuse University Press.

The National Military Strategy of the United States of America: A Strategy for Today, a Vision for Tomorrow. 2004. Washington, DC: Joint Chiefs of Staff.

O'Neil, Cathy. 2016. *Weapons of Math Destruction: How Big Data Increases Inequality and Threatens Democracy.* New York: Crown.

Panetta, Grace. 2019. "Here's Everything We Know about the Persistent but Unproven Rumors that Rep. Ilhan Omar Married Her Brother, which Trump Repeated at a Recent Rally." *Business Insider,* October 11. www.businessinsider.com/unproven -allegations-ilhan-omar-married-her-brother-explained-2019-7.

Puar, Jasbir, and Amit Rai. 2002. "Monster, Terrorist, Fag: The War on Terrorism and the Production of Docile Patriots." *Social Text* 20, no. 3: 117–48.

Rana, Junaid. 2016. "The Racial Infrastructure of the Terror-Industrial Complex." *Social Text* 34, no. 4: 111–38.

Razack, Sherene H. 2008. *Casting Out: The Eviction of Muslims from Western Law and Politics.* Toronto: University of Toronto Press.

Razack, Sherene H. Forthcoming. *Nothing Has to Make Sense: Anti-Muslim Racism, White Supremacy, and Law.* Minneapolis: University of Minnesota Press.

Roy, Samya Brata. 2021. Comment posted in the #Coded-bias channel of the Anti-Racist CCS Reading Group. *Discord,* February 19.

Salaita, Steven. 2015. *Uncivil Rites: Palestine and the Limits of Academic Freedom.* Chicago: Haymarket Books.

Scheer, Robert. 2015. *They Know Everything about You: How Data-Collecting Corporations and Snooping Government Agencies Are Destroying Democracy.* New York: Nation Books.

Shah, Nayan. 2001. *Contagious Divides: Epidemics and Race in San Francisco's Chinatown.* Berkeley: University of California Press.

Sharpe, Christina. 2016. *In the Wake: On Blackness and Being.* Durham, NC: Duke University Press.

Sheehi, Stephen. 2011. *Islamophobia: The Ideological Campaign against Muslims.* Atlanta: Clarity Press.

Stop LAPD Spying Coalition. 2018. "Before the Bullet Hits the Body: Dismantling Predictive Policing in Los Angeles." May 8. stoplapdspying.org/wp-content /uploads/2018/05/Before-the-Bullet-Hits-the-Body-May-8-2018.pdf.

Stop LAPD Spying Coalition and Free Radicals. 2020. "The Algorithmic Ecology: An Abolitionist Tool for Organizing against Algorithms." *Medium,* March 2. stoplapdspying.medium.com/the-algorithmic-ecology-an-abolitionist-tool-for -organizing-against-algorithms-14fcbdoe64do.

Trump, Donald J. 2017. "Executive Order Protecting the Nation from Foreign Terrorist Entry into the United States." Trump White House Archives, January 27. trumpwhitehouse.archives.gov/presidential-actions/executive-order-protecting -nation-foreign-terrorist-entry-united-states/.

Zuboff, Shoshana. 2019. *The Age of Surveillance Capitalism: The Fight for a Human Future at the New Frontier of Power.* London: Profile Books.

Tom J. Abi Samra

. . . .

Four Editorials from *Bint al-Nīl*

Abstract: This article is in two parts. The first part provides an overview of the life of the Egyptian feminist Doria Shafik by drawing extensively on the work of her biographer Cynthia Nelson. This allows readers unfamiliar with Shafik to understand her social, political, and cultural milieu. The second part consists of translations from the Arabic of four editorials that Shafik wrote in her feminist magazine *Bint al-Nīl*.

Biographical Sketch

Doria Shafik[1] was an Egyptian feminist, activist, scholar, poet, and novelist. She grew up in a traditional middle-class household in Mansura, and in 1915, at the age of seven, Shafik moved back to Tanta, where she was born, to live with her grandmother and attend the French missionary school Notre Dame des Apôtres (Nelson 1996: xxi–xxii). After that, she attended the "French mission school of St. Vincent de Paul, where she prepared for the elementary certificate known as the Brevet *élémentaire*" (Nelson 1996: 23). Shafik had a relentless desire to succeed, to be someone; therefore, she decided to take the French baccalaureate, known as the *bachot*. To study for the bachot, one had to attend the all-boys French lycée for two or three years. This was too much time for the teenage, knowledge- hungry Shafik; she decided to self-study for the bachot, and she passed with flying colors. She then decided to take the second part of the bachot, choosing the philosophy track (Nelson 1996: 24); this required a year of intense preparation with a tutor. It eventually paid off, and she was "awarded silver medal for

MERIDIANS · feminism, race, transnationalism   20:2 October 2021
DOI: 10.1215/15366936-9547907 © 2021 Smith College

attaining second highest marks in the country-wide exam" in 1924 (Nelson 1996: xxiii). By 1928, Shafik's desire for learning was unstoppable. She took matters into her own hands and wrote to Huda Shaarawi (1879–1947), who ran the francophone Egyptian feminist magazine *L'Égyptienne* (*The Egyptian Woman*) and founded both the Wafdist Women's Central Committee in 1920 and the Egyptian Feminist Union in 1923 (Sharawi Lanfranchi 2012). Shaarawi responded and invited her to Cairo. That same year, there was a contest for the best essay written in memory of Qāsim Amīn (1863–1908), an Egyptian intellectual whose book, *Taḥrīr al-mar'a* (*The Liberation of Women*, 1899), precipitated the debate regarding women's liberation in Egypt (Elsadda 2007). Shafik won the contest and read her essay aloud at Amīn's commemoration. At nineteen, this was the first time Shafik publicly declared her feminist vision.[2]

The day after her speech, Shafik earned a scholarship via the Ministry of Education to study in France. In 1932, she earned two degrees, a *licence libre* and *licence d'état* from the Sorbonne, and returned to Egypt (Nelson 1996). In 1936, she returned to the Sorbonne in Paris to complete her doctorate, also on an Egyptian government scholarship. She wrote two theses "in half the time it takes most other students" (Nelson 1996: 74). Furthermore,

> her choice of research topics reflected her own existential situation of living in the very different cultural and intellectual worlds of France and Egypt. Through her two theses she attempted to bridge these distinct traditions. On the one hand, she blended European aesthetic philosophy with a study of ancient Egyptian art, and on the other, she reconciled the question of women's rights with Islamic religion. In so doing she was also giving shape to her own modes of being-in-the-world—the poetic and the political. (Nelson 1996: 74)

She subsequently published her theses as *L'Art pour l'art dans l'Egypt antique* (Art for Art's Sake in Ancient Egypt) and *La femme et le droite Religieux dans l'Islam* (Women and Religious Law in Contemporary Egypt). The latter includes her liberal reading of Islam, in which she is indebted to Muḥammad 'Abduh (c. 1849–1905), the former Mufti of Egypt, "who was the principal representative of modern Muslim reformism in Egypt" (von Kügelgen 2007). She draws extensively on his writings to argue that, in Islam, men and women are considered equal, the veil is not a necessary item of clothing for women, and polygamy is not encouraged ([Shafik] Ragai 1940).

In 1945, Shafik was approached by Princess Chevikar (1876–1947), the first wife of the then–Egyptian king Fuad (1868–1936), to be editor in chief of La femme nouvelle, a magazine run by the princess's eponymous association. By that time, there occurred a rift among the Egyptian elite: Princess Chevikar, a descendant of Mehmet Ali (Arabic: Muḥammad 'Alī, 1769–1849), the Ottoman-Albanian ruler of Egypt, embodied the old, pre-nationalist elite, especially since she was divorced from the king; Huda Shaarawi, on the other hand, symbolized the new national Egyptian woman. As a result of Shafik taking up the princess's offer, she was alienated from Shaarawi, and, by extension, the women she wanted to resonate with most. Nonetheless, she saw in the princess's offer an opportunity to work toward that goal (Nelson 1996: 121–22). Shafik continued to be criticized by and alienated from the Egyptian Feminist Union that Shaarawi established (whose members included Marxists such as the painter Inji Efflatoun [see Nelson 1996: 116]), which considered her hypocritical for fighting for women's rights in a bourgeois environment (Nelson 1996: 123–24).

Due to the ongoing criticism against her, Shafik seriously considered leaving her position as editor in chief of La femme nouvelle, a francophone journal; however, she decided to stay, and in addition founded, in 1945, Bint al-Nīl, an arabophone journal. The journal's language was important for Shafik, for she wanted it to be "a vehicle for educating Egyptian and Arab women in the profound sense of that term—awakening their conscious-ness" (Shafik, qtd. in Nelson 1996: 125). She published the journal from November 1945 until 1957. In 1948, a few months after Shaarawi's death, Shafik founded the Bint al Nīl Union, "a new movement for the complete liberation of the Egyptian woman" (Nelson 1996: 147). The union aimed to bring together women from all social classes; she later established a school for illiterate grown women, in addition to

> training centers in other districts of Cairo as well as the major provincial capitals "where women were taught the rudiments of reading and writ-ing, some elementary hygiene, and a trade which they could work at in their homes to augment family income. . . . The goal is to wipe out illit-eracy in a few years." (Nelson 1996: 165–66)

After Princess Chevikar's death in 1947, Doria Shafik continued running La femme nouvelle, and its headquarters were moved to the Bint al-Nīl offices. If Shafik's audience for La femme nouvelle was the Western, francophone elite, her audience for Bint al-Nīl was Egyptian women themselves. As Nelson puts it,

If *La Femme Nouvelle* was Doria's aesthetic/cultural voice turned outward to
the Occident with the goal "of conveying the true image of Egyptian
greatness," then *Bint al-Nil* was Doria's activist/feminist voice turned
inward to the Egyptian and Arab women of the nascent middle-class
with the aim of "awakening woman's consciousness to her basic rights
and responsibilities" (Nelson 1996: 135).

In 1951, the year preceding the 1952 Egyptian Revolution, Shafik was further radicalized, and her activism extended to include all women, not just
the bourgeoisie. In February 1951, along with 1500 women, she successfully
stormed the Egyptian parliament, and did not leave before "extracting
from the president of the senate a verbal promise that parliament would
immediately take up the women's demands" (Nelson 1996: 169). After the
1952 revolution, she continued the fight for women's suffrage and voting
rights (Nelson 1996: 180–81). In 1954, Shafik organized a hunger strike at
the Press Syndicate to further protest for women's rights, given her disen-
chantment with the political situation (Nelson 1996, chapter 11). In 1954–
55, Shafik traveled extensively, and upon her return to Egypt, Gamal Abdel
Nasser (1918–70) had risen to power. As a result of Nasser's "centralist
bureaucratic philosophy and socialist experiment," "the state co-opted the
Bint al-Nil movement by taking over all the various women's organizations
and centralizing their activities through the Ministry of Social Affairs." As
a result of this, Shafik could no longer criticize the government and openly
advocate for change, at least not in the way she had desired or intended to
(Nelson 1996: 227). In January 1956, a new constitution was passed, and
although it gave women the right to run for office and vote, the women had
to be literate—a requirement that didn't apply to men. Naturally, Shafik
found that discriminatory and sought to advocate for equality. She publicly
confronted Nasser and his government, which increased the Bint al-Nīl
Union's isolation as the government continued its retaliation against it
(Nelson 1996: 234–37).

   The last nail in the coffin occurred in February 1957, when Shafik went
on a hunger strike in the Indian embassy in Cairo. She had two demands:
(1) that Israeli forces withdraw from Egyptian lands and solve the problem
of Arab refugees, and (2) that Egyptian authorities end the dictatory rule
that "is driving our country towards bankruptcy and chaos" (Nelson 1996:
238). After eleven days of fasting, she was taken to the hospital; she eventually ended her fast. Her fast was criticized by leftist feminists, who found

Shafik "too committed to the liberal-humanist values of the imperialist West, with its emphasis on legal reform and social transformation based on a democratic system of parliamentary government" (Nelson 1996: 249). After her hunger strike, she was placed under house arrest, yet she continued writing critical editorials in *Bint al-Nīl*. The last three editorials—the penultimate of which is translated below—were especially directed toward the proliferation of communism in Egypt. The government ruled "that her editorials would deter cordial relations between Egypt and her communist allies during this very critical period," and banned her from publishing *Bint al-Nīl* (Nelson 1996: 250). Since then, Shafik "withdrew into the shadows" until 1975, when she allegedly died by suicide after jumping from her sixth-floor balcony (Nelson 1996: 274).

A Selection of Editorials from Bint al-Nīl

The following passages are a selection of four editorials that Egyptian feminist Doria Shafik (1908–75) wrote in her feminist magazine Bint al-Nīl *(1945–57), translated from the Arabic.*

I.

IS IT A MIRAGE?

November 1948

Have our rights become a mirage—deceiving us and leaving us parched, without any water? Are we destined to lag behind other peoples of the world, simply because a certain class of individuals took control over the world and refuse to listen to us? With the rush of time, in Egypt, universities are established; academies are opened; train carriages are equipped with air-conditioning; various signs of civilization permeate most households; many of us become women lawyers, doctors, and soldiers; and even the most prominent of religious men in Egypt support our demands for equity. It is bizarre, O God, that despite all of this, there are some. . .

. . . who stand in our way. The House of Representatives—comprising our educated men [*shabābinā al-muthaqqaf*][3] for whom our people voted and whom they supported, both openly and privately—stands as an obstacle between us and our dreams.[4] This House is not committed to supporting women and their rights. Not even one of the House's men gives them as much as a glance, to the point that women's interests were debated by the Senate and not the House.[5] In any case, should the Senate members [*shuyūkh*], contend with us and stand in our way, they are excused, for they

هل هى سراب ؟..

هل أصبحت حقوقنا سرابا نمد اليه البصر ظامئات فلا نجده ماء ؟ هل ضرب
علينا أن نتخلف عن شعوب الارض طرا لان فئة ركبت رأسها فأبت أن تستمع
لنا أو تنصت الينا ؟ عجبا والله أن تسير عجلة الزمن فتنشأ فى مصر بدل الجامعة
جامعتان ، وتفتح معاهد ، وتكيف عربات السكك الجديدية بالهواء ، وتدخل أعظم
الوان الحضارة فى معظم البيوت ، ويكون منا محاميات وطبيبات ومجندات ،
ويؤازرنا فيما ندعو له من مساواتنا بالرجال كبير زعما الدين فى مصر ثم ٠٠٠
ثم يقف بيننا وبين تحقيق آمالنا مجلس النواب ، وهو مجلس فيه من شبابنا
المثقف نخبة بشرنا لها فى الخفاء والعلانية ، فاذا هى منصرفة عن تأييـــد المرأة
وتأكيد حقوقها ، ولم يبصدر عن شاب منها لفتة أو توجيه ، حتى ان التفكير فى
مصالحنا النسائية صدر عن مجلس الشيوخ لا مجلس النواب ، وللشيوخ عذرهم
ان خاصمونا وكافحوا خطانا ، فان جيلهم غير جيلنا ، ولكن وجه العجب أن يكون
موقف مجلس النواب منا هذا الموقف الذى لا يتفق وشبابه وهذه النخبة من
أعضائه وسامره ٠!

لقد عرضنا فى هذا المكان الى حقوقنا النسائية التى يجب أن تأخذ مكانها من
تفكير المسئولين ، وطالبنا بها مطالبة الهادى، الذى يعنى ما يقول ولا يستجدى
حقه من حابسيه ، وكنا ننتظر وفينا طبيعـة السلحفاة من الارجاء والتعطيل أن
يفرغ المسئولون ساعة أو بعض ســـاعة فى دورة البرلمان المـاضية فيتذاكروا
قضيتنا ، ويضعوها فى مناقشاتهم ولو الى جانب النظر فى شق قناة فى احدى
قرى مراكز مديرية القليوبية مثلا ٠٠٠ !! فان النظر فى حياة نصف الشعب
الادبية جديرة بملاحظة الرجال جدارة ملاحظتهم لتعيين شبخ خفراء ناحيـــة
من النواحى !!٠٠ والا كان المسئولون متعمدين احتقار مطالبنا والتخلف بالشعب
المصرى عن مكانه بين شعوب الارض ، حتى تلك التى لاتنيرها الكهرباء ولا تكيف
عربات السكك الجديد فيها بالهواء !! ٠٠

ترى ماذا يقول رجالنا فى باريز اذا سئلوا عن مكان المرأة المصرية من حياة
بلادها السياسية ؟ أيقولون ان الحريم فى قرارهم موجود فى مصر وان اختلفت
مظاهره عن أيام المماليك ؟ أيقولون ان المرأة تتعلم حتى القمة ولكنها لا تساوى
جدا أو نجارا لا يزال يبصم ورقة الانتخاب جهلا بالقراءة والكتابة ! ماذا يقولون
لو أحرجوا فى هذا السـؤال ؟ أيريد المسئولونأن نفزع الىالدنيا البعيدة لتحق
لنا حقوقنا ؟ اننا لا نرجو لانفسنا شيئا فان جيلنا ذاهب ، ولكننا نريد لجيلنـا
لا من النساء ــ بل من الرجال ــ أن يحفظ له التــــاريخ أجمل الذكرى ، ذكرى
تحقيق مطالب المرأة المصرية المشروعة ، وانا لنرجو أن يختم البرلمان دورته الاخيرة
بتحقيق هذا الحلم فيكتب فى سجله صفحة من أنصع الصفحات

العدد ٣٦

Figure 1. Editorial, "Is It a Mirage?" *Bint al-Nīl*, November 1948.

aren't of our generation.[6] But what is surprising is that the House assumes such an antagonistic stance that doesn't match its youthfulness and the Samaritan nature of its members.

On this platform, we have tackled our rights as women, a matter that should secure its place in our officials' minds more than it currently does. We have asked for what we want in a calm and straightforward manner, and without begging for our rights from those keeping us prisoners. As officials postponed and obstructed progress, we waited, with the patience of turtles,[7] hoping that they carve out an hour—or less—in the previous parliamentary session to consider our struggle, and to include it in their agenda, even alongside the issue of laying a new waterway in one of the villages of al-Qalyūbiyya, for example . . . [8] For these men, to consider the life [ḥayāt adabiyya][9] of half of the population is as worthy as appointing a random village sheikh someplace . . . The officials intentionally ridicule [iḥtiqār] our demands, thus causing Egyptian society to fall behind other peoples of the world—even those who have neither electricity nor air-conditioning in their train carriages.

What would our men say in Paris if they were to be asked about the role of the Egyptian woman in politics? Can they claim that the role of women [ḥarīm][10] in politics has changed since the times of the Mamluks?[11] Will they admit that the woman reached the peak of education but is as worthless as a shoe, or as illiterate carpenter who fingerprints the voting ballot?[12] What would they do if they are cornered with this question? Do the officials want to scare us into a faraway land for us to earn our rights? We are not wishing for anything; our generation is soon leaving this world, but we desire that our generation of women—but also of men—be fondly remembered in history for realizing the Egyptian woman's legitimate demands. And we urge the Parliament to conclude its final session by realizing this dream, for it would mark the brightest page of their time in office.
—Doria Shafik

II.

THE PROBLEMS OF THE EGYPTIAN FAMILY
January 1951
And now . . .

This is the same naive speech that expresses a true reality for most of Egyptian families, with their various deep-rooted problems. I won't be able to entertain in this space all of the issues that my miserable friend's speech tackled,[13] so I will limit myself to two important issues.

مشاكل الاسرة المصرية

والان ...

هذا هو الخطاب بنفس كلماته الساذجة التي تعبر عن واقع حقيقي لغالبيـة أسراتنا المصرية بمشاكلها المتعددة ذات الجذور المزمنة . ولن أستطيع فى هذا المقام أن أعرض لكل المشاكل التي أثارها خطاب الصديقة البائسة وانما سأقتصر على مشكلتين هامتين :

أولى هاتين المشكلتين هي انخفاض مستوى معيشة الاسرة المصرية الذى هو انعكاس لهبوط المستوى الاقتصادى للمجتمع كله وهذا بدوره نتيجة للنظم الاجتماعية السائدة والتي لا تسمح باطلاق كل قوى الشعب فى الانتـــاج والاستفادة منها استفادة كاملة فنحن لا زلنا نقف فى وجه تعليم الفتاة المصرية ونعتبر خوضها لميدان العمل عارا وبذلك نحبس نصف قوى شعبنا عن الانتاج وعن غزو الموارد الاقتصادية المعطلة والتي أكد الاقتصاديون مرارا انها لو استغلت استغلالا صحيحا لرفعت كثيرا من مستوى معيشتنا . وهكذا نجد أن هبوط المستوى الاقتصادى العام وبالتالى فقر الاسرة وما ينتابها من أمراض وعلل مرتبط ارتباطا وثيقا بتعليم المرأة المصرية واطلاقها نحو الانتـــاج والعمـــل .

والمشكلة الثانية هي الزواج . وهذه المشكلة مرتبطة فى جذورها بالمشكلة الاولى والواقع ان الكثيرين لا يزالون ينظرون الى الزواج نظرتهم الى صفقـة تجارية بطلاها بائع ومشتر لا انســان وانسانة يريدان العيش فى وحدة انسانية تفيض حياة آمنة سعيدة دستورها الكفاح المشترك من أجل لقمـة العيش والتفاهم والمحبة .

وأخيرا لا أريد أن تمر فرصة عرض خطاب هذه الصديقة دون أن أؤكد ضرورة خروجنا بمجتمعنا من الدائرة الضيقة المظلمة التي يقبع فيها الان الى دائرة أوسع من التقدم والتطور واطلاق نصف قواه المعطلة الى النور والعمل والحياة ..

ان العالم كله يسير الى الامام ونحن لا زلنا نقف فى جمود ثائر فى أعماقه هادىء فى مظهره .. ان الامام معناه الحياة ..

والجمود معناه التأخر .... معناه الموت .. ونحن النساء المصريات لا نريد الموت ..

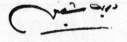

Figure 2. Editorial, "The Problems of the Egyptian Family," *Bint al-Nīl*, January 1951.

The first issue is the drop in the Egyptian family's standard of living, which is a reflection of the overall economic recession. This, in turn, is a result of the prevalent social structure that doesn't allow society to operate at, and benefit from, its full productive potential. We still oppose educating the Egyptian girl, and we consider her joining the workforce shameful. In doing so, we prevent half of our people's potential from participating in the economy and thus eliminating [*ghazū*] any dormant economic resources. Time and time again, economists confirmed that these resources, if well-exploited, would increase our standard of living. Therefore, we see that the economic recession, and consequently the poverty of the family and other related afflictions including diseases and deficiencies that afflict it, are deeply linked to the education of the Egyptian woman and her participation in production and work.

The second problem is marriage. This problem is, at its roots, tied to the first one. The reality is that many still see marriage as an economic transaction, its protagonists a buyer and a seller—not a man and a woman[14] wishing to live in unity, safety, and happiness, and whose constitutive purpose is a joint struggle to make a living, to be understanding of each other, and to love.

Lastly, I wouldn't want to discuss this dear friend's speech without underscoring how important it is that we, as a society, exit our constricted, dark circle in which we are jailed, into society—into a wider circle of progress and advancement, catapulting, as a result, half of society's dysfunctional capabilities into light, work, and life . . .

The whole world is moving forward, while we are at a standstill—rebelling at our core but calm in our appearance . . .

Moving forward means life . . . and stagnancy means falling behind . . . means death . . . and we Egyptian women do not want death. —Doria Shafik

III.

OUR GOALS AND STRATEGIES

February 1951

After many years of struggle, with partial success, to gain her literary and moral rights [*ḥuqūq adabiyya*, lit. "literary rights"],[15] the Egyptian woman must now turn toward attaining her political rights to ensure her equality with men.

The Egyptian woman is not asking for something heretical or absurd, and she isn't ahead of her time or deviant from the current state of things.

Her counterparts in the rest of the civilized world have secured and enjoyed these rights for a while now. This enabled them to contribute to their societies to lead their governments toward the good.

There is no room for those who oppose a woman's activities and stand in the way of her development to debate her talents and abilities. With the very little opportunity she was given, she has demonstrated her drive and competence; she is different from man in neither drive nor competence. Though this is not to say that she doesn't even surpass him sometimes . . .

So, our aim is to achieve realistic and just goals. Our pusuit of these goals is further buttressed by reason and by the world's natural tendency toward development and achieving wholeness.

But one might ask, "What are the woman's strategies to realizing these goals?" I would answer by saying that our means for achieving these goals are the tools of every claimant demanding justice: to be powerfully prepared and to be perseverant in their struggle.

This power we derive from within ourselves. Every person's [insān] power is in their education, willingness, and ability to exercise their rights . . .

The educated woman is the ideal woman for enjoying her political rights, for she knows what is happening around her and can discern good from evil.

That's why my colleagues [zamīlātī] and I, in the Bint al-Nīl Union, decided to take a practical step toward equipping the Egyptian woman for this near future: we initiated our project to educate women and combat illiteracy among women. We established our first school in Būlāq as a pilot, and it succeeded, thanks be to God. Then, we continued in this direction by establishing schools of the same kind that educate the mothers of today, who, otherwise, are too old to attend school. They will then be able to exercise their political rights once we attain them soon, God willing.

There are now twelve such schools. They teach women reading, writing, cultural principles, wellness, child-rearing, and civics. And I noticed with enthusiasm and delight that women of all social classes embraced these schools, which is reassuring for the near future that we are striving for— namely, educating mothers and eradicating illiteracy among women of various social classes.

These are some, but not all, of the strategies we adopt to achieve our goals. As for our other strategies, they include fighting with all legitimate means and seeking with tireless zeal to snatch our political rights from those who begrudge them.[16]

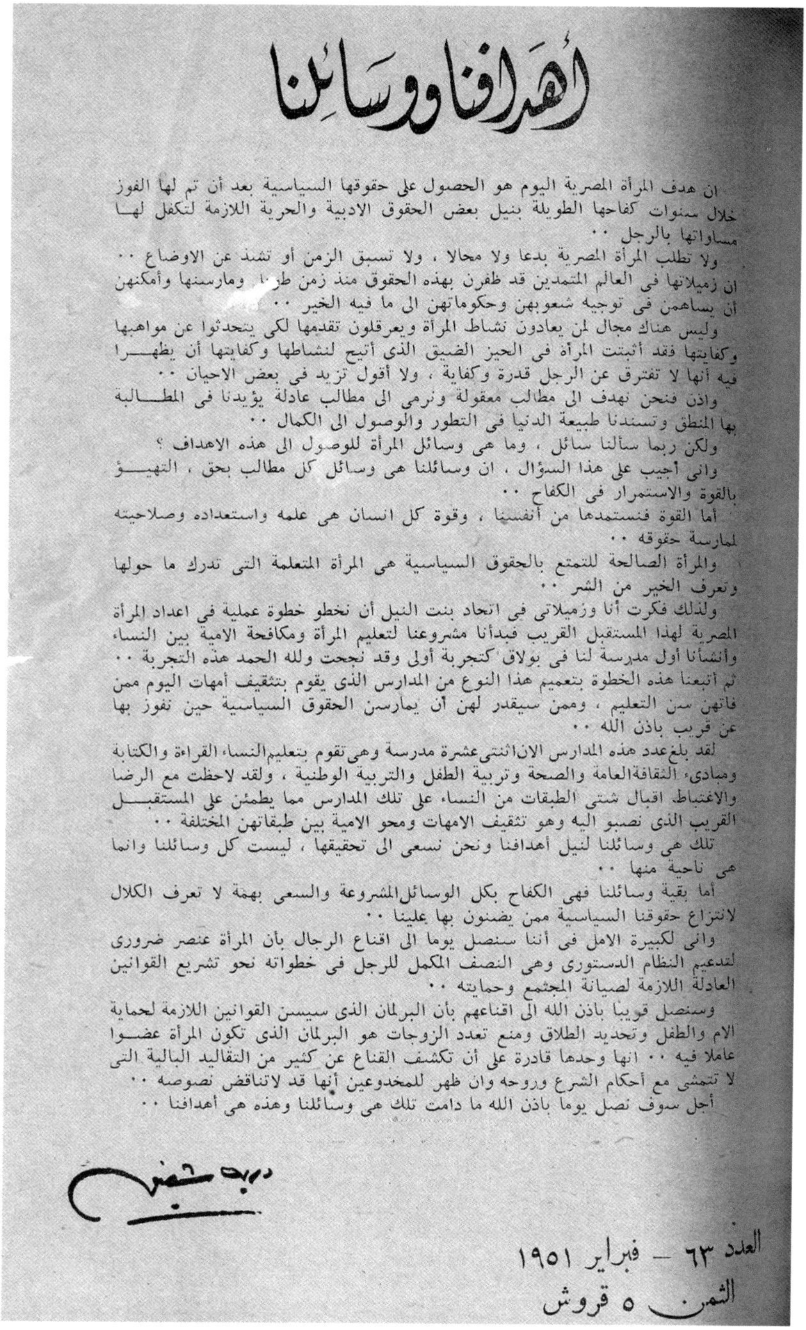

اُهدافنا ووسائلنا

ان هدف المرأة المصرية اليوم هو الحصول على حقوقها السياسية بعد ان تم لها الفوز خلال سنوات كفاحها الطويلة بنيل بعض الحقوق الادبية والحرية اللازمة لتكفل لها مساواتها بالرجل ٠٠

ولا تطلب المرأة المصرية بدعا ولا محالا ، ولا تسبق الزمن او تشذ عن الاوضاع ٠٠ ان زميلاتها في العالم المتمدين قد ظفرن بهذه الحقوق منذ زمن طويل ، ومارسنها وامكنهن ان يساهمن في توجيه شعوبهن وحكوماتهن الى ما فيه الخير ٠٠

وليس هناك مجال لمن يعاندون نشاط المرأة ويعرقلون تقدمها لكي يتحدثوا عن مواهبها وكفاءتها فقد اثبتت المرأة في الحيز الضيق الذي اتيح لنشاطها وكفاءتها ان تظهـــرا فيه انها لا تفترق عن الرجل قدرة وكفاية ، ولا اقول تزيد في بعض الاحيان ٠٠

وادن فنحن نهدف الى مطالب معقولة ونرمي الى مطالب عادلة يؤيدنا في المطالبة بها المنطق وتسندنا طبيعة الدنيا في التطور والوصول الى الكمال ٠٠

ولكن ربما سألنا سائل ، وما هي وسائل المرأة للوصول الى هذه الاهداف ؟

واني اجيب على هذا السؤال ، ان وسائلنا هي وسائل كل مطالب بحق ، التهيــؤ بالقوة والاستمرار في الكفاح ٠٠

اما القوة فنستمدها من انفسنا ، وقوة كل انسان هي علمه واستعداده وصلاحيته لممارسة حقوقه ٠٠

والمرأة الصالحة للتمتع بالحقوق السياسية هي المرأة المتعلمة التي تدرك ما حولها وتعرف الخير من الشر ٠٠

ولذلك فكرت انا وزميلاتي في اتحاد بنت النيل ان نخطو خطوة عملية في اعداد المرأة المصرية لهذا المستقبل القريب فبدأنا مشروعنا لتعليم المرأة ومكافحة الامية بين النساء وانشأنا اول مدرسة لنا في بولاق كتجربة اول وقد نجحت ولله الحمد هذه التجربة ٠٠ ثم اتبعنا هذه الخطوة بتعميم هذا النوع من المدارس الذي يقوم بتثقيف امهات اليوم ممن فاتهن سن التعليم ، وممن سيقدر لهن ان يمارسن الحقوق السياسية حين تفوز بها عن قريب باذن الله ٠٠

لقد بلغ عدد هذه المدارس الاثنتي عشرة مدرسة وهي تقوم بتعليم النساء القراءة والكتابة ومبادئ الثقافة العامة والصحة وتربية الطفل والتربية الوطنية ، ولقد لاحظت مع الرضا والاغتباط اقبال شتى الطبقات من النساء على تلك المدارس مما يطمئن على المستقبل القريب الذي نصبو اليه وهو تثقيف الامهات ومحو الامية بين طبقاتهن المختلفة ٠٠

تلك هي وسائلنا لنيل اهدافنا ونحن نسعى الى تحقيقها ، ليست كل وسائلنا وانما هي ناحية منها ٠٠

اما بقية وسائلنا فهي الكفاح بكل الوسائل المشروعة والسعي بهمة لا تعرف الكلال لانتزاع حقوقنا السياسية ممن يضنون بها علينا ٠٠

واني لكبيرة الامل في اننا سنصل يوما الى اقناع الرجال بان المرأة عنصر ضروري لتدعيم النظام الدستوري وهي النصف المكمل للرجل في خطواته نحو تشريع القوانين العادلة اللازمة لصيانة المجتمع وحمايته ٠٠

وسنصل قويبا باذن الله الى اقناعهم بأن البرلمان الذي سيسن القوانين اللازمة لحماية الام والطفل وتحديد الطلاق ومنع تعدد الزوجات هو البرلمان الذي تكون المرأة عضـوا عاملا فيه ٠٠ انها وحدها قادرة على ان تكشف القناع عن كثير من التقاليد البالية التي لا تتمشى مع احكام الشرع وروحه وان ظهر للمخدوعين انها قد لاتناقض نصوصه ٠٠

اجل سوف نصل يوما باذن الله ما دامت تلك هي وسائلنا وهذه هي اهدافنا ٠٠

درية شفيق

العدد ٦٣ — فبراير ١٩٥١
الثمن ٥ قروش

Figure 3. Editorial, "Our Goals and Approaches," *Bint al-Nīl*, February 1951.

I am very hopeful that we will one day convince men that the woman is essential to reinforce the constitutional system. She is the half that completes the man in his steps toward passing new, just laws to maintain and protect society . . .

God willing, we will soon manage to convince men that the Parliament that will enact the necessary laws to protect the mother and the child, curtail divorce, and ban polygamy, is the Parliament in which the woman is an active member. Only the woman is able to debunk many of our obsolete traditions that are not compatible with Islamic shari'a law [ahkām al-shar'] and its essence [rūhihi]—although some were deceived and thought that these traditions contradict the shari'a.

Yes, God willing, we will one day make it as long as these are our means and strategies. And these are our goals.

—Doria Shafik

IV.

COMMUNIST COLONIALISM

May 1957

One of the ways communism obscures its true mission is by claiming that there is no risk whatsoever in its pervading influence in the Arab world,[17] since it does not have intentions to colonize or exploit.

The most significant counterpoint to this claim is the terrible recent events in Hungary, and the methods that communism adopted there.[18] These incidents and their details were kept from Arabic readers until they were discussed in a recently published book in Arabic.

This splendid book's telling of this history and the communists' atrocities must be celebrated by every loyal nationalist in the Arab world, for it is the best evidence that international communism poses the greatest colonial threat.

We must welcome this detailed publication because it is the best refutation of the claims of international communism, in which it maintains that it works to achieve peace and resist colonialism; it is also the best evidence for those who deny the influence and permeation of international communism in the Arab world.

All these claims are just deceptive talk that would eventually be forgotten once communism dominates. People would then be poisoned as a result of the agony and oppression they would endure.

Is the Arab world closer to communism's heart than Hungary, such

الاستعمار الشيوعي

من أساليب الدعاية التي تموه بها الشيوعية أنه لاخطر اطلاقا من تغلغل نفوذها في
الشرق العربي لانها ليست لها غايات استعمارية ولا أهداف استغلالية فيه ·

ولعل أبلغ دليل للرد على ذلك هو الحوادث الفظيعة والوسائل التي اتبعتها الشيوعية
اخيرا في المجر فقد ظل أمر هذه الحوادث وتفاصيلها بعيدا عن قراء العربية حتى نشرت
في كتاب صدر اخيرا باللغة العربية ·

ونشر هذه الحوادث والفظائع الشيوعية في المجر عمل جليل يجب ان يرحب به كل
وطني مخلص في الشرق العربي لانه أبلغ دليل على أن الشيوعية الدولية تمثل خطرا
استعماريا أبلغ من أي خطر ·

وهذا النشر التفصيلي يجب أن نرحب به جميعا لانه أبلغ رد على دعاوى الشيوعية
الدولية التي تنادي بأنها تعمل للسلام وتقاوم الاستعمار وأبلغ رد على بعض الذين يرون
الاخطار هناك على الشرق العربي من تغلغل نفوذها فيه ·

ذلك أن كل هذه الدعاوى ماهي الا مظاهر خادعة تنسى بعد ان يتم للشيوعية السيطرة
ثم تسام الشعوب بعد ذلك من ألوان العذاب والاضطهاد الشيء الكثير ·

وهل الشرق العربي أعز على الشيوعية من المجر حتى تدلله وتربت على كنفه يوم أن
توطد أقدامها فيه ؟

الجواب طبعا لا ٠٠ لان المجر وهي بلد شيوعي طالب بقسط من الحريات فنال جزاء
ذلك مانال واستعملت معه أشد وسائل العنف وأهله شيوعيون من طبقة العمال الذين
تدعي الشيوعية انها قامت لحمايتهم وتأمين حياتهم ·

حدث كل هذا لمجرد انهم طالبوا بقسط ضئيل من الحريات ·

فكيف يكون الحال عندما يتم للشيوعية السيطرة على الشرق العربي ؟

المقطوع به أننا سنعامل معاملة أسوأ بكثير من معاملة الروس للمجريين أو البولنديين
أو غيرهم من الشعوب التي في حوزتها وهي شعوب أقرب اليها منا ·

اننا نبغض الاستعمار من أي لون ومن أي نوع يكون ونتمسك باستقلالنا وحريتنا
ولكن حذار من أن نفتح للشيوعية في شرقنا العربي الابواب لتنفذ منها ، فانهــــا تريد
استعماره وعندئذ لايجدي الندم ولا نعرف الطريق الى الخلاص ·

درية شفيق
رئيسة التحرير

العـــدد ١٣٩ ــ مايو ١٩٥٧ ـالثمن ١٥ قرشا

Figure 4. Editorial, "Communist Colonialism," *Bint al-Nīl*, May 1957.

that it would pamper the Arab world and pat its back after it establishes itself in it?

Of course not . . . Hungary—which is a communist state—asked for a share of its freedoms only to be punished by communists in the most violent of ways, even though the people are working class communists, whom communism claims to defend and provide for.

All this happened merely because they asked for a minute portion of their rights.

So what would it be like if communism controls the Arab world?

To be sure, we will be treated much worse than the Russians' treatment of the Hungarians, Poles, or other peoples who fall within its territory; and they are peoples who are much more like the Russians than we are.

We despise colonialism in all its colors or kinds, and we hold on to our independence and freedom. Watch out! We must not open the door for communism to carry out its project in the Arab world. It wants to colonize us. At that point, it would be futile to be regretful, and we would not be able to identify the path to redemption.

—Doria Shafik

....

Tom J. Abi Samra is currently an MA student in comparative literature at Dartmouth College. He has a BA in literature, with an emphasis on Arabic literature, from New York University Abu Dhabi. His translations and essays have appeared in ArabLit Quarterly, ASAP/J, and Protean Magazine, among others.

Notes

1   Arabic words and names have been transliterated according to the International Journal of Middle East Studies guidelines. I have not changed the transliterations of names adopted by authors who write in either English or French (e.g., Shafik, not Shafiq). I have transliterated names to conform as closely as possible to common usage. Arabic words and proper names widely used in English, such as Quran and Cairo, are left in the familiar form. I offer a biographical sketch based on Nelson 1996, which is a book-length biography of Shafik. For an alternative, summarized version of her biography, see, for instance, Nelson 1991.

2   I have not been able to access this speech in the original French; it was published as "Un petit mot" in 1928 in the thirty-fifth issue of L'Égyptienne. For an English translation of the speech, see Nelson 1996: 28–29; Nelson and Rouse 2000: 101–3.

3   Muthaqqaf can also be translated as "learned" or "cultured." Shabābinā, here translated as "our men," connotes youthfulness; the word shābb, as an adjective, means "young" or "youthful."

4   The parliamentary structure in Egypt at the time, as dictated by the 1923 Egyptian Constitution, was bicameral. The Egyptian Parliament was composed of two houses, (1) the House of Representatives (Arabic: *Majlis al-nuwwāb*), and (2) the Senate (*Majlis al-shuyūkh*). The House of Representatives was fully elected by popular vote; two-fifths of the Senate, on the other hand, was appointed by the king, and the remaining three-fifths was also elected by popular vote. See "Royal Decree No. 42 of 1923 on Building a Constitutional System for the Egyptian State" (art. 74; art. 82). For an overview of the 1923 Egyptian Constitution, see (in Arabic), Al-Ardawi and Al-Mosawi 2018.

5   There is in this statement an implicit criticism of the Egyptian monarchy, and at the same time a criticism of the House of Representatives. Her argument is that although one would have expected the Senate—two-fifths of which is appointed by the king—to be less progressive when it comes to women's issues, even this body has proven more interested in women's rights than the democratically elected House of Representatives.

6   I translate the word *shuyūkh* (plural of "sheikh") at the beginning of the sentence to "Senate members," since the Senate in Arabic is called *Majlis al-shuyūkh* (literally, "assembly of the sheikhs"). This isn't to be confused with religious sheikhs.

7   This is a literal translation; this simile compares the women's patience to turtles' speed.

8   This statement is supposed to be sarcastic, equating the importance of the women's struggle with the digging of a waterway in al-Qalyūbiyya, a rural area in Egypt.

9   For a discussion of the polysemy of the words *adab* and *adabiyya*, see note 17 below.

10   Here, she uses the word *ḥarīm*, which may have been read as somewhat derogatory.

11   This is a peculiar statement to make since the first Mamluk ruler was a woman, known as Shajarat al-Durr (ruled 1250 CE). For more on Shajarat al-Durr, see Ammann 2012. That said, Shafik's point, of course, is that women at the time did not have rights. I am thankful to one of the anonymous reviewers for pointing this out to me.

12   Here, of course, Shafik does not agree that women are as worthless as a shoe, but rather is describing the status quo in society; despite their high educational attainment, women are still treated not only as if they are secondary, but also as if they are illiterate.

13   Unfortunately, I have been unable to identify the speech she is responding to here.

14   "Man and woman" in the Arabic is *insān wa-insāna*. It is worth noting that they share the same root in Arabic.

15   The phrase "*ḥuqūq adabiyya*" is ambiguous, due to the word *adabiyya*'s (from *adab*) polyvalency. In the modern Arab world, it became roughly equivalent to "literary" (and "*adab*" to "literature"); see Allan 2012. However, the word *adab*

also means apposite social conduct and behavior. Even more, these two "definitions" of *adab* were not entirely separate—the literary and the worldly frequently intersected. I translate "*ḥuqūq adabiyya*" literally as "literary rights," and I leave it up to the reader to interpret the phrase in light of this information I provide. For more on the modern transformation of *adab*, see Allan 2012; and Hallaq 2014. For more on the premodern usage of *adab*, see Hämeen-Anttila 2014; and Kilpatrick 1998.

Another way to translate this phrase is "moral rights," if we are to understand the phrase as a demand for intellectual property rights. A more ambitious and interpretive, if also risky, way to translate this phrase is "freedom of speech/expression," for "*ḥuqūq adabiyya*" also encompasses the political and public aspects of *adab* that "literary rights" doesn't necessarily foreground. However, "freedom of expression/speech" opens another can of worms—namely, the relationship between free speech and secularism in the non-Western world (see Asad et al. 2009). Thus, I prefer to translate the phrase literally. I would like to thank one of the anonymous readers for pointing out that "literary rights" is inadequate—hence this footnote.

16 I am thankful for an anonymous reviewer's correction of my translation of this line.

17 She uses the phrase *al-sharq al-'arabī*, whose literal translation is "the Arab East." I choose to use "the Arab world" instead to avoid associating this text with Orientalist connotations that the literal translation might invoke, for the original Arabic does not invoke this same Orientalism.

18 This is a reference to the Soviet intervention in Hungary in October and November 1956.

Works Cited

Al-Ardawi, Hameed Shaheed Hussein, and Rabee Hayder Yaher Al-Mosawi. 2018. "The Constitutional Developments in Egypt in 1923 (A Historical Study)." *Islamic College University Journal* 50, no. 1: 147–86. www.iasj.net/iasj/article/156385.

Allan, Michael. 2012. "How *Adab* Became Literary: Formalism, Orientalism, and the Institutions of World Literature." *Journal of Arabic Literature* 43, nos. 2–3: 172–96.

Ammann, L[udwig]. 2012. "Shadjar al-Durr." In *Encyclopaedia of Islam*, edited by P. Bearman, Th. Bianquis, C. E. Bosworth, E. van Donzel, and W. P. Heinrichs. 2nd ed. Brill Online. dx.doi.org/10.1163/1573-3912_islam_SIM_6738.

Elsadda, Hoda. 2007. "Amīn, Qāsim." In *Encyclopaedia of Islam*, 3rd ed., edited by Kate Fleet, Gudrun Krämer, Denis Matringe, John Nawas and Everett Rowson. Brill Online. dx.doi.org/10.1163/1573-3912_ei3_SIM_0215.

Hallaq, Boutros. 2014. "Adab e) modern usage." In *Encyclopaedia of Islam*, 3rd ed., edited by Kate Fleet, Gudrun Krämer, Denis Matringe, John Nawas, and Everett Rowson. Brill Online. dx.doi.org/10.1163/1573-3912_ei3_COM_23653.

Hämeen-Anttila, Jaakko. 2014. "Adab a) Arabic, early developments." In *Encyclopaedia of Islam*, 3rd ed., edited by Kate Fleet, Gudrun Krämer, Denis Matringe, John Nawas, and Everett Rowson. Brill Online. dx.doi.org/10.1163/1573-3912_ei3_COM_24178.

Kilpatrick, Hilary. 1998. "adab." In *Encyclopedia of Arabic Literature*, edited by Julie Scott Meisami and Paul Starkey, 54–56. London: Routledge.

Nelson, Cynthia. 1991. "Biography and Women's History: On Interpreting Doria Shafik." In *Women in Middle Eastern History: Shifting Boundaries in Sex and Gender*, edited by Nikki R. Keddie and Beth Baron, 310–33. New Haven, CT: Yale University Press.

Nelson, Cynthia. 1996. *Doria Shafik, Egyptian Feminist: A Woman Apart*. Cairo: American University in Cairo Press.

Nelson, Cynthia, and Shahnaz J. Rouse. 2000. "Gendering Globalization: Alternative Languages of Modernity." In *Situating Globalization: Views from Egypt*, edited by Cynthia Nelson and Shahnaz J. Rouse, 97–158. Bielefeld: Transcript.

"Royal Decree No. 42 of 1923 on Building a Constitutional System for the Egyptian State [1923 Egyptian Constitution]." *constitutionnet.org*. constitutionnet.org/sites /default/files/1923_-_egyptian_constitution_english_1.pdf.

[Shafik] Ragai, Doria. 1940. *La femme et le droit religieux de l'Égypte contemporaine* [Women and religious law in contemporary Egypt]. Paris: P. Geuthner. doria -shafik.com/image-egyptian-feminist/pdf/La%20Femme%20Et%20Le%20Droit %20Religieux.pdf.

Shafik, Doria. 1928. "Un petit mot." *L'Égyptienne* 35: 12–14.

Shafik, Doria. 1948. "*Hal hiya sarāb?* [Is it a mirage?]" *Bint al-Nīl*, November. dar .aucegypt.edu/handle/10526/1936.

Shafik, Doria. 1951a. "*Ahdāfunā wa-wasā'ilunā* [Our goals and approaches]." *Bint al-Nīl*, February. dar.aucegypt.edu/handle/10526/2123.

Shafik, Doria. 1951b. "*Mashākil al-usra al-miṣriyya* [The problems of the Egyptian family]." *Bint al-Nīl*, January. dar.aucegypt.edu/handle/10526/2125.

Shafik, Doria. 1957. "*Al-Istiʿmār al-shuyūʿī* [Communist colonialism]." *Bint al-Nīl*, May. dar.aucegypt.edu/handle/10526/2208.

Sharawi Lanfranchi, Sania. 2012. *Casting Off the Veil: The Life of Huda Shaarawi, Egypt's First Feminist*, edited by John Keith King. New York: I. B. Tauris.

von Kügelgen, Anke. 2007. "'Abduh, Muḥammad." In *Encyclopaedia of Islam*, 3rd ed, edited by Kate Fleet, Gudrun Krämer, Denis Matringe, John Nawas, and Everett Rowson. Brill Online. dx.doi.org/10.1163/1573-3912_ei3_COM_0103.

Elora Shehabuddin

. . . .

Between Orientalism and Anti-Muslim Racism:
Pakistan, the United States, and Women's Transnational
Activism in the Early Cold War Interlude

Abstract: This article explores some of the ways in which, in the early years of
the united Pakistan experiment, elite educated Muslim East Bengali women
experienced and narrated their relationship to the new Pakistan nation as
they navigated the international stage as citizens of a new sovereign
Muslim-majority state. In the context of the nascent Cold War and the Pakistani state's efforts to develop its own relationship with the United States,
one that was distinct from that of India and yet motivated almost entirely
by concerns about the greater military might of this large neighbor, Pakistani women from both wings were quickly pulled into the orbit of US- and
Soviet-sponsored women's organizations targeting women around the
world. In this article, the author focuses on the relationship between Pakistani and US women in the 1950s that emerges from the memoirs, biogra-
phies, and writings of Bengali Pakistani women active in this period, as well
as from the archives—housed in Smith College's Sophia Smith Collection—
of one of the first formal US women's groups to establish contact with East
Bengali women leaders: the New York-based Committee of
Correspondence.

In November 1949, the teenager Mushfequa Rahman (later, Mahmud),
then living in Chittagong in East Bengal, the eastern wing of Pakistan,
reminisced about the August 1947 birth of Pakistan in an article in the
magazine *Begum*. The veteran journalist Muhammad Nasiruddin had

MERIDIANS · feminism, race, transnationalism   20:2 October 2021
DOI: 10.1215/15366936-9547921 © 2021 Smith College

founded *Begum* mere weeks before partition and the independence of Pakistan and India, envisioning it as an illustrated Bengali-language weekly magazine devoted entirely to women's issues and concerns. *Begum* was still based in Calcutta in what was now the Indian state of West Bengal when Rahman published her piece, but in 1950 it would move to the East Bengali capital of Dacca, on the heels of many of its Muslim writers who emigrated to what they saw as a new homeland for South Asia's Muslims (Akhtar 2012: 114; Gupta 2009).

In her essay Rahman described the birth of independent Pakistan as the day on which "we cast off the shackles of servitude" and emerged as "*azaad* [free] inhabitants of an *azaad* Pakistan." She recalled that the moment of independence at the stroke of midnight had been preceded by five minutes of "blackout" in her neighborhood to mark the end of almost two centuries of British colonial rule in the Indian subcontinent. Although, in her words, she was just a schoolgirl at the time and "didn't understand anything about politics," she was overcome by the excitement, joy, and enormous pride she felt that day, as well as by her somber recollection of the many who had sacrificed so that she might now partake in this new national freedom. She remembered how she was unable to sleep the rest of that night. All she could think about was how, where once her compatriots had felt the need to lower their heads in shame when meeting foreigners from independent nations, today "we had been liberated from that humiliation and now we will be able to hold our head up high and walk alongside the rest of the world as we move forward." These thoughts occupied her until dawn broke and it was time to attend a ceremony of the hoisting of the new flag (Begum 2006, 1:53–54; Shehabuddin 2021: 169).

Given the history of South Asia over the following seven decades—and, indeed, the power of the nationalist historiographies of the region and popular memories of that era—such enthusiasm for Pakistan on the part of an East Bengali might elicit some surprise today. Tensions had already erupted between the two wings of the new nation by the time Rahman submitted her article. In March 1948, Mohammad Ali Jinnah, who had led the movement for Pakistan and then become its governor-general, had informed a crowd of a half-million people in Dacca that Urdu, spoken by a small fraction of even West Pakistan's population, would be the country's state language. Bengalis, a numerical majority in united Pakistan, had vociferously protested, energizing the *bhasha andolan* or "language move-ment" that had been simmering quietly for several months. East Pakistani protests against cultural, political, and economic inequalities perpetrated by the West Pakistani–dominated central regime in the coming years, and the regime's violent repression of these protests, would culminate in 1971 in East Pakistan's declaration of independence and the creation of yet another new South Asian state, Bangladesh.

Rather than assume Bengali resentment toward West Pakistan and the inevitability of Bangladesh's birth from the moment of partition in 1947, I explore in this article some of the ways in which, in the early years of the united Pakistan experiment, elite educated Muslim East Bengali women experienced and narrated their relationship to the new Pakistan nation as they navigated the international stage as citizens of a new sovereign Muslim-majority state. The Pakistan period or *Pakistan amal*, as Bangladeshis refer to it today, coincided with the beginning of the Cold War and with the Pakistani state's efforts to develop its own relationship with the United States, one that was distinct from that of India and yet motivated almost entirely by concerns about the greater military might of this large neighbor. Soon anointed as a strategic US ally, the Pakistani state also engaged in often repressive efforts to unify its population. It was in this larger context that Pakistani women from both wings, even as they worked to define their own agendas for change, were quickly pulled into the orbit of US- and Soviet-sponsored women's organizations targeting women around the world. As I show elsewhere, US women would visit East Pakistan throughout the 1950s and 1960s, as journalists, consultants (for example, for the new home economics college), Peace Corps volunteers, and as representatives of women's groups, and they would also sponsor visits by Pakistani women to the United States (Shehabuddin 2021). In this essay, I focus on the relationship between Pakistani and US women in the 1950s that emerges from the writings of Bengali Pakistani women active in this period as well as the archives, housed in Smith College's Sophia Smith Collection, of one of the first formal US women's groups to establish contact with East Bengali women leaders, the New York–based Committee of Correspondence (hereafter, CoC). Generously funded from the very beginning by the Central Intelligence Agency (CIA)—though not all committee members would learn of this until a 1967 exposé—the committee's primary concern was the cultural and political threat it perceived from the Soviet Bloc (Laville 2002; Wilford 2009).

This project contributes to the rich and growing body of scholarship on Muslim women's agency and activism. While work on Muslim women's piety and religious practice over the past two decades has posed important challenges to older narrow Western liberal feminist ideas about what constitutes power and agency (e.g., Deeb 2006; Mahmood 2005; Jamal 2013), I'm interested here in non-religious forms of public activism and engagement with politics in a particular historical period by women who identified as Muslim—and as Bengali and Pakistani. The Bengali Muslim women of East Pakistan whose memoirs and letters inform this article were well-educated and well-traveled. They also saw themselves as empowered citizens and nation builders at a time of hope and postcolonial possibility. They were generally of an elite class background that was similar to that of the American women with whom they interacted, and like them, they were enmeshed in a variety of familial, professional, national, and international concerns that were often connected to but also extended beyond their religious identity. The juxtaposition of these Bengali and US women serves to complicate the Otherness that is often attached to Muslim women to the exclusion of power, history, politics, and economics, and to such an extent that their "Muslimness" overshadows all other aspects of their lives.

This essay also provides broader historical and geographical context against which to understand current forms of imperial and colonial feminism as well as transnational solidarities and networks. Specifically, it contributes to the emerging literature on transnational feminism between accounts of the "international first wave" (the mobilization around women's suffrage around the world in the early twentieth century) and the many transnational organizations that emerged in the Global South in the late twentieth century. Bringing the different contexts of East Pakistan, West Pakistan, and the United States into one transnational analytical frame allows me to contribute to the growing field of gendered histories of the Cold War, and to do so from the vantage point of the Third World and its interactions with the superpowers (McMahon 1994; de Haan 2010; de Haan 2012; Rotter 2013; Armstrong 2016).

By examining women's activism in both Pakistan and the United States, I am able to find moments of exchange and collaboration that pose a contrast to the European civilizing mission impetus of the formal colonial period as well as to more recent US and European anti-Muslim foreign and domestic policy. At the same time, given clear asymmetries of power, such collaborations cannot be reduced to notions of global sisterhood that gained currency in the 1970s and 1980s. In the Pakistan *amal*, power asymmetries characterized relations not only between women in the United

States and Pakistan, but also between women in East and West Pakistan, urban and rural women within Pakistan, and those with access to formal education and the English language and those without.

Historians of the US women's movement have challenged popular memories and older scholarly depictions of the early post–World War II years as marked by stagnation in the US women's movement, an era of "doldrums" between the winning of women's suffrage in 1920 and the rise of the so-called second wave of feminism in the 1960s. But despite recent work on the activism and public presence of large numbers of US women in the postwar years, there remains a need for attention to their active engagements with women from what came to be called Third World countries and to the local histories and specificities of the women from these newly decolonizing contexts (Rupp and Taylor 1987; Meyerowitz 1993; Leslie 2011; Laville 2013; Pieper-Mooney and Lanza 2013; McGregor 2016; Kim 2019). Long before the Danish economist Ester Boserup's groundbreaking *Women's Role in Economic Development* (1970) directed policymakers in donor nations to pay serious attention to women's distinct needs in development planning, elite Muslim East Pakistani women who visited the United States or the Soviet Union in the 1950s and 1960s expressed interest in the idea of "modernization" and voiced their openness to lessons from these wealthier countries that they deemed useful to help build their own new nation. In addition, the Muslim Bengali women visitors' assessments of US society provide an important contrast to the well-circulated essay by the Egyptian Islamist Sayyid Qutb about his stay in Greeley, Colorado, in 1949, which is often taken as the iconic Muslim representation of the United States in that period (Calvert 2000).

Rallying to "Counteract Communist Propaganda"

In April 1952, ten patrician women (of whom nine were white, one Black) gathered at the Women's University Club in New York to discuss, "What steps should be taken to rally the women of the free world to counteract communist propaganda?" (Committee of Correspondence [CoC] "Minutes," April 16, 1952; Laville 2002: 24, 172). Rose Peabody Parsons (usually referred to as Mrs. William Barclay Parsons in the committee's documents) had convened this first meeting of a group that initially called itself the Anonymous Committee. The women present had prior experience with major organizations such as the Woodrow Wilson Foundation, the Young Women's Christian Association, the Girl Scouts, and the National

Council of Negro Women. Parsons herself had worked with the Red Cross in both world wars and held leadership positions in the International Council of Women and its American affiliate, the National Council of Women. In 1946, she had founded Women United for the United Nations (WUUN), a coalition of US-based women's nongovernmental organizations that supported the newly established United Nations and its efforts toward peace (CoC "Asian Workshop, 1957"). WUUN survived the hostile McCarthyist scrutiny by pitching itself as a liberal voluntary educational organization that did not contradict the era's feminine ideal of domesticity, in sharp distinction and, indeed, outright opposition, to radical, action-oriented organizations such as World Organization of Mothers of All Nations, American Women for Peace, or the recently shuttered US Congress of American Women (Laville 2002; Weigand 2002; de Forest 2005; Gore 2011; Armstrong 2019).

Parsons brought this "safe" liberal internationalist approach to the new committee, which chose the name Committee of Correspondence at its August 1952 meeting. According to the minutes from that meeting, this was "the name given in Colonial days to committees in various colonies which kept each other informed of measures they were taking to cope with their mutual problems" with the hope that "our committee might some day be corresponding with similar committees in other parts [of] the free world." Thus the mid-twentieth century committee set out to counter Communist ideas through direct and personal correspondence with women around the world (CoC "Minutes," August 22, 1952; Laville 2002). Committee member Anna Lord Strauss, who had recently served as president of the National League of Women Voters, assured everyone that, based on her inquiries, no other group was doing similar work (CoC "Minutes," May 20, 1952).

Bolstered by an anonymous donation of $25,000 in early 1953, the committee began to plan its future activities with great enthusiasm. It decided that its upcoming "newsletters should be pegged to the three forthcoming Communist events," among them International Women's Day (March 8); International Children's Day (June 1); and the World Congress of Women, the conference of the Women's International Democratic Federation (WIDF), to be held in Copenhagen in June (CoC "Minutes," January 27, 1953). It also confirmed that its objective was to "establish mutual friendship and trust among women throughout the world who believe that a free society can minister to the news of mankind spiritually, intellectually and materially better than any other form of society." It would "establish channels of direct communication with responsible women leaders abroad" through not only letters, but also news bulletins and other forms of information "which give a forceful presentation of the above beliefs" and encourage these correspondents to keep the committee apprised of the "effectiveness of adverse propaganda in their communities" and suggest ways to "neutralize this propaganda" (Hester 1953: 2). The introductory letter that would be sent to "foreign contacts" would "give our friends the tools with which they can combat anti-American propaganda." The committee members insisted, predictably, that the information they themselves shared would be "factual . . . , not propaganda" (CoC "Minutes," February 24, 1953).

In April 1953, the Committee sent a news bulletin, a questionnaire, and a letter introducing itself to some 750 overseas contacts. The inaugural news bulletin focused on "The Emotional, Social, and Spiritual Growth of the World's Children," in anticipation of the Soviet Bloc's celebration of International Children's Day. The bulletin included not only US statements and efforts on behalf of American children, but also reports on the topic from the United Nations, a conference in Bombay, India, and—strategically—a Czechoslovakian child expert who clearly disapproved of Communist regimes' plans for families (CoC News Bulletin, April 1953). Ruzena Palentova, who was described in the bulletin as an "internationally known expert in the field of Child Welfare," had served as first deputy mayor of Prague until the Communists took over. Her recent lectures in the United States, such as one at a parent-teacher association meeting at Wandell School in Saddle River, New Jersey, were sponsored by the Crusade for Freedom, which also operated Radio Free Europe as part of its efforts to "encourage and enlighten the captive peoples behind the Iron Curtain" (Sunday News, February 15, 1953: 5). In the committee's bulletin, Palentova wrote of plans by "the Communist State" to shatter the "traditionally strong family ties in Czechoslovakia" and "disrupt family life by forcing the mother to work outside the home," thereby rendering the children vulnerable to being molded "into the pattern of well-disciplined little robots" to serve the Soviet system. This, according to the bulletin, was in sharp contrast to the approach to families in the Free World, as represented by the Bombay conference, which stressed the need "to preserve and strengthen family life, since a happy home life is essential to the greatest growth and development of every child" (CoC News Bulletin, April 1953; Laville 2002: 177–78).

The committee then turned its attention to composing a new letter that it hoped to send the following month to as many as "1000 women abroad" with the clear objective of taking "the wind out of the sail" of the upcoming Copenhagen congress (CoC "Minutes," April 28, 1953). Ultimately sent to 770 women in 72 countries and 100 US-based organizations, the committee's May 6 letter set out to provide "accurate information as to the sponsorship, aims and purpose of that congress," through a history of the leadership and activities of the left-leaning WIDF (CoC May 6 letter; Van Voris 1989: 7). At a late May meeting, Anne Hester was pleased to report that "the response" to the letter had been "excellent"—for example, the largest newspaper in Chile had translated and published the letter and the Committee for Free Asia had reported that it was "put . . . to good use" (CoC "Minutes," May 26, 1953).

The committee's vice-chair Dorothy Bauman attended the WIDF congress in Copenhagen and shared her observations on her return to New York. Bauman was one of the most widely traveled members of the committee: as a journalist she had covered the first free elections in Italy and the war in Greece (both in 1948) and more recently, in 1952, had traveled "in eighteen countries in Europe and the Middle East in four and one-half months." She was very well connected, not only to women like Rose Parsons but also to the State Department which, following her 1952 tour, sought her recommendations, as she later recalled, on "how the United States could respond to the Soviet effort to enlist women in their cause all over the world" (Bauman 1974: 137). Bauman herself had been responsible for facilitating the "anonymous" $25,000 donation from the CIA. In the summer of 1953, she spent almost seven weeks in Europe, where she encountered great concern over the "totalitarian techniques of Senator McCarthy and the trial of the Rosenbergs." She attributed the concern to "misinformation or lack of information" and Communist efforts, but conceded, at least when she wrote her memoirs two decades later, that even non-Communists "believed justice had been miscarried." She was surprised to find growing anti-Americanism in friendly or neutral cities like Paris and Geneva (Bauman 1974: 143). She reported to the committee that the WIDF congress in Copenhagen, held June 5–10, was "impressive" and "dramatically staged" and that the "Congress pledged itself to infiltrate women's organizations . . . in the free countries." She was particularly struck by the "considerably lower" average age of the women at the congress—thirty-nine—than of women involved in US organizations.

From Copenhagen, she had traveled on to Berlin and was there for the out-break of a massive uprising of East German citizens against the Socialist Unity Party on June 17. Ever committed to her larger agenda, she "regretted that the West had not exploited the propaganda opportunities presented by the revolt" (CoC "Minutes," June 30, 1953: 3).

In August 1953, the committee's executive director, Anne Hester, pro-posed a change in strategy. She was concerned that anti-Americanism, hostility, and "resentment in Asia, South America and the Middle East," as well as in Europe, arose as much from "US foreign policy—economy, social or political" as from Communist propaganda. She called therefore on the committee to "contribute to the restoration of confidence in the US, the leader of the free world." This new direction would lead the committee to produce articles with titles such as "Typical Days in the Lives of Five Amer-ican Women" to combat prevalent international—and Hollywood—portrayals of American women as "selfish idlers" (CoC *News Bulletin*, Feb-ruary 1955; Laville 2002: 178).

The committee also decided to address the issue of race relations in the United States in its bulletin. Anna Lord Strauss recalled how, on a 1949 Round the World tour with America's Town Meeting of the Air while she was still president of the League of Women Voters, their team had repeat-edly faced the same question from audiences across Asia: "In country after country, we heard the same theme song. It wasn't so much that commu-nism would bring greater satisfaction to the people. It was that in the United States, which boasted of its freedom and many advantages, how was it there was discriminations against the Negroes, that lynchings still occurred" (Laville and Lucas 1996: 570). In Karachi, Pakistan, a question about "the Negro problem" had come up at a meeting of the women of the Town Meeting group with leaders of the newly founded All Pakistan Women's Association. Edith S. Sampson, who in 1950 would become the first Black US delegate to the United Nations, had responded by sharing her own story, concluding that "America is making great progress in solving this problem; we have a long way to go yet, but my nieces are having an easier time than I had in getting an education. I am proud to be an Ameri-can" (Decker 1950: 196–197).

The committee decided to devote its October 1953 bulletin to the ques-tion of "The Negro in the United States of America" as a response to the "many inquiries received" on this topic. Accompanied by a cover letter from lawyer Eunice Carter, the committee's sole Black member, it included excerpts from reports and speeches of several Black leaders of the time who, in the 1950s, actively supported the US government's limited efforts toward racial equality, such as Lester B. Granger, Walter White, Mary McLeod Bethune, Ralph Bunche, and Edith S. Sampson. Conspicuously absent were Black leaders such as Eslanda and Paul Robeson who had been blacklisted for their outspoken criticism of the US government's progress on civil rights and their open support for anticolonial movements in Africa and Asia (CoC *News Bulletin*, October 1953; Von Eschen 1997; Duberman 2005; Ransby 2014).

A Congress "For Equality, for Happiness, for Peace"

The 1953 WIDF World Congress of Women in Copenhagen that Bauman attended attracted nearly two thousand women from sixty-seven countries, among them peasants, teachers, office workers, journalists, artists, members of parliament, "housewives," and "mothers of families some of them with 10 or 12 children." Among those unable to attend were Koreans who, with the Korean War still underway, were "suffer[ing] from the immense grief brought by the American aggression, and because they are courageously fighting for peace and the happiness of the new generation." The support enjoyed by the WIDF was reflected in a successful resolution proposed by the Indian delegation "emphasising . . . the incontestable authority of the WIDF in the international women's movement and the confidence which the women of the world have in it" (WIDF 1953: 3–4, 266).

The Pakistani delegate to the congress was the renowned leftist Punjabi women's rights activist Tahira Mazhar Ali. Following the 1947 partition, she had served on committees to establish peace between India and Pakistan and founded the Democratic Women's Association, which was affiliated with the Communist Party of Pakistan of which she was an active member. In 1971, the Pakistani state would label her a traitor because she was among the few West Pakistanis to protest against its violent military action in East Pakistan following the eastern wing's declaration of independence (Jalil 2015; Malik 2013: 523; Mohsin 2015).

In her speech in Copenhagen, Ali forcefully denounced the "twin evils of feudalism and foreign control" and expressed her apprehension regarding US interests in her country and of the "danger" of Pakistan becoming "embroiled in the western powers' plans for World War III." She continued: "There is talk of food gifts and loans, and simultaneously of bases and manpower supplies in the drive to make 'Asians fight Asians,' and there is

talk of Pakistan's participation in the Middle East Defense organisation—
an organisation intended to make Pakistan defenceless against the foreign
exploiters and their local agents." She concluded, "The women of Pakistan
will resist any attempt to use Pakistan as a power in the warmongers' game,
like all women all over the world" (WIDF 1953: 207–8). Tahira Mazhar Ali's
fears were soon realized. Less than a year after the WIDF congress, Pakistan's leaders became formally "embroiled" in Western treaties and mach-
inations. In 1954, Pakistan and the United States signed a Mutual Defense
Assistance Agreement and in 1955, Pakistan joined the Baghdad Pact
alongside Turkey, Iran, Iraq, and Great Britain.

A Tale of Two Wings

Pakistan was not even a decade old when the Committee of Correspondence began sending letters to women around the world. Although Pakistan
was founded in 1947 ostensibly as a homeland for the Muslims of the Indian
subcontinent, some thirty million Muslims remained in India and as many
non-Muslims in Pakistan. Moreover, the populations in the two wings of
the new country, separated by over a thousand miles across northern India,
shared little beyond being predominantly Muslim. As the US political scientist Hans J. Morgenthau observed in those early years, "It is as if after the
Civil War Louisiana and Maryland had decided to form a state of their own
with the capital in Baton Rouge. In fact, it is worse than that" (Morgenthau
1962: 261). East Bengal's clear demographic advantage, as well as its history
of progressive, even radical, politics worried the central government then
based in Karachi, West Pakistan (Toor 2011). The government's efforts to
forge a nation out of geographically divided and culturally and linguisti-
cally diverse peoples, with such misguided policies as the proposal to
impose Urdu as the national language, had already led to protests and, in
February 1952, several deaths in Dacca.

The committee seemed unaware of these tensions between the two
wings. The largest organization for women in Pakistan—and the committee's main contact—was the All Pakistan Women's Association (APWA),
founded in February 1949 by Raana Liaquat Ali, the wife of then–Prime
Minister Liaquat Ali Khan. Its headquarters were in Karachi with provincial
headquarters in Lahore, West Pakistan, and Dacca, East Pakistan. As was
also the case with women's organizations founded in Iran, Turkey, and
elsewhere in this period, APWA had strong government backing and most
of its members were female relatives of the predominantly male civil

servants and politicians (Chipp 1970; Ansari 2009; Jalal 1991). Given the glaring imbalance in the distribution of high-ranking positions in the civil service (and military) in favor of West Pakistanis, this meant that most leadership positions in APWA went to West Pakistani women. Not surprisingly, the committee's carefully maintained lists of correspondents (with their addressees, occupations, activities, and history of travel to the United States) reveal that most of its correspondence was directed to women leaders in West Pakistan or to West Pakistani women based in East Pakistan. It is telling that when APWA hosted Eleanor Roosevelt for a weeklong visit in February 1952, she spent only seven hours in East Bengal (Shehabuddin 2014).

In its early years, APWA received generous support from the Committee for Free Asia, which was renamed the Asia Foundation in 1954, with its goal to "support peace, independence, personal liberty, and social progress in Asia, and to foster mutual respect and understanding between Asia and the West." The foundation's board comprised the Pulitzer Prize–winning author James Michener, the university presidents of Stanford; the University of California, Los Angeles; Columbia; and Brown; and several business and foreign policy leaders. It set up offices in Lahore, Karachi, and Dacca (Asia Foundation 2014; Blum 1956). Throughout the 1950s, the Asia Foundation funded the travel of Pakistanis to attend different training workshops and conferences, including the Committee of Correspondence's first international workshop in 1956, "The Responsibilities of Freedom," directed primarily at correspondents from Asian countries. The "selection process" for workshop participants followed "careful criteria" and, in the matter of South Asia, reflected a concern with parity between India and Pakistan that proved paramount. The committee invited two correspondents each from India and Pakistan to the 1956 workshop. Both the Pakistanis invited, however, were from West Pakistan. Whether to redress this injustice or simply by accident, the committee invited three guests from East Pakistan and one from West Pakistan to its second Asian Workshop in 1957 (CoC "Asian Workshop, 1956"; CoC "Asian Workshop, 1957").

Pakistan through US Eyes

At this time, Pakistan was beginning to emerge as a friendly, even potentially "modern" country in US eyes. An August 1951 *Time Magazine* article had identified Turkey and Pakistan as the only two Muslim-majority countries where Islam might be able "to adapt itself to the changes that must come" and the then–Pakistani premier Liaquat Ali Khan (who would be assassinated in October 1951) as "probably the ablest Moslem political leader in office today" (*Time*, August 13, 1951: 33). News of the February 1952 killings in Dacca did make it to several regional US newspapers, courtesy of the United Press, but as a story about "language riots"; the *New York Times* devoted two short paragraphs to the crisis on page 2.

Some well-circulated mid-twentieth-century US representations of Bengal continued in the tradition of earlier nineteenth-century British depictions. British colonial officials, while appreciative of Bengal's great riches, had seen its people, to quote Thomas Macaulay ([1830] 1910: 39), as "enervated by a soft climate and accustomed to peaceful employments." Bengalis, he wrote,

> bore the same relation to other Asiatics which the Asiatics generally bear to the bold and energetic children of Europe. . . . Whatever the Bengalee does he does languidly. His favourite pursuits are sedentary. He shrinks from bodily exertion; and, though voluble in dispute, and singularly per-tinacious in the war of chicane, he seldom engages in a personal conflict, and scarcely ever enlists as a soldier. . . . There never, perhaps, existed a people so thoroughly fitted by nature and by habit for a foreign yoke.

In an article in the November 1952 issue of *National Geographic Magazine* on Pakistan's "first five busy years," authors and photographers Jean and Franc Shor wrote of "the muggy stillness of the East Bengal jungles" and of its rice paddies and jute fields (Shor and Shor 1952: 637). In March 1955, the Shors devoted an entire article to East Pakistan, this time under the title "East Pakistan Drives Back the Jungle: A Land of Elephant Roundups, Bengal Tigers, and a Bamboo Economy Takes Big Strides toward Becoming a Modern Nation." They wrote too of the East Pakistanis' "somewhat casual attitude toward work" (Shor and Shor 1955: 426). Alongside these fairly Orientalist and predictable invocations of elephants, Bengal tigers, snake charmers, and a poor work ethic, the Shors acknowledged the significance of East Pakistan's exports to "Pakistan's national solvency," mentioned the "jeeps, airplanes, rafts, dugout canoes and river steamers" they traveled on, and underscored the "high priority" given to women's education by the government and US aid programs (Shor and Shor 1955: 399, 402). They concluded that as citizens of an independent country, and therefore no longer colonial subjects, Bengalis were finding "inspiration" powerful enough to change attitudes toward work—and to lead East Pakistan "out of the jungle" (Shor and Shor 1955: 426). Against this backdrop of continued Western Orientalizing of Pakistan and Pakistanis (specifically East Pakistanis), the communications between the privileged women of Pakistan and of the Committee of Correspondence offer a glimpse into a different kind of relationship.

An Exchange of Ideas

The committee kept close track of replies to its mailings by country. The highest response rates were from Canada and Western Europe. By the time of the August 1953 report, six responses had arrived from Pakistan, representing 23 percent of letters mailed to that country. One early letter on file from East Pakistan was from Syeda Jahan Ara Karim. The committee's December 1953 news bulletin, focused on "Education for Peace: Through the International Exchange of Persons," reproduced the following excerpt from her letter in a section titled "Comments from our Correspondents":

> I have been to your country for higher studies in economy at Columbia University. . . . I was very much impressed with the educational system. . . . The ideas and friendly treatment I received in the USA . . . are working deep in my mind. I have been thinking of maintaining . . . relationships . . . with the women of America. I believe this will help in the betterment of our relationships with the USA and therefore the development of the peace throughout the world. (CoC *News Bulletin*, December 1953: 4)

Karim had recently returned from the United States with a masters in economics and was then a professor at Eden Girls' College in Dacca (Lamia Karim, pers. comm., January 2, 2021). She was also general secretary of the East Pakistan branch of APWA, which she described in her letter as having "similar aims and views" to the committee. She saw value in corresponding with the committee for the information the news bulletins might provide on the "progress made by women of other countries" since she "firmly believe[d]" that it was only through the "exchange of ideas" that "we can clarify misunderstandings prevailing among us and bring peace in this world" (CoC "Pakistan: Correspondence, General").

In all the excerpts selected for the bulletin, the focus was on the correspondents' views regarding the United States rather than regarding their own countries. A correspondent from South Africa who had visited recently after a gap of ten years claimed to have observed improvements in "race tension" in the United States while one from India wrote how she, while in the United States, had initially struggled against local customs but enjoyed herself much more after she resolved to "try to understand why Americans did things the way they did" (CoC *News Bulletin*, December 1953: 4).

Printed below these excerpts were US women's comments on the exchange program, in which they shared how their travels had revealed to them their prior ignorance and prejudice about other parts of the world. Peripatetic committee member Dorothy Bauman described how her travels to the Arab world had helped disabuse her of her old ideas about "the romantic colors of the Arabian Nights and other fiction." She had discovered, for example, how the 1921 Rudolf Valentino film "*The Sheik* misrepresent[ed] life in those areas as much as many of our own films misrepresent American life to others." Gladys Gilkey Calkins, then vice president of the World's YWCA, wrote of her visit to Equatorial Africa: "I went . . . expecting to find only jungles and primitive, illiterate people. I came back with the realization that I had seen a new civilization emerging." Eleanor Roosevelt, for her part, noted how her own travels had "enriched her understanding of other countries and other peoples," and how visitors "from the Middle East and India have told me frequently that they were impressed by the friendliness of the people they met in the United States" (CoC *News Bulletin*, December 1953: 4).

Shamsun Nahar Mahmud of Dacca, East Pakistan, received her first letter from the Committee of Correspondence in the fall of 1953. She didn't know how this Mrs. Parsons had learned of her or tracked down her address in order to write to her. In her October 1953 reply to Parsons, Mahmud pointedly asked her as much, after politely thanking her for her letter and the committee's news bulletins, and assuring her that she would be "very glad to be in close touch in future with your Committee." Mahmud also made clear that she herself had attended numerous international meetings focused on women's issues and concerns and understood not only "the similarity of our problems throughout the world," but "also the importance of [a] united effort to solve them." She wrote too of her own long experience in "the field of social welfare" and of her curiosity regarding women's efforts in other countries. Rose Parsons responded a few weeks later, explaining that Mrs. Rickard, "a personal friend of our Executive Director" had suggested Mahmud's name. Ada Thomas Rickard, who had passed on Mahmud's name to Executive Director Anne Hester, was then living in Karachi, West Pakistan, with her husband Samuel H. Rickard of the

Committee for Free Asia (CoC "Pakistan: Correspondence, General";
Washington Post, May 21, 1998: B8). Personal connections and networks such
as these, of course, proved crucial to the creation of the Committee of Correspondence as well as its efforts to connect with women around the world
between 1952 and 1969.

"A Truly 'Hardship Post'"

Committee of Correspondence members—and their friends and
supporters—regularly traveled to different parts of the world to learn about
the work of current correspondents and to recruit new ones. Elizabeth
Halsey, for example, visited Dacca, East Pakistan, in June 1955. She was a
consultant for the Carrie Chapman Catt Memorial Fund, a research and
educational fund established by the League of Women Voters. Halsey
reported that she arrived "prepared for the worst," having heard from colleagues that East Pakistan was "a truly 'hardship post,'" due to its "highly
developed insect life" as well as its "lack of contact with other countries"
and low literacy rate, all of which contributed to "slow progress." In letters
from her subsequent stop in Colombo, she admitted that it was "perhaps a
little disappointing" to have then found herself in a fine hotel in Dacca, the
new Hotel Shahbagh, with "private baths, hot and cold running water, and
perfectly palatable food," not to mention "taxis, hundreds of bicycle drawn
rickshaws and dial telephones." She had arrived in June rather than early
May because she had been advised to avoid the month of Ramadan, marked
by fasting and reduced social activity when "men go much oftener to the
temples [*sic*], and women stay quietly at home" (Halsey 1955).

Halsey's time in Dacca also forced her to revisit long-standing misconceptions about veiling and seclusion. Although she insisted that purdah—
the practice of seclusion and modest dress—still posed an obstacle to
women's desires to improve their condition, the institution was "no mysterious, bejeweled enslavement of women held behind locked doors await-
ing their master's pleasure." Purdah women, she wrote, came from all
walks of life, "from beggars to wives and daughters of government officials.
Their average of charm, beauty, enjoyment of life is about the same as those
of any other group of women anywhere." She found the Dacca University
students she met to be "very much like our own college girls without undue
shyness, or the repressions still so common to their mothers." She met
women leaders like Shamsun Nahar Mahmud and visited the recently

established Dacca Ladies' Club, which had received funding from the Asia Foundation for the construction of its new clubhouse. Other educated women she met included "a PhD from Yale and . . . the only nuclear physicist in Pakistan," which would have been Dr. Amina Rahman (Halsey 1955; *Pakistan Affairs* 1951: 8)

Halsey tried on several occasions to initiate a discussion about purdah, but found the Dacca women activists uninterested. It was not a priority for them and articles from this time in *Begum* also downplayed the salience of purdah as an obstacle for women. These elite Bengali women were, Halsey noted, far more concerned with the issue of polygamy. Just months earlier, the prime minister's second marriage had re-energized the national women's campaign against polygamy and, despite the resentment toward the West Pakistani–dominated central government's policies, Bengali women activists had started working with their West Pakistan counterparts to curb Muslim men's license to take multiple wives (Halsey 1955; Shehabuddin 2021: 183–186).

From her conversations, Halsey also quickly understood the emerging sense of bitterness among Bengalis regarding their relationship with West Pakistan. Just eight years after independence, they already felt that East Pakistan was like a "step-child," denied the "same consideration, privileges" accorded the western wing (Halsey 1955; Shehabuddin 2021: 183).

US committee members attended follow-up workshops organized by the women they had brought to the United States. For instance, the Asian delegates to the 1956 Asian Workshop organized their own workshops throughout South and Southeast Asia in late 1957 and committee member Anna Lord Strauss attended every one of the fifteen workshops held that fall. In a letter to her colleagues in New York from Dacca, dated October 9, 1957, Strauss remarked, "One great advantage of East Pakistan is that both in the center and in the villages there is a desire to learn, less apathy than in some other countries. This despite the fact that many women are still in purdah and go out only when covered from head to foot in a burkah notwithstanding the humid heat" (CoC "Member Files: Strauss, Anna Lord, 1953–66").

Like many of her fellow committee members, Strauss had long believed that the United States had a responsibility to provide global leadership on women's issues. The granddaughter of abolitionist and suffrage movement leader Lucretia Mott, Strauss had served as president of the League of

Women Voters and as a member of the US delegation to the United Nations before joining the Committee of Correspondence. Significantly, while she was president of the League of Women Voters the organization established the Carrie Chapman Catt Memorial Fund, envisioned, in the words of a fundraiser, as no less than what "might be called a 'little Marshall Plan' in the field of political education for women all over the world." Such efforts were deemed particularly vital to combat the manner in which women were "being bombarded with propaganda on the left side," and to encourage them instead to turn "to the U.S. to learn the political know-how" (Leslie 2011: 295).

The Asian Workshop of 1956

The US visit of thirteen Asian women in April–May 1956 was the committee's first major program beyond written correspondence. Between 1956 and 1963, the committee would bring in over 130 international visitors for eight annual workshops. Committee member Elizabeth Wadsworth would later describe the workshops as forums for generating and sharing ideas, as an opportunity to "give people information they could take home with them and use" (Van Voris 1989: 15).

The first workshop was designed precisely to tackle "the battle of ideologies under way in much of Asia" and, to quote a *New York Times* article on that month-long workshop, "to strengthen leadership among women in the non-Communist world" (Teltsch 1956). Committee members had decided that "the first invitations should go entirely to Asian lands, and to civic leaders whose influence could reach Asia's 750,000,000 women." Of course, the visitors had their own motivations for undertaking the long journey. While there were differences among them, they generally sought out what interested them most and made their own inferences from what they were formally shown by the committee. As Raksha Saran, a high-ranking activist from India, put it: "We in Asia are sensitive about aid given in a patronizing way or aid given with strings attached." Both the Pakistani guests spoke of their particular interest in the important role played by American women volunteers in a variety of settings (Teltsch 1956).

The West Pakistani physician Zarina Fazelbhoy later recalled that they had had the opportunity to meet human rights activist Eleanor Roosevelt, Frank Graham (who, among other things, had served as UN mediator in the Kashmir dispute), and Dorothy Height (civil rights activist and longtime president of the National Council of Negro Women). Although they did not meet Martin Luther King Jr. himself, "We had one of his helpers come and talk to us about civil rights." In an interview conducted decades later, Fazelbhoy expressed appreciation that this visit, her first to the United States, had not been as "an ordinary tourist," but rather "through the eyes of a group like this." She also valued the access their hosts provided to a variety of "social welfare and medical agencies—for the blind, the deaf, the old people, family planning, the whole works." She reminisced too about the contrast in the colors favored by the American and foreign guests, the former looking "so drab in their black suits" (upgrading merely to navy blue once spring arrived) while the latter were attired in "flashing silks, turquoise blue, peacock blue saris" (CoC "Oral Histories—Transcripts and Biographical Material, 1987–88").

Tazeen Faridi, Zarina Fazelbhoy's fellow West Pakistani delegate to the first workshop, would go on to assume a top leadership position in APWA and remain a steadfast proponent of intercultural exchanges. In a booklet she published in 1960 on the changing role of Pakistani women, for example, she argued: "There still remains a great gap in communication with women in other lands. We can still do so much to get to know each other better. One is often amazed by the questions put to one abroad!" (Faridi 1960).

International workshop participants reported also on their impressions of American society. Some, for instance, expressed surprise that most American women, "even university graduates," devoted themselves to their home and family after marriage. The Ghanaian journalist Edith Wuver and the Indian journalist Kamla Mankekar, who would attend the April 1961 workshop, would both comment at length on the extent of racial prejudice in the United States. Mankekar was particularly surprised "to find a people, going out of their way to buy the friendship of the world, so narrow-minded in their own country" (Van Voris 1989: 12, 21–22).

A Study of US Women's Lives

Shamsun Nahar Mahmud arrived in the United States for her own visit several months after the Asian Workshop of spring 1956, as a participant in the Foreign Leader Program of the International Educational Exchange Service at the US State Department. The American Council on Education's biographical sheet in preparation for her visit was shared with the

Committee of Correspondence. The sheet described her as "one of the first Muslim women graduates of undivided Bengal" with a "brilliant academic career" and "one of the pioneers of women's education and emancipation movement among the Muslims of undivided Bengal." It listed in detail the numerous positions she had held before and since partition, noted her long history of writing and publishing, and described her "knowledge of English" as "good." At the time of her visit, Mahmud held the post of president of the East Pakistan branch of APWA as well as leadership positions in several organizations and institutions (American Council on Education 1956). Mahmud's carefully planned US itinerary reflected attention to her areas of interest. Over the course of almost three months, between August 19 and November 10, 1956, she traveled widely and made some twenty stops throughout the country (Mahmud 2001: 140). In a July 1957 letter to the Committee of Correspondence, she reported that she had found the "coast to coast tour . . . very enjoyable and instructive" and would "never forget the kindness with which I was received everywhere in your wonderful country" (CoC "Pakistan: Correspondence, General").

In her journal, Mahmud described being particularly struck by how hard and productively US women worked, both inside and outside the home. She lamented how so many of the women in "our country," by comparison, remained confined to household tasks, trapped in a cycle of cooking and cleaning. She thought the higher education system in the United States to be superior to that of Great Britain in terms of access. While only a chosen few could attend university in Britain, she sensed that in the United States it was quite normal for everyone, men and women, to at least strive to study beyond high school. In reality, of course, the more than two million veterans that had attended college and university—courtesy of the original GI Bill that expired that same year—had been overwhelmingly white and included relatively few African Americans (Katznelson 2006).

Mahmud recognized the obstacles that US women had had to overcome not so long ago in order to attain the opportunities they now enjoyed and what she identified as equality with men in all spheres of life. She recalled her awed reaction to her experience of walking down the street in Hartford, Connecticut, just as the workday came to an end: the street was lined with banks and "flocks" of women poured out onto the street in such large numbers that it made it difficult for her to pass.

Even as college students, Mahmud marveled, American women worked and earned an income. She mentioned one Mr. Bietz she met, a widower whose daughter earned $600 working as a typist and stenographer during her vacation, and the many female students who worked in restaurants and cafeterias. The high regard accorded to all forms of work was clear, according to Mahmud, in the easy manner in which the women could switch from being a waitress to joining friends for a meal in that same establishment. This lack of rigid distinction and hierarchy between people doing different jobs was reinforced by the lack of difference in clothing that she observed among women of different socioeconomic backgrounds on the campus of the University of California, Berkeley.

Mahmud admitted that, before her visit, she had harbored the misconception that all US women involved in social welfare work were paid employees. She was surprised to discover in the many social welfare organizations she visited that innumerable volunteers, women and men, worked alongside the small salaried staff. She wrote of elderly women she saw in Red Cross offices, devoting hours to sewing in support of relief efforts, and younger women who took on driving shifts for Red Cross vehicles. She understood Americans' enthusiasm to help out in any capacity as a reflection of their deep love for their country. She remarked too that the position and rank of a woman's husband seemed to have little bearing on her position in her organization—in contrast perhaps to the situation with leadership positions in APWA. As an example, she pointed to one Mrs. Cooke who had been recently elected president of the League of Women Voters in Cincinnati even though her husband was an "ordinary" employee at Proctor and Gamble. Mahmud understood from her conversations with other league members that it was Cooke's own hard work and personality that had led to her rise to her present position.

Mahmud remarked that American women had been especially drawn to married life after the end of the Second World War, with many getting married while still in college, and that universities had had to respond by providing housing for married students. She noticed that while most families had no more than two children in the recent past, there was greater interest after the war in having three. The divorce rate remained high because, according to US men and women she spoke with, once a woman started to earn an income, she was less likely to put up with any bad behavior from her husband. Mahmud quickly added, however, that she saw no discord whatsoever among the couples she met. Also, she noted approvingly, since only the very wealthy in the United States could afford domestic help, no matter what a woman's responsibilities outside the home, she did not shirk her work at home. Of course, technological advances had made household work in the United States significantly easier. Rather than needing to stand over a stove all day to prepare the daily meals, the woman could have the food ready in "two minutes." That was why, Mahmud reported an American woman explaining to her, "we can work so much outside the home." Mahmud noted that the San Francisco Red Cross Society offered parenting classes to fathers, so that they would not be completely uninformed if ever called upon to assume responsibility (Mahmud 2001: 149–50).

Nonetheless, Mahmud reported, older US women she spoke with complained that younger women would do well to devote a little more energy and time to their children and household responsibilities. They suggested that it was precisely because US women had been confined to the home for so long that, now that they had their independence, they had lost all interest in household work. When Mahmud informed them that in her country, it was believed that bearing children and molding their characters was still the primary duty of women, even if they were highly educated, they warmly congratulated her.

Mahmud's interest in what she described as the particularly Western problem of juvenile delinquency led her to spend several hours observing proceedings at the San Francisco Juvenile Court on Woodside Avenue. While she certainly saw a relationship between juvenile delinquency and the fact that both parents worked outside the home, she did not think the problem was women working outside the home—as the American juvenile court judge claimed. Rather, Mahmud believed that the problem lay in the fact that, unlike places like Bengal, US society lacked the large extended families and the many relatives who could step in to help raise the children of working parents (Mahmud 2001: 150–51).

In an interview with a local newspaper during her five-day visit to Oxford, Ohio, Mahmud spoke of how pleased she was with her American tour, "despite the still wide differences in our way of living." Although in Pakistan, "we feel that a woman's first responsibility is her home and family . . . we are beginning to feel more and more that every person should be doing something of community service." She particularly appreciated how nursery schools had made it possible for US mothers to undertake "community service without slighting their responsibilities at home." She explained how "many people in my country felt that I should visit a country whose background and customs are more like ours, but I have seen many things here which we can adapt." She was also "quite impressed" with the questions the young children posed to her during her visits to schools in Oxford and elsewhere and their level of knowledge about her own background: "They not only asked about our form of government, but they followed up with correct comments on what other countries had similar governments. Many for them could point directly to Pakistan on the map—even to its separate parts, which I found quite pleasing!" (Howard 1956).

Toward the end of her visit, with the tumult of the 1956 presidential election over, Mahmud spent a few days in New York where she met with members of the Committee of Correspondence. She also received an invitation to have tea with Eleanor Roosevelt. They had first met in February 1952 during Roosevelt's brief visit to East Pakistan. Mahmud reported that her extended stay in the United States had only confirmed her previous sense that Roosevelt was a true representative of American women. Time and again, throughout the country, men and women alike shared with Mahmud their deep respect and admiration for the former first lady and human rights leader. Many even seemed quite open to her running for president (Mahmud 2001: 147–49).

As she assessed what she had learned from her tour of the United States, Mahmud lamented that her own country lacked the facilities necessary to impart civic training to its younger citizens on the order of what she had observed in elementary schools across the United States. Upon visiting several elementary and middle schools, she had noted the early responsibilities students took on—as school safety patrollers who assisted other students to cross intersections or as class librarian—as well as the nature of the training they received in civic practices, through student government, for example.

At the same time, she conceded that there were significant differences in the social structures of the two countries. After all, the close-knit and affectionate nature of families in her country meant that children were protected from the many dangers and temptations within reach of American children. Americans had spoken openly to her of how they looked on with envy at the good fortune of families in her society. Recognizing the advantages and disadvantages of both American and Pakistani societies, she concluded, "In building our state and nation, we will accept from foreign countries only that which is good for us. If we are careful on this point, we will be able to steer clear of many dangers. Many of their problems will not even be able to raise their heads in our society" (Mahmud 2001: 152–54).

Before the Demonization of Muslims

There is little doubt that Cold War concerns—the need to maintain stability and support for the United States in the developing world and keep Communism at bay—influenced the US individuals and organizations, scholars, foundations, and policymakers who engaged in a range of efforts to connect with women in the Third World. Modernization ideology clearly permeated all aspects of the US-Pakistan relationship in this period, from support for the military government down to the Peace Corps volunteers sent to Pakistan in 1961, the very first year that the corps was launched. And yet, the material presented in this article allows us a more nuanced perspective on that era, complicating both the traditional narratives of that period as well as the histories of imperial/colonial feminism and anti-Muslim racism.

US efforts targeting Bengali women in the early Cold War period were significantly different from the civilizing mission discourse of the colonial era. The goal was no longer to destroy the local culture—through religious conversion or imperial secularization—in order to save local women. In these early postwar years, the United States sought to distance itself from the old European colonial powers by celebrating the new sovereignty of the recently decolonized states and courting the leaders of Muslim-majority countries such as Pakistan, Saudi Arabia, and Iran to persuade them to join the US fight against Communism. An April 1952 *New York Times Magazine* article titled "Peace May Be in Moslem Hands" captured well the new strategic significance of these Muslim countries in European and US eyes: "The attitude of the Moslem countries toward the West might easily determine the future of every American, Britisher or Frenchman" (Landau 1952; Jacobs 2006).

In their own contributions to these US outreach efforts, members of the Committee of Correspondence (and associated organizations such as the League of Women Voters and Carrie Chapman Catt Memorial Fund) were careful in how they approached their work with foreign correspondents. Committee members were hopeful and optimistic about their ability to change the lives of the women around the world and to lure them away from Communism by presenting them with the example of their own privileged lives and opportunities. This required them, unsurprisingly, to downplay racist attitudes and institutions, including Jim Crow, as well as the fair amount of gender discrimination that structured US society.

Remarkably, Islam and Muslim identity did not appear in US writings about Pakistani women as a problem to be overcome. US organizations and policymakers saw Islam as no greater an obstacle to modernization than any other "traditional" worldview. In other words, in the 1950s and 1960s, they considered Muslims just as capable of being "modernized" as any other people in the Third World. They did not see Muslims as uniquely backward, or Muslim women as singularly oppressed. This would begin to change in the 1970s when second-wave feminism in the US would coincide with growing anti-Muslim sentiment in both the government and the general population, following the oil embargo of the early 1970s, the emergence of a voting bloc of Muslim countries at the United Nations on the question of Palestine and Zionism in 1975, and the Iranian Revolution of 1979 (Said 1997: 5–6; Aydin 2017: 210–11; Shehabuddin 2021).

Bengali East Pakistani leaders like Shamsun Nahar Mahmud, for their part, were clearly eager to learn about US society and institutions, but their detailed descriptions of life in America reveal a lack of either defensiveness or a sense of inferiority. In these early years of the Pakistan *amal*, they were still basking in the pride of liberation from the "humiliation" of colonial rule. They approached the United States and US women, to again quote the words of the young Mushfequa Rahman, holding "our head up high" and with aspirations of "walk[ing] alongside the rest of the world as we move forward." On their visits to the United States, these confident representatives of a new sovereign nation admired much of what they saw and reflected carefully on what might work in their own society and what would not. Mahmud's own records of her US trip confirm what urban educated women in East Pakistan had already long been articulating in the pages of *Begum* and elsewhere regarding what they considered to be obstacles to their own desires to study, work, and lead meaningful lives, and about their strategies to effect change. They found US-style day cares very attractive, but they also understood that the extended family structure in Pakistan made them less urgent a priority there. Similarly, while it was important for women to work outside the home and contribute to nation-building, it did not follow that they needed to uncover their heads to do so (Begum 2006).

Finally, revisiting this period allows us to appreciate how the nature of Muslim women's activism has been shaped by local and global political contexts as well as by changing Western ideas about Muslim women. Much of the politically urgent writing on imperial feminism by postcolonial feminist scholars following 9/11 and the invasion of Afghanistan argued, and assumed, that the West has always viewed Muslim women as oppressed by Islam. I've tried to show here that this was not the case in the 1950s. That is, because Muslims were not the main enemy (yet) in US eyes, US policymakers and organizations who engaged in public diplomacy in the 1950s and 1960s did not see the religion of Islam, or its teachings and practices, as a particular obstacle to modernization nor did they regard Muslim women as oppressed specifically by Islam. The early years of the Cold War period were marked, undoubtedly, by US racism and condescension toward the populations of Asia and Africa—but, significantly, not by the distinct and overt anti-Muslim and anti-Arab racism of the late– and the post–Cold War eras. This created a space for Muslim women in countries like Egypt, Indonesia, and Pakistan to mobilize to change the Muslim Personal laws that governed them (regardless of their personal relationship to Islam) without the constraints of the double bind that many Muslim women find themselves in today, in an age of anti-Muslim attacks often couched in feminist discourse.

. . . .

Elora Shehabuddin is professor of transnational Asian studies and core faculty, Center for the Study of Women, Gender, and Sexuality, at Rice University. She is author of *Sisters in the Mirror: A History of Muslim Women and the Global Politics of Feminism* (2021).

Works Cited

Akhtar, Shirin. 2012. "East Bengal Women's Education, Literature, and Journalism: From the Late Nineteenth Century through the 1960s." In *Women's Activism: Global Perspectives from the 1890s to the Present*, edited by Francisca de Haan, Margaret Allen, June Purvis, and Krassimira Daskalova, 106–20. New York: Routledge.

American Council on Education. 1956. "Biographical Data on Mrs. Shamsun Nahar Mahmud." Sophia Smith Collection, Smith College Library.

Ansari, Sarah. 2009. "Polygamy, Purdah, and Political Representation: Engendering Citizenship in 1950s Pakistan." *Modern Asian Studies* 43, no. 6: 1421–61.

Armstrong, Elisabeth. 2016. "Before Bandung: The Anti-imperialist Women's Movement in Asia and the Women's International Democratic Federation." *Signs: Journal of Women in Culture and Society* 41, no. 2: 305–31.

Armstrong, Elisabeth. 2019. "Peace and the Barrel of the Gun in the Internationalist Women's Movement, 1945–49." *Meridians* 18, no. 2: 261–77.

Asia Foundation. 2014. "The Asia Foundation Celebrates Sixty Years in Pakistan." Islamabad: Asia Foundation. asiafoundation.org/publication/the-asia -foundation-celebrates-60-years-in-pakistan/.

Aydin, Cemil. 2017. *The Idea of the Muslim World: A Global Intellectual History.* Cambridge, MA: Harvard University Press.

Bauman, Dorothy. 1974. "Memories," manuscript, Sophia Smith Collection, Smith College Library.

Begum, Maleka, ed. 2006. *Nirbachito Begum: Ordhoshatabdir somajchitro, 1947–2000* [Selections from Begum: A half century of social portraits, 1947–2000]. 3 vols. Dhaka: Pathak Somabesh.

Blum, Robert. 1956. "The Work of the Asia Foundation." *Pacific Affairs* 29, no. 1: 46–56.

Calvert, John. 2000. " 'The World Is an Undutiful Boy!': Sayyid Qutb's American Experience." *Islam and Christian-Muslim Relations* 11, no. 1: 87–103.

Chipp, Sylvia A. 1970. "The Role of Women Elites in a Modernizing Country: The All Pakistan Women's Association." PhD diss., Syracuse University.

Committee of Correspondence (CoC) Archives, Sophia Smith Collection, Smith College Library, available at *Women Organizing Transnationally: The Committee of Correspondence, 1952–1969,* link.gale.com/apps/collection/3XNW/GDSC?u= txshracd2542&sid=GDSC; accessed through Rice University, January 4, 2021.

Decker, Mary Bell. 1950. *The World We Saw with Town Hall.* New York: Richard R. Smith.

Deeb, Lara. 2006. *An Enchanted Modern: Gender and Public Piety in Shi'i Lebanon.* Princeton, NJ: Princeton University Press.

de Forest, Jennifer. 2005. "Women United for the United Nations: US Women Advocating for Collective Security in the Cold War." *Women's History Review* 14, no. 1: 61–74.

de Haan, Francisca. 2010. "Continuing Cold War Paradigms in Western Historiography of Transnational Women's Organisations: The Case of the Women's International Democratic Federation (WIDF)." *Women's History Review* 19, no. 4: 547–73.

de Haan, Francisca. 2012. "The Women's International Democratic Federation (WIDF): History, Main Agenda, and Contributions, 1945–1991." Alexandria, VA: Alexander Street. search.alexanderstreet.com/view/work/bibliographic_entity% 7Cbibliographic_details%7C2476925.

Duberman, Martin. 2005. *Paul Robeson: A Biography.* London: The New Press.

Faridi, Tazeen. 1960. *The Changing Role of Women in Pakistan.* Karachi: Department of Advertising, Films, and Publications, Government of Pakistan.

Gore, Dayo F. 2011. *Radicalism at the Crossroads: African American Women Activists in the Cold War.* New York: New York University Press.

Gupta, Sarmistha Dutta. 2009. "*Saogat* and the Reformed Bengali Muslim Woman." *Indian Journal of Gender Studies* 16, no. 3: 329–58.

Halsey, Elizabeth. 1955. "Letter from Elizabeth T. Halsey to Carrie Chapman Catt Memorial Fund, September 15, 1955." In *Women and Social Movements, International—1840 to Present,* edited by Kathryn Kish Sklar and Thomas Dublin. Accessed through Fondren Library, Rice University, https://library.rice.edu//, March 26, 2021.

Hester, Anne. 1953. "Report on the Committee of Correspondence, March 1–August 31, 1953." In *Women Organizing Transnationally: The Committee of Correspondence, 1952–1969*, link.gale.com/apps/collection/3XNW/GDSC?u=txshracd2542&sid=GDSC; accessed through Rice University, January 4, 2021.

Howard, Robert T. 1956. "Women's Leader from Pakistan Likes Questions of Small Children, She Says during Oxford Visit." *Hamilton Journal—The Daily News*, October 27.

Jacobs, Matthew F. 2006. "The Perils and Promise of Islam: The United States and the Muslim Middle East in the Early Cold War." *Diplomatic History* 30, no. 4: 705–39.

Jamal, Amina. 2013. *Jamaat-e-Islami Women in Pakistan: Vanguard of a New Modernity?* Syracuse, NY: Syracuse University Press.

Jalal, Ayesha. 1991. "The Convenience of Subservience: Women and the State of Pakistan." In *Women, Islam and the State*, edited by Deniz Kandiyoti, 77–114. Philadelphia: Temple University Press.

Jalil, Xari. 2015. "Tahira Mazhar Ali's Death a Profound Loss to Many." *Dawn*, March 24. www.dawn.com/news/1171442.

Katznelson, Ira. 2006. *When Affirmative Action Was White: An Untold History of Racial Inequality in Twentieth-Century America*. New York: W. W. Norton.

Kim, Suzy. 2019. "The Origins of Cold War Feminism during the Korean War." *Gender and History* 31, no. 2: 460–79.

Landau, Rom. 1952. "'Peace May Be in Moslem Hands': Proud, Religious, and Nomadic, These People Will Judge Us Friends or Foes by Our Works." *New York Times Magazine*, April 6.

Laville, Helen. 2002. *Cold War Women: The International Activities of American Women's Organisations*. Manchester: Manchester University Press.

Laville, Helen. 2013. "Gender and Women's Rights in the Cold War." In *The Oxford Handbook of the Cold War*, edited by Richard H. Immerman and Petra Goedde, 523–39. Oxford: Oxford University Press.

Laville, Helen, and Scott Lucas. 1996. "The American Way: Edith Sampson, the NAACP, and African American Identity in the Cold War." *Diplomatic History* 20, no. 4: 565–90.

Leslie, Grace Victoria. 2011. "United for a Better World: Internationalism in the U.S. Women's Movement, 1939–1964." PhD diss., Yale University.

Macaulay, Thomas Babington. (1830) 1910. *Essay on Lord Clive*. London: Harrap.

Mahmood, Saba. 2005. *Politics of Piety: The Islamic Revival and the Feminist Subject*. Princeton, N.J.: Princeton University Press.

Mahmud, Mushfequa. 2001. *Begum Shamsun Nahar Mahmud, Ekti pramanyo jiboni* [Begum Shamsun Nahar Mahmud: An authoritative biography]. Dhaka: Bulbul Publishing House.

Malik, Anushay. 2013. "Alternative Politics and Dominant Narratives: Communists and the Pakistani State in the Early 1950s." *South Asian History and Culture* 4, no. 4: 520–37.

McGregor, Katharine. 2016. "Opposing Colonialism: The Women's International Democratic Federation and Decolonisation Struggles in Vietnam and Algeria, 1945–1965." *Women's History Review* 25, no. 6: 925–44.

McMahon, Robert J. 1994. *The Cold War on the Periphery: The United States, India, and Pakistan.* New York: Columbia University Press.

Meyerowitz, Joanne. 1993. "Beyond the Feminine Mystique: A Reassessment of Postwar Mass Culture, 1946–1958." *Journal of American History* 79 (March): 1455–82.

Mohsin, Jugnu. 2015. "Tahira Mazhar Ali Khan, 1925–2015." *Friday Times,* March 27. www.thefridaytimes.com/tahira-mazhar-ali-khan-1925-2015/.

Morgenthau, Hans J. 1962. *The Impasse of American Foreign Policy.* Chicago: University of Chicago Press.

Pakistan Affairs. 1951. "Pakistan Claims First Woman Atomic Scientist in Asia." *Pakistan Affairs,* August 3, 1951, 8.

Pieper-Mooney, Jadwiga E., and Fabio Lanza. 2013. *De-centering Cold War History: Local and Global Change.* London: Routledge.

Ransby, Barbara. 2014. *Eslanda: The Large and Unconventional Life of Mrs. Paul Robeson.* New Haven, CT: Yale University Press.

Rotter, Andrew J. 2013. "South Asia." In *The Oxford Handbook of the Cold War,* edited by Richard H. Immerman and Petra Goedde, 212–29. Oxford: Oxford University Press.

Rupp, Leila J., and Verta Taylor. 1987. *Survival in the Doldrums: The American Women's Rights Movement, 1945 to the 1960s.* Oxford: Oxford University Press.

Said, Edward W. 1997. *Covering Islam: How the Media and the Experts Determine How We See the Rest of the World.* Rev. ed. New York: Vintage.

Shehabuddin, Elora. 2014. "Feminism and Nationalism in Cold War Pakistan." *Südasien–Chronik* [South Asia Chronicle], no. 4: 49–68.

Shehabuddin, Elora. 2021. *Sisters in the Mirror: A History of Muslim Women and the Global Politics of Feminism.* Oakland: University of California Press.

Shor, Franc, and Jean Shor. 1955. "East Pakistan Drives Back the Jungle: A Land of Elephant Roundups, Bengal Tigers, and a Bamboo Economy Takes Big Strides toward Becoming a Modern Nation." *National Geographic Magazine* 107, no. 3 (March): 398–99, 402, 410–11, 420–23, 426.

Shor, Jean, and Franc Shor. 1952. "Pakistan, New Nation in an Old Land." *National Geographic Magazine* 102, no. 5 (November): 637–42, 654–55, 658, 664, 666–67, 672–75.

Sunday News. 1953. "Parent-Teachers to Hold Meeting Wednesday Night." *Sunday News,* Ridgewood, New Jersey, February 15, 5.

Teltsch, Kathleen. 1956. "Twelve Asian Women Study Life in U.S.: Their Visit Is Designed to Aid Female Leadership in the Anti-communist World." *New York Times,* April 29.

Time. 1951. "The Moslem World." *Time Magazine* 58, no. 7: 28–33.

Toor, Saadia. 2011. *The State of Islam: Culture and Cold War Politics in Pakistan.* London: Pluto Press.

Van Voris, Jacqueline. 1989. *The Committee of Correspondence: Women with a World Vision.* Northampton, MA: Sophia Smith Collection, Smith College.

Von Eschen, Penny M. 1997. *Race against Empire: Black Americans and Anticolonialism, 1937–1957.* Ithaca, NY: Cornell University Press.

Washington Post. 1998. "Ada Thomas Rickard: Churchwoman." *Washington Post,* May 21, B8.

Weigand, Kate. 2002. *Red Feminism: American Communism and the Making of Women's Liberation.* Baltimore: Johns Hopkins University Press.

WIDF. 1953. *As One! For Equality, for Happiness, for Peace.* Berlin: Women's International Democratic Federation.

Wilford, Hugh. 2009. *The Mighty Wurlitzer: How the CIA Played America.* Cambridge, MA: Harvard University Press.

Amina Jamal

The Entanglement of Secularism and Feminism in Pakistan

Abstract: In many Muslim-majority societies, including Pakistan, liberal pro-gressive subjects who espouse feminism and gender equality do so through the language of universal human rights and political secularism. This brings them into conflict not only with anti-secular rightwing conservatives within their own societies but also with progressive scholarly critics of secularism in other contexts. To clear the space for a nuanced understanding of femi-nist secularism in Pakistan, the author examines a unique style of politics that may be described as "secular" among middle-class Muslim women interviewed by the author in Karachi and Islamabad. She argues that the espousal of secularism by feminists as a political cultural discourse in South Asia can initiate a politics that challenges hegemonic notions of self, com-munity, and nation that are gaining strength in Pakistan. This position mili-tates against simplistic understandings of secular feminism in this Muslim-majority society as the politics of colonized subjects or as a hegemonic nexus for reproducing the discursive power of Eurocentric and universalist discourses.

Introduction

During the course of my ongoing research on women's struggles in Paki-stan I was invited to give a talk at a major Islamic university for women whose stated mission is to promote Islamic knowledge while producing scholars who can contribute to the economic, social, political, and other development needs of Muslim societies.[1] Since I had just completed a study

MERIDIANS · feminism, race, transnationalism   20:2 October 2021
DOI: 10.1215/15366936-9547932 © 2021 Smith College

involving women activists of a politico-religious movement, Jamaat-e-Islami (JI), I thought it would be appropriate to speak about the struggles of Islamist women to this audience of mostly hijab- and niqab-wearing female students and teachers.[2] In addition to the political, social, and religious activities of the Jamaat women, I mentioned that a key project of the Jamaat was to transform Pakistan into an Islamic state by erasing all laws and principles that made it "too secular." I was surprised at the response in the room to this characterization of the Pakistani state. Many hands went up and an energetic discussion followed. Despite their evidently deep attachment to Islam and their meticulous observance of what are considered to be Islamic practices in Pakistan, such as prayers, veiling, and gender segregation, my audience was clearly opposed to a state dedicated to stamping out "secularism." They saw strong resonances of the "Islamic" in much of what was deemed to constitute "secular" in the context of liberal politics in Pakistan, for example, equal rights for all citizens regardless of gender or faith, non-sectarianism among Muslims, respect and tolerance for religious minorities, modern economic development, women's rights and mobility, and parliamentary democracy. As someone immersed in the historical and political interplay between notions of "secularism" and the "Islamic" in the South Asian Muslim context, it was evident to me that these religiously identified women did not privilege secularism simplistically as a more egalitarian political ideology since they, like many Muslims, believed in the ability of Islam to deliver equally democratic and egalitarian principles. Indeed, theirs was a measured response to the discursive constructions of "secular" and "Islamic" within intra-Muslim and intracommunity politics in South Asia due to which they were unwilling to support the kind of "Islamic" state envisioned by some politico-religious groups, in particular the Jamaat-e-Islami.[3] Yet their leniency toward the terms *secular* and *secularism* surprised me, since in Pakistan secularism is a political-cultural ideology widely discredited as un-Islamic, suspected of foreign affiliation, and largely associated with feminism. It is "feminists" who, like their counterparts in many Muslim-majority societies, are seen to espouse secularism through their persistent demands for gender equality and universal human rights and through their relentless challenging of hegemonic projects of religious purity and cultural authenticity.

My experience at the Islamic university reaffirmed for me that secularism is not simply an analytical category for social scientific analysis; rather, it is a normative discourse, as ably theorized by scholars such as Talal Asad

(2003), Saba Mahmood (2005), Sherene Razack (2008), and other critical theorists. Critical scholarship in the wake of Michel Foucault theorizes secularism as an encompassing form of power associated with the modern state that produces secular subjectivities through discourses of freedom, rights, and equality.[4] In the aftermath of 9/11 and increased Islamophobia in many secular societies—Euro-American, for instance, as well as India under the current regime—postcolonial and critical race scholars emphasize that contemporary global politics of secularism are constructed, shaped, and deployed in opposition to Islam and Muslim subjectivities. They make the persuasive argument that secularism as a globalizing discourse serves to install a dividing line between "modern" and premodern subjects and civilizations that furthers Western imperialist agendas toward Muslim societies and also toward Muslim communities in Western societies (Asad 2003; Chatterjee 1993; Scott and Hirschkind 2006; Razack 2007). Furthermore, ever since the groundbreaking work of Saba Mahmood (2005), critical postcolonial feminist discourse acknowledges that many Muslim women may agentively privilege faith-defined and communitarian norms, rather than individualizing secular ones, in order to accomplish individually and collectively fulfilling lives.[5] A burgeoning literature from postcolonial feminists of Muslim and Arab descent, but also from authoritative Western feminists such as Judith Butler (2004), Joan Scott (2007), and Sara Farris (2017), has drawn upon Mahmood's theory to critically examine the complex relationship of secular feminisms everywhere and Islamophobic politics in Euro-American societies since the start of the US-led war on terror in October 2001. This literature has exhaustively examined the possibilities and limitations of secularism as a feminist project, and explored political differences among feminist struggles at various historical moments and across transnational sites. Clearly, secular feminism not only irks right-wing and religious conservatives in Pakistan but also discursively challenges critical progressive scholarship on secularism in many other contexts (e.g., Calhoun, Juergensmeyer, and Vanantwerpen 2011).

Acknowledging the normative character of secularism and the possibility of feminist complicity in secularism's circulation as an Islamophobic discourse is troubling for transnational feminist scholars like myself who seek to challenge racialized forms of secularism in Western liberal societies but also reject gender-oppressive politics posing as "Islamic." This makes it necessary to understand why prominent feminists and mainstream feminist movements in Pakistan, the world's largest Islamic State, might espouse "secularism," and why they see it as a route to social, particularly gender, equality and democratic freedom.

This essay seeks to bring under scholarly scrutiny the entanglement of feminism and secularism in Pakistan by an examination of feminists' own understanding of "secularism" and "Islam" and their explanations of feminism's individual and collective engagement with secularism as a political project and as a lifestyle, when counterposed against politically and ideologically dominant notions of the "Islamic." Further, my project has an explicitly feminist agenda since I argue that a "secular" attitude, when embraced as an admixture of defiance and defensiveness by feminists in Pakistan, denotes and enables modes of identification and political activism that may escape notice when secularism and Islam are simply posited in a dichotomy of secular-versus-religious, as subjectivities, gender performativity, or political positions. While informed by the extant feminist literature on secularism, Islam, and gender, this essay diverges significantly from existing scholarship by drawing scholarly attention to the complex cultural-political and affective struggles of Muslim women in Pakistan who are caught between universalist discourses of secular emancipation and parochial assertions of "Islamic" citizenship. I draw on the notion of transnational feminist practices advocated by scholars such as Inderpal Grewal (Grewal and Kaplan 1994, 2000) and Gayatri Spivak (2004, 1993), and others in their wake, who have expanded Foucauldian theories of power and subject-formation to conceptualize women as multiply interpellated subjects of scattered and dispersed cultural, political, and economic discourses. These insights expand opportunities to discern modes of enactment, subjectivities, gender performativity, and political positions beyond identitarian notions of secular-versus-religious.

In the following discussion, I will introduce my research project and situate it within Pakistan's ongoing military and political involvement in the US-led war in Afghanistan (1979 to the present), which has dramatically shifted the relationship of gender, secular nationalism, and Islam and intensified political and cultural divisions in society. Following Fennella Cannell's (2010: 100) advice to treat secularism as "a form of ethnographic datum," I will describe the divergent understandings of and attitudes toward "secularism" and the "secular" in Pakistani society and among liberal feminists. Since my task is to clear the space for a nuanced understanding of feminist "secularism" in Pakistan, my discussion throughout this essay will intertwine women, gender, and nation with the social-cultural history of Islam in South Asia along with the discourses of anti-colonial nationalism in this region.[6]

The Project

The arguments in this paper are based on my interviews with fourteen Muslim women in Karachi and Islamabad who may be described as feminist and secular.[7] These women were diverse in terms of regional affiliation, ethnic background, age, sections of the "middle class," educational achievement, bodily performativity, relationship to Islam, and linguistic preferences. The majority of them had been active participants in the initial phase of what is termed the "women's movement," a highly vocal public activism by individuals and groups against the Pakistani state in its aggressively Islamizing period (1978–88). I enlisted these women through the use of "snowball sampling," which enables the researcher to access a particular social network and tap into its "social knowledge," defined by feminists as knowledge that is dynamic, processual, and accumulative and aligns with poststructuralist challenges to the notion of a Cartesian Subject as a container of knowledge.[8] Widely used by feminist researchers to access members of marginalized groups, I found this method useful for my project since, despite the social class location of individual participants, the subjectivity of "feminist" is neither normative nor prestigious in Pakistani society, nor in many societies in the contemporary neoliberal era.[9] Avoiding distinctly religious or self-identified secular atheists, I purposefully selected women for whom the Islam/secular dichotomy would be likely to pose political and personal challenges due to their (in my understanding) somewhat ambiguous positioning in both "Islam" and "secularism." That is, I tried to recruit women who were associated with feminist projects or movements that have publicly pursued a secular, rights-based politics and whose enactment of their Muslim identity was not publicly evident (that is, they did not wear hijab, niqab, etc.).[10] I also purposefully eliminated women who are publicly associated with a religious movement or politico-religious party or enact what Mahmood has termed a "pious" subjectivity (Mahmood 2005).[11] On the other hand, I did not deliberately seek out individuals who had publicly declared themselves to be antireligious or atheist.[12] In short, I wanted to interview self-identified feminist Muslim women of the middle classes who through political, social, or cultural activism demand a secular state and society as a key principle of their project for gender equality and religious pluralism. The embodied feminist performativity enabled by the entwining of "secular," "feminist," and "Muslim" that emerged through this study may be encapsulated in the words of my interlocutor Kiran, who said: "Many of the feminists I come across say they are atheist but they are not against religion. For me my religion is my personal life and that is how it should be and that is how it was at one time— now it has become everybody's business whether I am a good Muslim or a bad Muslim, whether I practice my religion at home and how I practice it— this is what bothers me."[13]

While I used a set of guidelines to ensure the commonality of topics across interviews and to provide coherence to the larger project, the actual "interviews" invariably turned into a discussion rather than a question-response format that might be controlled by the researcher. I have attempted to transcribe the words of my interlocutors as faithfully as possible, although their comments have been edited for readability.

Feminism, Secularism, and Islamization

Few women in my research were interested in offering a definition of secularism when prompted to do so; instead, they juxtaposed the "secular" against the oppressiveness of a singularly defined state-implemented version of "Islamic nation" imposed on a society they considered to be permeated with heterogeneous religious and cultural traditions and practices. Sana, a scholar who has acquired a global reputation as an analyst of the Pakistani state and its institutions, signaled toward this when she said: "In this day and age in Pakistan the minute you say the word *secular*, people kind of boil over . . . not even bothering to understand what it means; that, in fact, secularism could be a very Islamic concept. People are just not willing, you know, to hear that." Sana, who was strongly in support of a secular state in Pakistan, called for a separation of religious identity and citizenship rights by drawing on her extensive knowledge of Islamic history to emphasize instances where there was a clear distinction between political and legal administration and community identity. She deplored the fact that changes in the ideological character of the state had enabled the differentiation of citizens based on their religious and sectarian identification. Indeed, almost all my interlocutors claimed the previous existence of a more "tolerant" and "pluralistic" Muslim culture in South Asian society, which they argued could only be restored by a "secular" state in Pakistan—that is, one that did not prioritize Islam over other religions.

They almost always elaborated this argument with references to their individual or women's collective political and cultural response to "Islamization," a religio-military project aimed at promoting Sunni religious nationalism to serve the objectives of the state's foreign policy and militaristic ambitions. Although these tendencies existed since the creation of the state in 1947, Islamization was officially named as state policy during the military regime of General Mohammed Zia-ul-Haq (1977–88), who implemented wide-ranging changes in law, politics, the economy, education, and media, and drastically altered the citizenship status of women and religious minorities (Mumtaz and Shaheed 1987; Weiss 1986a; Khan 2006; Jahangir and Jilani 1990). The institutionalization of a hitherto ambiguous state-religion relationship reinvigorated questions of secularism versus Islam in Pakistan, with middle-class women's groups at the forefront of the opposition to state-prescribed Islamic national identity and culture. In sum, as explained by my interlocutors, in the context of Pakistani politics secularism was seen to imbue gendered subjects with the propensity to trouble all kinds of political, social, and cultural orthodoxies.

General Zia's Islamization project acquired global militaristic significance when his regime allied itself with the United States against the Soviet Union in a proxy war in Afghanistan (1978–89). Constructed as an alliance of Western liberalism and Islam against "Godless" Communism, and with a strong backing by Saudi Arabia, this coalition significantly bolstered General Zia's regime financially and ideologically. Unlike neighboring Iran, where a popular revolution had brought about an Islamic government, there was very little international outrage as a military regime, accomplished by ousting a democratically elected leader, imposed repressive regulations under the guise of Islamization in Pakistan mostly through presidential ordinances and directives for an entire decade.[14] This alliance also opened the way for Pakistan becoming a key center of both US-led counter-terrorism and Muslim terrorism in the present time (Rashid 2001, 2008). These connected events speeded the expansion of narrower and more prescriptive interpretations of Islam in Pakistani society, with devastating effects for the constitutional rights and human rights of women, gender-queer persons, and sectarian and religious minorities. Substantial scholarship by Pakistani scholars has recorded the ongoing effects of state-imposed Islamization, as successive governments have lacked the political weight or the moral will to modify some of the most detrimental laws and measures introduced under its cover. Not the least of these are the controversial Hudood Ordinances, which have effectively reduced the status of women and religious minority citizens below that of the Sunni Hanafi male citizen-subject (Mumtaz and Shaheed 1987; Khan 2006; Jahangir and Jilani 1990; Mehdi 1994; Said Khan, Saigol, and Zia 1994; Shaheed and Mumtaz 1990; Shakir 1997; Weiss 1986a; Zia 2018; Toor 2011; Jamal 2013). In this regard, it is imperative to draw attention to a point repeatedly emphasized by feminist historians and by the interlocutors of my study: the transformation of middle-class women from beneficiaries of the state's benevolent cultural nationalism into a strong force for secular rights and universal equality against state-imposed Islamization (Mumtaz and Shaheed 1987; Hussain, Mumtaz, and Saigol 1997; Weiss 2003; Jamal 2013; Toor 2007; Zafar 1991). Literature by and on the women's movement of this period claims it as the key moment for "secular" and "feminist" consciousness in Pakistan (Mumtaz and Shaheed 1987; Said Khan 1994; Haq 1996; Toor 1997).

In marked contrast with India, the concept of "secularism" had never really functioned as a topic in serious debates about the possibilities for organizing social, political, and ethical life in Pakistan; however, since the 1980s it has become an effective epithet to delegitimize the claims of equity-seeking groups. Of the multiplicity of ongoing conflicts and divisions resulting from failed domestic economic development, misguided regional and global alliances, militaristic ambitions, neoliberal cultural consumerism, and other secular projects, it is feminism and feminist projects that most vehemently draw charges of the un-Islamic foreignness associated with secularism (Charania 2014).

Indeed, is by revisiting secularism as constitutive of the interrelationship of gender, community, nation, and state that some critical South Asian feminists invoke the notion of "secularism" to unsettle the hegemonic citizen-subject that is bolstered by anxieties about gender, class, caste, ethnicity, and sectarianism in this region (Jalal 2014; Needham and Sunder Rajan 2007; Tejani 2008; Zia 2018). These feminist scholars discursively dismantle the "secular" from its Eurocentric mooring as the antithesis of "religion" and explicate the diverse meanings and functions associated with secularism at different historical moments in South Asia. For example, Anuradha Needham and Rajeswari Sunder Rajan (2007) refer to the Hindu right-wing assault on the secular character of the Indian state and argue that the key issue concerning secularism in South Asia is not its relationship with religion but rather the role of religion as a basis of individual and group identity, and of politics related to that identity. Their argument finds support in the ideas of the Pakistani historian Ayesha Jalal (1999: 83), who emphasizes that since colonial rule, religions have functioned as social demarcators aimed "specifically at establishing boundaries with other communities."

While cognizant of the colonial genealogy of secularism, these feminist scholars and activists direct us toward a social-cultural use of secularism for building new types of national community, a distinctive project from Western nation-states that invoke secularism to emphasize the universalistic principles of constitutional democracy. It is apt that Needham and Sunder Rajan (2007) reiterate this by reference not to the history of Indian secularism but to the founding father of Pakistan, Mohammed Ali Jinnah, who made a historic statement about the community that would populate the state carved out specifically to preserve the interests of Muslims in the subcontinent. In a much cited first presidential address to the Constituent Assembly of Pakistan on August 11, 1947, Jinnah said:

> If you change your past and work together in a spirit that every one of you, no matter to what community he belongs, no matter what relations he had with you in the past, no matter what is his color, caste, or creed, is first, second, and last a citizen of this State with equal rights, privileges, and obligations, there will be no end to the progress you will make. (qtd in Asghar Khan 1985: 136)

Overall these scholars ask us to understand secularism through the ideas it generates, the kinds of struggles it initiates, and the vision of community it enables. It may be argued that the Muslim secular in South Asia is better thought of as an *ethos*—a term ubiquitous among South Asian users of English to describe the "secular." *Ethos* is defined by the Cambridge English Dictionary as "the set of beliefs, ideas, etc. about the social behavior and relationships of a person or group,"[15] and it is in this sense that it is the preferred term of scholars and writers to promote the idea of secularism: "Jinnah's preference was for the state of Pakistan to be governed on the basis of a pluralist and secular ethos" (Akbar 1999: 194); or Bangladesh's "inclusive and soil-loving ethos" (Bennett 2012: 224).[16] *Ethos* in this usage may not only be understood as "performative," from Judith Butler's theory of performativity as simultaneously naming and doing a gendered subjectivity; it also has the potential to bring together human subjectivity, actors, contexts, terrain, behaviors, relationships, and beliefs (Butler 2004, 2010).

Such approaches enable a different kind of accounting for feminist struggles in Muslim majority societies.

Feminist Trouble and Activist Citizenship

As this essay makes evident, liberal feminist calls for a secular state in Pakistan draw not only from theories of modern citizenship and universal human rights conventions. They also rely on traditions and memories related to anticolonial nationalist and postcolonial histories, as well as uniquely South Asian Islamic and cultural traditions. Agreeing with Charania (2014), who has critically examined the use of the epithet "Westernized" as a way to delegitimize women's struggles in Pakistan, I reiterate that it is a mistake to construe these struggles as a mindless replication of Euro-American feminisms as an economic, political, and social model for all women's emancipatory movements. Indeed, if Pakistani women demand personal autonomy and bodily security as well as economic and political opportunities, they are as much in line with the long-standing traditions of women's struggles in South Asia as with gender-based struggles in many societies internationally.

In South Asia under colonial rule, women of the elite and upper-middle classes were upheld, and self-identified, as markers of the secular development and progress of the Muslims and other communities (Grewal 1999; Mumtaz and Shaheed 1987: 6; Ahmed 1992: 236; Gole 2008: 296; Chatterjee 1993; Ikramullah 1963: 290). In present-day Pakistan, the notion of the "modern Muslim woman" is highly contested due to a widening and expansion of the class and social status of women who are expected to occupy women's modern roles as doctors, teachers, lawyers, and even political leaders (Husain 2020; Mallick 2018; Maqsood 2017). Increasing urbanization, the flow of foreign aid for gender development projects, remittances from overseas workers, and cultural changes related to media proliferation have enabled easier access for a variety of hitherto excluded groups of women—lower middle class, religiously identified, culturally conservative—to political, social, cultural, and professional spaces. Indeed, the demand for women's greater economic mobility, enhanced political and public participation, consumerism, and even sexual freedom is no longer confined to the Westernizing upper-middle classes or elites. Yet regardless of class or social-cultural location, any calls for women's rights when articulated through the label "feminism" become suspect for their vulnerability to "un-Islamic" and "foreign" sources of cultural, social, and political manipulation and are retrospectively termed *elite* and *secular*. What has changed in Pakistan since the 1980s is not simply the intensification of opposition to women's struggles but also the institutionalizing of misogynist and sectarian agendas of specific politico-religious groups in the name of Islamization. Consequently, women's struggles for their rights have veered further toward universalist and human rights language, and due to this, feminism looms larger in the social, cultural, and political landscape than warranted either by its agenda or numbers—posing a kind of "feminist trouble" to a variety of religious, political, social, and cultural orthodoxies.[17]

Sara Ahmed (2014: 185) draws on Judith Butler's concept of "gender trouble"—i.e., the difficulties encountered while tying together gender identities, sexual desires, and physical bodies—to propose a notion of "feminist trouble." She defines feminist trouble as the trouble that feminism is seen to pose to society, the kind of trouble feminists are asked to stay out of, and the kind of trouble that feminists can create in society. In the case of Pakistan, feminist trouble is a mode not only for women's groups but also for a host of other progressive and equity-seeking groups to challenge narrow and prescriptive attempts to install a singular concept of the citizen as a Hanafi, Sunni Muslim patriarch.

Tying Ahmed's notion of feminist trouble to a notion of citizenship conceptualized by Engin Isin makes it possible to argue that feminist politics in Pakistan may be understood as an activist type of citizenship, something Isin (2009: 370–71) defines as "those deeds by which actors constitute themselves (and others) as subjects of rights." Isin identifies what he calls "activist citizens," who seek to transform the boundaries between different kinds of rights, and contrasts these with "active citizens," a concept used to denote activities such as voting, taxpaying, and so on that are associated with conventional accounts of citizenship. Isin's theory disrupts the notion of citizenship, since he relates it not to those acts that fulfill the conventional obligations of citizenship but to acts that call into question the obligations and responsibilities that make citizenship oppressive and exclusionary. Isin's intervention allows us to further expand Ahmed's gloss on feminist trouble, since it enables a conceptualizing of a mode of citizenship that feminists are obliged to enact in the context of Pakistani society. Further, Isin, like Butler, disentangles acts from subjectivity, habitus, and other concepts that refer to the relatively stable disposition of individuals in a social order and its transformation.

Secularism and Feminist Politics

To illustrate how feminism and secularism may come together to constitute a politics of "activist" citizenship in Pakistan, I will focus on my interlocutors' responses to different forms of the questions, "Would you
describe yourself as secular?" and "What do you mean when you say you
want a secular state?" Reflecting the intensified tensions around feminism
and culturalist nationalism, many women positioned themselves as defi-
ant and contrary to imposed notions of gender, culture, religion, and
nation. Although this was a common thread in all the interviews, it was
most evident for those who were active members of organized feminist
politics. Thus, in response to the question, "What do you mean when you
say you want a secular state?" Hala recalled her own gendered experiences
of the changing relationship of Islam, state, and society. She said:

> *Mazhab* [religion] was always around in Pakistan but it never really both-
> ered me. Even though I am not religious, I do believe in freedom of ideas.
> My mother was very religious and she prayed five times a day. *Ramzan*
> [Ramadan] and *milads* [birthday celebration of the Prophet Muhammad]
> were part of religion. People prayed and fasted but no one imposed these
> things on me or others. And I never cared whether others fasted or
> prayed or not—I would happily go to a *milad* or *kunda* [feast for the sixth
> Shia Imam, Jaffar-e-Sadiq, celebrated by many Sunnis in South Asia].

Hala, who is a member of a women's activist movement, grew up in rural
Sindh province and now lives in Karachi. She is a well-known writer and
poet and has published stories and plays in Urdu and Sindhi, some for
radio and TV serials. Many of her works including her autobiography have
been translated into English. She emphasized that all her writing was
based on the experiences of women in Pakistan, adding that rather than
this being a self-imposed project it was due to "who I am and how I feel
internally [and] my vision, my ideas are oriented this way." Hala, who
spoke in Urdu, used the English words *feminist* and *secular* to refer to herself.
Like almost all my interlocutors, Hala drew attention to the qualitative
changes she noticed in people's attitude toward faith and its practices, and
said this angered her:

> This bitterness toward [puritanical/state-imposed] religion that we now
> feel began after the 1970s and the breakup of the Soviet Union and the
> rise of religious extremism in our society. General Zia-ul-Haq imposed

strict religious laws and regulations on us and it was at that time that religious extremists were nurtured like serpents. . . . [For example,] people always kept a beard and it never bothered me. Indeed, my father himself had a beard—and I never disliked beards but now the way it is spread [*phel gaya*] it is something else. It bothers me; it is another kind of religion with which I have a problem.

Relating individual experience to national politics, Bina, a professor of politics at a large public university in Pakistan, explained feminist calls for a secular state by describing the wide-ranging legal and political changes that were legitimized by recourse to Islam. She stated:

Some religious scholars are saying they have the authority to interpret and tell us what our rights are and they will decide what this entire international discourse of human rights means. [They say] "this is Islam and we will tell you how Islam defines people's rights, whether it's women or minorities and so forth." We [feminists/secularists] say "no"— look at the people of this country and ask women what rights they want.

She elaborated:

This whole notion of secularism takes place within particular contexts. For us this remains a useful concept. . . . It defines what we want to say. What we are saying is that fatwas will not decide, nor will a higher authority in Islam nor whichever Mullah.

It is noteworthy that Pakistani feminists' experiences of both "Islam" and "secularism" not only differ from those of feminists in Western liberal democracies but also diverge from what is represented in the feminist literature from Middle Eastern Muslim societies such as Egypt, Turkey, and Iran (Ahmed 1992; Abu Lughod 1998; Gole 2008; Haddad and Esposito 1997). The early leadership of the Pakistani state never adopted the aggressive secularizing policies, such as banning of religious symbols or exclusion of religious parties, that were associated with many Muslim-majority states in the Middle East into the 1970s and 1980s. In contrast, despite proclaiming its Islamic character, the Pakistani state of the 1940s–1970s allowed itself a great deal of ambiguity about the implications of this identity. Furthermore, since religious forces were never banned from political participation, they largely damaged their moral credentials by aligning with authoritarian political and military setups. Thus, unlike

Iran, Turkey, or Egypt, the rise of Islamism or claims to state power by religiously identified groups, when they did gain some momentum in the 1980s, were neither as fiercely a reaction to state secularism nor as passionately populist or organic. This history was a recurring theme among my interlocutors, who deeply resented the ascendance of religious conservatives within the state and society, mostly as a result of strategic political and military alliances (Mumtaz and Shaheed 1987).

Kiran, who is a founding member of a feminist group and deeply involved in human rights advocacy in Pakistan, described her political struggles, saying: "We are in a mess today and it's all because of having religion in politics and being part of the state." Another feminist, Sana, similarly bewailed the differing interpretations of Islamic principles among the state, the military, and "Islamic" politico-religious parties, as well as within and across the diverse Islamic theological and jurisprudence traditions including within the majority Muslim Sunni Hanafi sect. She noted: "Pakistan tops the list in many ways among countries where there is disharmony among religious sects. It is the country which is suffering the most in the name of religion because we have so many sects of religion which are fighting among themselves and against the state. Pakistan has become a dangerous country in the name of religion."

Not surprisingly, the most vehement condemnation of the military/state project of Islamization came from Juhi, who at the time of this study was an elected representative of a largely urban populist party, the Mohajir Qaumi Movement (MQM). The MQM at that time garnered near-monopolistic support from Urdu-speaking *mohajirs* or those Muslims who migrated to Pakistan from India following partition in 1947. This party has repeatedly called for a secular state in Pakistan on the same lines as India and is a key rival to the mainstream Islamist political party Jamaat-e-Islami (JI). Emerging in the 1980s, the MQM successfully wrested away large numbers of voters in Pakistan's largest city, Karachi, by promoting mohajir cultural and ethnic politics against the nationalist religious politics of the JI. In addition to being a leader of the MQM, Juhi is a well-known public speaker due to her eloquence in Urdu; although she is also proficient in English, this interview was conducted in Urdu. Beyond her party's principles, Juhi invoked the history of her father's involvement in the anticolonial struggle for Pakistan to emphasize the legitimacy of a liberal and progressive understanding of Islam, which, she said, was "never suffocating":

> I do not believe that there is anything "religious" in the basis of our society. What did Quaid-e-Azam [Mohammed Ali Jinnah] say? Where does Islam come into it? Quaid did not say "I am trying to create a country where people are engaged all their time in prayers and bowing their heads on the *musalla* [prayer mats]" or that women should be covered in hijab or that men should be in *topis* [caps].

She added:

> From what I read and heard and understood from my childhood and what I learnt about Quaid and two-nation theory . . . the Quaid was a very liberal, progressive man—there was no kind of *ghuttan* [suffocation/stifling] in his vision [of faith].[18]

Asked what she understood by the concept of a secular state, Juhi dwelled on the history of the anticolonial Pakistan Movement from 1940–47. Reiterating her party's stance, Juhi said that Pakistan was never meant to be a state exclusively for Muslims but rather one that would promote tolerance for all religions, adding: "Church bells should ring, *mandir* bells should ring, and *azan* should be heard loudly." These sentiments speak to Juhi's unmistakably South Asian understanding of secularism, as expounded by early national leaders in India and Pakistan as well as by social and political scientists: the state's responsibility to protect many faiths instead of privileging either Islam or Hinduism. Her antipathy for a mono-religious state is palpable in her emotional proclamation below:

> Religious parties and extremists use *mazhab* [faith] as a crutch to save their political projects. When their *nayya* [boat] starts to sink they begin interfering in politics. What business do religious leaders have in parliament? They should be leading prayers in mosques, teaching and *tabligh* [preaching]. What purpose do they have in parliament? Indeed, religious parties should be banned in parliament. They should be banned in the parliament of Pakistan!

The Secular Ethos of South Asian Muslim Culture

Beyond reacting to recent history, many of my interlocutors, like South Asian feminists generally, also claimed a longer social-cultural history that entangles with and even prevails over the political and religious. The uppermost concern for these feminists was the disintegration of what they consider to be South Asia's secular Muslim culture that flourished for over a century of Muslim presence in India. As described by the poets, writers, and also activists, South Asian Muslim culture seemed to encompass local and regional affective expressions of faith, ethno-poetical and narrative projects, assorted cultural embodiments and practices, modes of dressing, political ideologies, linguistic claims, music, and dance, to name just a few "secular" expressions that have emerged from the mixing of Islam's Arab roots with South Asian, Central Asian, and non-Arab Middle Eastern traditions (Robinson 2000; Metcalf 2009; Alam 2004; Eaton 1985). These self-proclaimed secular feminists lamented the oppressiveness of a singularly defined, state-implemented version of the "Islamic" over a society they associated with heterogeneous religious and cultural traditions and practices. Their responses were rich with descriptions of a social and cultural history replete with women and other dissident characters who populate the literary, cultural, and political imagination in South Asia. I was reminded of the unruly woman or girl that was a significant trope in the literature by feminist members of the Progressive Writers' Movement of the early twentieth century in South Asia (Jalil 2014). My interlocutors' comments, explicitly at times but implicitly always, challenged prescriptive religion in a manner that was resonant of the poetry of feminists such as Fehmida Riaz and Kishwar Naheed, whose highly popular poems "Chaddar aur char deewari" ("A Cloak and Four Walls") and "Hum gunahgaar auraten" ("We Sinful Women") mocked the Islamization project in the 1990s (Mahwash 2009). More recently, these feminists challenged the Taliban and extremist Hindu nationalism in their poems "Wo jo bachiyon se bhi dar gaye" ("Those Who Fear Young Girls") and "Tum bilkul ham jaise nikle" ("Turns Out You Are No Better Than Us") (Mir 2014).

Such construction of gendered selves through a dissenting genealogy of faith, politics, and history, along with feminist "troubling" of community, culture, and society, was uppermost in the remarks of feminist poets, artists, and writers in my study.[19] This self-positioning was eloquently explained by Hamida,[20] an iconoclastic writer and feminist poet who during her lifetime publicly associated herself with "secular" forces and was widely deemed to be an exemplar of "secularism" in Pakistani society. She told me:

> *Secularism* is an English word. I do not know much about the roots of this term and Pakistan is a country of Muslims—I have always considered myself as part of this society. But every society is inhabited not only by its

followers [adherents] but also its critics. The society itself creates its own critics—they are part of the society and they are created by the society because it is ready for change—it wants to be changed. And this is why these [secular] people are born. They bring about change.

Elaborating on her iconic status as a "secular feminist," Hamida said:

Putting this word [secularism] aside, the fact is that I belong to a society which has always been a mixed society, there has been religious diversity in it, and in that society traditionally the followers of all religions have always been free to do their own way of worship. This wasn't something which ever had to be declared or imposed [by a state].

This widely read South Asian feminist poet, author, and cultural critic lamented that Pakistani society had been transformed by the ascendance of a "totally bigoted and tyrannical version of Islam." She insisted that it was the right of Pakistani women to own as our inheritance "the aggregate experiences and struggles of human beings all over the world."

Hamida's sentiments were reflected in a comment by the other poet and writer featured earlier in this article, Hala, who stated simply: "Religion should be joined with culture as it was until the 1970s."

In a poignantly personal musing, Hala said:

Just as I was a feminist by birth so I had these ideas about religion by birth. I was a village girl living in a village. I came later to understand through study that my thinking may be called secular. One does not need to acquire all knowledge through books—I had this within myself. Just as I can say I was a feminist child in my village, I can also say that I was a secular child in my village.

The loss of what these women considered to be a culturally secular Islamic and Muslim identity was also present in the social experiences of Ghazala, a well-known leader of the Human Rights Commission of Pakistan (HRCP), who noted: "I grew up in the 1960s and I don't remember anyone ever lecturing me on religion. I mean, forget about my family, not even family friends, or relatives or in school, college."

Ghazala came from a professional middle class family, was educated at convent schools, and grew up with a fluid understanding of Islam. She became involved with the women's movement in the 1980s when the Women's Action Forum was formed to fight the Islamization of laws by the government of General Zia. She later became very active in wider issues of human rights in Pakistan and occupied a leadership role in HRCP. Speaking in English interspersed with Urdu, Ghazala described her family as "moderately religious," explaining that although her mother was "deeply religious" and her father somewhat less so, her parents did not enforce practices such as five daily prayers, fasting, or covering onto the children. She said the atmosphere in the house was such that "you had your space." Ghazala said that General Zia's Islamization policies had "turned her away from religion," even though she conceded that "secular" or liberal leaders had also historically used Islam to reinforce their authoritarian power:

> For example, [General Zia] introduced this ordinance of *Ehteram Ramaz* [Respect for Ramadan] under which you could be fined for eating and drinking in public places and restaurants. Earlier in the 1970s restaurants would be open in Ramzan and they would just put a curtain or something so that people could go in and have their meals.

Ghazala noted that some of these regulations had eased after the end of Zia's regime, but the official narratives of Islamization continued to pervade society. However, like many of the other women in this study, Ghazala made it clear that she would not yield to imposed ideas about Islam, gender, or Pakistani national identity.

　　This cohort of women who began to identify as feminist and secular in the 1990s against the religio-military project of Islamization are keepers of a collective feminist memory of women's activism and a repository of experiences testifying to the state's renegement from the self-avowed egalitarian argument that accompanied the creation of Pakistan. The intertwining of secularism with feminism is part of their strategy to keep alive, indeed to reignite, the possibilities of a heterogeneous Pakistan and Islam and an enriched Muslim social culture in South Asia. I discerned a similar sentiment in my interview with Yasmin, a professor of English literature at the Islamic institution for women that I referenced earlier in this article. Although she was not included in my initial list because of my own assumptions about her affiliation with a self-identified Islamic institution, I decided to interview Yasmin after my talk. I wanted to explore why women in this institution, especially hijab-wearing women like herself, were comfortable advocating for secularism even though this concept is so viscerally opposed by many in Pakistan. Yasmin explained that she had derived her own understanding of secularism from her scholarly engagement with

Muslim rational philosophers, especially Al-Ghazali and Ibn Khaldoun, as well as critical Western philosophers including Talal Asad and Michel Foucault. She clarified that while she rejected "irreligiousness" she embraced the open-mindedness, intellectual rationality, and tolerance that she associated with modern secularism, which also resonated with her study of Islam's epistemological traditions. She said:

> My understanding of the term *secularism* is that it doesn't mean "irreligious." . . . The secularist or secular intellectual doesn't mean an irreligious person or an atheist. It means, perhaps, looking at all things from a more enlightened perspective.

Yasmin went on to explain:

> I don't think there is any restriction on the part of the religion [Islam] that says we cannot accommodate ourselves into the way society changes and development occurs. And if we adapt ourselves to these changes, [and] these developments within the framework of religion, then that means a [kind of] secularism for me and it's not anti-religious.

While there were ambiguities and differences among my interlocutors' accounts of secularism as a feminist project and their self-understanding as secular subjects, their responses make it clear that middle-class feminist "secularism" cannot be theorized without a keen understanding of the complex histories of both secular and religious politics in South Asia. Feminism and secularism are normative projects that coalesced not simply as legacies of Eurocentric modernity bequeathed by British colonialism; in addition to their appropriation by anticolonial nationalists, they are narrated and lived social, cultural, and political experiences of gendered subjects in South Asian society amid ongoing attempts by the region's postcolonial states to reform and deform those histories.

Conclusion
This essay has attempted to clear a space for theorizing the political, cultural, and affective struggles of middle-class Muslim feminists in Pakistan who invoke "secularism" as a strategy against the normative categories of religion, class, gender, and nation prescribed by the military-dominated state, patriarchal nationalism, and Islamist leaders.

Privileging feminist narratives and women's self-understanding over overarching theorizations of "secularism" or "secular feminism" enables me to invoke other understandings of secularism and religion that are in friction with the colonial genealogy of these concepts. It is worth noting that feminist secularism in Pakistan as expressed by my interlocutors differed from accounts by scholars of Middle Eastern Muslim societies, especially Iran, Turkey, and Egypt, where secular feminists have been criticized for their antipathy toward native culture and tradition in favor of secular modernization. In contrast, Pakistani feminists, while demanding universal human rights and equal citizenship for women, claimed to speak on behalf of, not in opposition to, the genealogies of local and regional cultures, which they saw as being erased through an Arab-centric ideology of Islamic tradition—in particular the Salafi-centric traditions of Islam that are encapsulated in Pakistan by the term *Wahabism*. All of the women who experienced the regime of General Zia-ul-Haq (1977–89) described their response to his unambiguously Salafi-Wahabi-centric project of Islamization as a "shock" to their previous experiences of Islam or Muslim identity. In their understanding of secularism, many of my interlocutors referred to long-standing and oft-cited modes of cultural and spiritual dissent in the manner of poets, artists, and mystics of South Asia. This indicates that, despite its colonial genealogy, secularism may animate a different kind of feminist politics in Pakistan, where the interrelationship of Islam, the secular, and gender has not been the same as in Western and Middle Eastern societies. Thus, as noted for Turkey by Nilofer Gole (2008), secularism is a women's issue in Pakistan; but, as emphasized by many South Asian feminists, it is also an issue that is densely entangled in historical, material, religious, and social concerns that call for a situated feminist analysis as well as one that addresses transnational feminist projects (Needham and Sunder Rajan 2007; Jalal 2014).

Postcolonial Muslim scholars, especially in diasporic locations, are persistently invited by Eurocentric hegemonies and nationalist patriarchies to choose between religiously defined "community/nation" and universalistic narratives of "feminism" and "gender." This precludes any notice of the interrelationship of gender, power, and desire that are integral to meaningful debates about community and nation. By commending the authenticity of some performances of gendered Muslim subjectivity and not others, patriarchal secular and religious authorities obstruct recognition of shared desires for freedom and autonomy among differently positioned women. I found this to my surprise in the diversity of political desires evinced by women whom I had homogenized as Islamic-not-secular based on their institutional affiliation in the introduction to this essay. To engage the diversity of the vast majority of Pakistani women who are unlikely to identify exclusively with oppressive forms of religiosity or anti-Muslim secularism, we need painful and painstaking ethnographies of secularism in religious spaces and of the presence of religion in secular spaces. As my interlocutors' accounts indicate, Islam, piety, and secularism are different kinds of entangled traditions in South Asia and elsewhere, with their own discourses and counter-discourses as well as diverse gendered embodiments and enactments.

Amina Jamal is associate professor of sociology at Ryerson University, Toronto. She has authored a monograph, *Jamaat-e-Islami Women in Pakistan: Vanguard of a New Modernity?* (2013). She writes in the areas of women, Islam and modernity, transnational and postcolonial feminism, violence against women, and Muslim women's struggles in Pakistan and Canada.

Notes

Acknowledgment: This article draws on research funded by the Social Sciences and Humanities Research Council of Canada (SSHRC).

1   I do not include the institutional name as this college has been the target of bombing by the Tehreek-Taliban-Pakistan (TTP) for not following their particular understanding of what is "Islamic."

2   I use the term *Islamist* to refer to those who seek to use the power of the modern state to bring about a political and legal order that meets their particular interpretation of *Islamic*. These are not necessarily militants or terrorists though they might have linkages with some militant groups.

3   For a study of the Jamaat-e-Islami, see Reza Nasr 1994. For Jamaat women's politics, see Jamal 2013.

4   For a quick recapitulation of Foucault's arguments, see Foucault 1982. For further analysis, see Gordon 1991; Dean 1999.

5   Mahmood's (2005) influence is evident in the various categorizations of Muslim feminists that have circulated in recent works: e.g., "imperialist/secular feminism," "Islamist or religious rights-based feminism," "Muslim feminism," "critical piety," etc.

6   For the specificity of Islam in South Asia see, for example, Metcalf 2009; Alam 2004; Robinson 2000; Jalal 2001. For some Pakistani feminist-secularist interpretations of Muslim anticolonial nationalism in South Asia, see Jalal 2014; Weiss 1986b; Hussain, Mumtaz, and Saigol 1997; Mumtaz and Shaheed 1987.

7   This article is drawn from a larger research project. The research was conducted from 2010–14 in Canada and South Asia. I use the terms *feminist* and *secular* together since scholars such as Jamal and Ahmed indicate that, unlike in the Middle East, the concept of Islamic feminism is ambiguous in Pakistan.

Women who join movements like the Jamaat-e-Islami or Al Huda define their struggles for women's rights in opposition to feminism and feminists and not as Islamic feminists.

8　For an interesting discussion of the interrelationship between feminist perspectives on sampling, social knowledge, and research, see Noy 2008; for the usefulness of snowball sampling in anti-racist feminist research, see Woodley and Lockard 2016.

9　For a scholarly study, see Anastosopoulos and Desmarais 2015. For a popular, globally circulated example, see University Wire 2014; for the Pakistani context, see Charania 2014.

10　See Mahmood 2005; Hoodfar 2001; Alvi, Hoodfar, and McDonough 2003. In truth, body and face covering by women in Pakistan is related to many other aspects of women's lives such as class, employment, urban/rural culture, status, education, and personal style. It is not simply an expression of piety or anti-imperialist stance or religious identity as described by scholars in other contexts.

11　According to Mahmood (2005), a pious Muslim woman practices self-abnegation and embraces pain and shameful experiences in contrast to secular subjects who are self-affirming and seek freedom from pain and suffering.

12　Since this might constitute blasphemy and therefore a death sentence in Pakistan, this clarification is more relevant to the portions of the project related to Canada and India.

13　Pseudonyms have been used throughout this article.

14　General Mohammed Zia-ul-Haq deposed the elected government of Prime Minister Zulfiqar Ali Bhutto in a military coup and declared martial law on July 5, 1977. After an extremely controversial trial for allegedly authorizing the murder of a political opponent, Bhutto was found guilty by the Pakistan Supreme Court and executed on April 4, 1979. For more information see Malik 2008; Coll 2005.

15　Cambridge Academic Content Dictionary, s.v. "ethos," accessed June 15, 2020, https://dictionary.cambridge.org/dictionary/english/ethos.

16　Bangladesh was formerly "East Pakistan" and one of two wings of the Pakistani state created in 1947. A revolutionary uprising against oppression of Bengalis successfully resisted a brutal crackdown by the Pakistani military and established a separate state for Bengalis in 1971. The former "West Pakistan" is now "Pakistan."

17　For an insightful analysis that situates the feminist women's movement within the political landscape of Pakistan, see Saigol 2016.

18　Mohammed Ali Jinnah is officially referred to in Pakistan as *Quaid-e-Azam*, Leader of the Nation.

19　There is an expansive literature on the long history of social and political struggles against communitarian and colonial patriarchies by and about women in South Asia, including Muslim women as individuals and members of social, cultural, and political organizations. For some sources relevant to Pakistan, see Mumtaz and Shaheed 1991.

20 Although I have used pseudonyms throughout this article, I decided to use a thinly disguised name for this iconic feminist poet who died in 2019 a few years after this interview, in order to pass on the inspiring legacy of this great Urdu feminist poet of modern South Asia. For more information, see Jalil 2014; Mir 2014.

References

Abu Lughod, Lila. 1998. *Remaking Women: Feminism and Modernity in the Middle East.* Princeton, NJ: Princeton University Press.

Ahmed, Leila. 1992. *Women and Gender in Islam: Historical Roots of a Modern Debate.* New Haven, CT: Yale University Press.

Ahmed, Sara. 2014. *Willful Subjects.* Durham, NC: Duke University Press.

Akbar, M. K. 1999. *Pakistan Today.* Delhi: Mittal Publications.

Alam, Muzaffar. 2004. *The Languages of Political Islam: India, 1200–1800.* Chicago: University of Chicago Press.

Alvi, Sajida, Homa Hoodfar, and Sheila McDonough. 2003. *The Muslim Veil in North America: Issues and Debates.* Toronto: Women's Press.

Anastosopoulos, Vanessa, and Serge Desmarais. 2015. "By Name or by Deed? Identifying the Source of the Feminist Stigma." *Journal of Applied Social Psychology* 45, no. 4: 226–42.

Asad, Talal. 2003. *Formations of the Secular: Christianity, Islam, Modernity.* Stanford, CA: Stanford University Press.

Asghar Khan, Omar. 1985. "Political and Economic Aspects of Islamization." In *Islam, Politics, and the State: The Pakistan Experience,* edited by Mohammed Asghar Khan, 127–163. London: Zed Books.

Bennett, Clinton. 2012. "Bangladeshi Sufism: An Interfaith Bridge." In *South Asian Sufis: Devotion, Deviation, Destiny,* edited by Clinton Bennett and Charles M. Ramsey, 211–32. London: Continuum.

Butler, Judith. 2004. *Precarious Life: The Powers of Mourning and Violence.* New York: Verso.

Butler, Judith. 2010. "Performative Agency." *Journal of Cultural Economy* 3, no. 2: 147–61.

Calhoun, Craig, Mark Juergensmeyer, and Jonathan Vanantwerpen. 2011. "Introduction." In *Rethinking Secularism,* edited by Craig Calhoun, Mark Juergensmeyer, and Jonathan Vanantwerpen, 3–30. Oxford: Oxford University Press.

Cannell, Fennella. 2010. "The Anthropology of Secularism." *Annual Review of Sociology* 39: 85–100.

Charania, Moon. 2014. "Feminism, Sexuality, and the Rhetoric of Westernization in Pakistan: Precarious Citizenship." In *Routledge Handbook of Gender in South Asia,* edited by Leela Fernandes, 318–32. London: Routledge, 2014.

Chatterjee, Partha. 1993. *The Nation and Its Fragments: Colonial and Postcolonial Histories.* Princeton, NJ: Princeton University Press.

Coll, Steve. 2005. *Ghost Wars: The Secret History of the CIA, Afghanistan, and Bin Laden, from the Soviet Invasion to September 10, 2001.* New York: Penguin Books.

Dean, Mitchell. 1999. *Governmentality: Power and Rule in Modern Society.* London: Sage.

Eaton, Richard. 1985. "Approaches to the Study of Conversion to Islam in India." In *Approaches to Islam in Religious Studies*, edited by Richard C. Martin, 107–23. Tucson: University of Arizona Press.

Farris, Sara. 2017. *In the Name of Women's Rights: The Rise of Femonationalism*. Durham, NC: Duke University Press.

Foucault, Michel. 1982. "The Subject and Power," translated by Leslie Sawyer. *Critical Inquiry* 8: 777–795.

Gole, Nilufer. 2008. "Secularism Is a Woman's Affair." *New Perspectives* 25, no. 2: 35–37.

Gordon, Colin. 1991. "Government Rationality: An Introduction." In *The Foucault Effect: Studies in Governmentality*, edited by Graham Burchell, Colin Gordon, and Peter Miller, 1–51. Chicago: University of Chicago Press.

Grewal, Inderpal. 1999. "'Women's Rights as Human Rights': Feminist Practices, Global Feminism, and Human Rights Regimes in Transnationality." *Citizenship Studies* 3, no. 3: 337–54.

Grewal, Inderpal, and Caren Kaplan. 1994. "Introduction: Transnational Feminist Practices and Questions of Postmodernity." In *Scattered Hegemonies: Postmodernity and Transnational Feminist Practices*, edited by Inderpal Grewal and Caren Kaplan, 1–33. Minneapolis: University of Minnesota Press.

Grewal, Inderpal, and Caren Kaplan. 2000. "Postcolonial Studies and Transnational Feminist Practices." *Jouvert: A Journal of Postocolonial Studies* 5, no. 1, legacy.chass.ncsu.edu/jouvert/v5i1/con51.htm.

Haddad, Yvonne Yazback, and John L. Esposito. 1997. *Islam, Gender, and Social Change*. Oxford: Oxford University Press.

Haq, Farhat. 1996. "Women, Islam, and the State in Pakistan." *Muslim World* 86, no. 2: 158–75.

Hoodfar, Homa. 2001. "The Veil in Their Minds and on Our Heads: Veiling Practices and Muslim Women." In *Women, Gender, Religion: A Reader*, edited by Elizabeth A. Castili, 420–46. New York: Palgrave Macmillan.

Husain, Fauzia. 2020. "Halal Dating, Purdah, and Postfeminism: What the Sexual Projects of Pakistani Women Can Tell Us about Agency." *Signs: Journal of Women in Culture and Society* 45, no. 3: 629–52.

Hussain, Neelam, Samiya Mumtaz, and Rubina Saigol, eds. 1997. *Engendering the Nation-State*. Vol. 1. Lahore: Simorgh Women's Resource and Publication Centre.

Ikramullah, Shaista Suharwardy. 1963. *From Purdah to Parliament*. London: Crescent.

Isin, Engin F. 2009. "Citizenship in Flux: The Figure of the Activist Citizen." *Subjectivity* 29: 370–71.

Jahangir, Asma, and Hina Jilani. 1990. *The Hudood Ordinances: A Divine Sanction?* Lahore: Rhotas Books.

Jalal, Ayesha. 1999. "Identity Crisis: Rethinking the Politics of Community and Region in South Asia." *Harvard International Review* 21, no. 3: 82–85.

Jalal, Ayesha. 2001. *Self and Sovereignty: Individual and Community in South Asian Islam since 1850*. Lahore: Sang-e-Meel.

Jalal, Ayesha. 2014. *The Struggle for Pakistan: A Muslim Homeland and Global Politics*. Cambridge, MA: Harvard University Press.

Jalil, Rakshanda. 2014. *Liking Progress, Loving Change: A Literary History of the Progressive Writers' Movement in Urdu*. New Delhi: Oxford University Press.

Jamal, Amina. 2013. *Jamaat-e-Islami Women in Pakistan: Vanguard of a New Modernity?* Syracuse, NY: Syracuse University Press.

Khan, Shahnaz. 2006. *Zina, Transnational Feminism, and the Moral Regulation of Pakistani Women*. Vancouver: University of British Columbia Press.

Mahmood, Saba. 2005. *Politics of Piety: The Islamic Revival and the Feminist Subject*. Princeton, NJ: Princeton University Press.

Mahwash, Shoaib. 2009. "Selections from the Poetry of Kishwar Naheed." *Pakistaniaat: A Journal of Pakistan Studies* 1, no. 1: 82–97.

Malik, Iftikhar H. 2008. *The History of Pakistan*. Westport, CT: Greenwood Press.

Mallick, Ayyaz. 2018. "Urban Space and (the Limits of) Middle Class Hegemony in Pakistan." *Urban Geography* 39, no. 7: 1113–20.

Maqsood, Ammara. 2017. "Meet Pakistan's Modern Middle Class." *New York Times*, September 24. www.nytimes.com/2017/09/24/opinion/pakistan-modern-middle-class.html.

Mehdi, Rubya. 1994. *The Islamization of the Law in Pakistan*. Surrey, UK: Curzon Press.

Metcalf, Barbara D. 2009. *Islam in South Asia in Practice*. Princeton, NJ: Princeton University Press.

Mir, Shabana. 2014. "Fahmida Riaz on Fundamentalism on Both Sides." *Koonjblog*, April 11. koonjblog.wordpress.com/2014/04/11/india-awash-in-fundamentalism-hail-fellow-well-met.

Mumtaz, Khawar, and Farida Shaheed. 1987. *Women of Pakistan: Two Steps Forward, One Step Back?* Lahore: Vanguard Books.

Mumtaz, Khawar, and Farida Shaheed. 1991. "Historical Roots of the Women's Movement: A Period of Awakening, 1896–1947." In Zafar 1991: 3–25.

Needham, Anuradha Dingwaney, and Rajeswari Sunder Rajan, eds. 2007. *The Crisis of Secularism in India*. Durham, NC: Duke University Press.

Noy, Chaim. 2008. "Sampling Knowledge: The Hermeneutics of Snowball Sampling in Qualitative Research." *International Journal of Social Research Methodology* 11, no. 4: 327–44. doi:10.1080/13645570701401305.

Rashid, Ahmed. 2001. *Taliban: The Story of the Afghan Warlords*. London: Pan Books.

Rashid, Ahmed. 2008. *Descent into Chaos: The US and the Disaster in Pakistan, Afghanistan, and Central Asia*. New York: Penguin.

Razack, Sherene. 2007. "The 'Sharia Law Debate' in Ontario: The Modernity/Premodernity Distinction in Legal Efforts to Protect Women from Culture." *Feminist Legal Studies* 15, no. 1: 3–32.

Razack, Sherene. 2008. *Casting Out: The Eviction of Muslims from Western Law and Politics*. Toronto: University of Toronto Press.

Reza Nasr, Seyyed Vali. 1994. *The Vanguard of the Islamic Revolution: The Jama'at-i Islami of Pakistan*. Berkeley: University of California Press.

Robinson, Francis. 2000. *Islam and Muslim History*. New Delhi: Oxford University Press.

Said Khan, Nighat. 1994. "Reflections on the Question of Islam and Modernity." In *Locating the Self: Perspectives on Women and Multiple Identities*, edited by Nighat Said Khan, Rubina Siagol, and Afiya Shehrbano, 77–95. Lahore: ASR.

Said Khan, Nighat, Rubina Saigol, and Afiya Shehrbano Zia. 1994. "Introduction." In *Locating the Self: Perspectives on Women and Multiple Identities*, edited by Nighat Said Khan, Rubina Siagol, and Afiya Shehrbano, 1–19. Lahore: ASR.

Saigol, Rubina. 2018. *Feminism and the Women's Movement in Pakistan: Actors, Debates, and Strategies.* Friedrich-Ebert-Stiftung Pakistan Office. library.fes.de/pdf-files/bueros /pakistan/12453.pdf.

Scott, David, and Charles Hirshckind, eds. 2006. *Powers of the Secular Modern: Talal Asad and His Interlocutors.* Stanford, CA: Stanford University Press.

Scott, Joan Wallach. 2007. *The Politics of the Veil.* Princeton, NJ: Princeton University Press.

Shaheed, Farida, and Khawar Mumtaz. 1990. "Islamization and Women: The Experience of Pakistan." *New Blackfriars* 71, no. 835: 54–64.

Shakir, B. 1997. "The State and the Minorities of Pakistan." In *Engendering the Nation-State*, edited by Neelam Hussain, Samiya Mumtaz, and Rubina Saigol, vol. 1, 260–66. Lahore: Simorgh Women's Resource and Publication Centre.

Spivak, Gayatri Chakravorty. 1993. "Scattered Speculations on the Question of Cultural Studies." In *Outside in the Teaching Machine*, 255–84. New York: Routledge.

Spivak, Gayatri Chakravorty. 2004. "Terror: A Speech after 9-11." *boundary 2* 31, no. 2: 81–111.

Tejani, Shabnum. 2008. *Indian Secularism: A Social and Intellectual History, 1890–1950.* Bloomington: Indiana University Press.

Toor, Saadia. 1997. "The State, Fundamentalism, and Civil Society." In *Engendering the Nation-State*, edited by Neelam Hussain, Samiya Mumtaz, and Rubina Saigol, vol. 1, 111–46. Lahore: Simorgh Women's Resource and Publication Centre.

Toor, Saadia. 2007. "Moral Regulations in a Postcolonial Nation-State: Gender and the Politics of Islamization in Pakistan." *International Journal of Postcolonial Studies* 9, no. 2: 255–75.

Toor, Saadia. 2011. *The State of Islam: Culture and Cold War Politics in Pakistan.* London: Pluto Press.

University Wire. 2014. "Emma Watson Addresses Feminist Stigma." October 16.

Weiss, Anita M. 1986a. "Implications of the Islamization Program for Women." In *Islamic Reassertion in Pakistan*, edited by Anita M. Weiss, 97–113. Syracuse, NY: Syracuse University Press.

Weiss, Anita M. 1986b. "The Historical Debate on Islam and the State in South Asia." In *Islamic Reassertion in Pakistan*, edited by Anita M. Weiss, 1–20. Syracuse, NY: Syracuse University Press.

Weiss, Anita M. 2003. "Interpreting Islam and Women's Rights: Implementing CEDAW in Pakistan." *International Sociology* 18: 581–601.

Woodley, Xetura M., and Megan Lockard. 2016. "Womanism and Snowball Sampling: Engaging Marginalized Populations in Holistic Research." *Qualitative Report* 21, no. 2: 321–29.

Zafar, Farida, ed. 1991. *Finding Our Way: Readings on Women in Pakistan.* Lahore: ASR.

Zia, Afiya S. 2018. *Faith and Feminism in Pakistan: Religious Agency or Secular Autonomy?* Sussex, UK: Sussex Academic Press.

Tatiana Rabinovich

Becoming "Black" and Muslim in Today's Russia

Abstract: Global anti-Muslim racism takes new and specific forms in contemporary Russia by mobilizing the shifting meanings of "Blackness" to stigma-
tize vulnerable populations. Stemming from the tsarist and Soviet pasts,
these meanings of "Blackness" (and "whiteness") have been refracted by
the dramatic socioeconomic and political shifts since the collapse of the
Soviet Union. This article draws on the accounts of working-class devout
Muslim women, with whom the author conducted ethnographic fieldwork
in Saint Petersburg between 2015 and 2017, to elucidate their experiences of
how anti-Muslim racism operates as a tool of exclusion, deployed along
racial, religious, ethnic, class, and gender lines. The women's daily
responses to anti-Muslim racism suggest how solidarities might sustain
communities targeted by racism, while laying the foundations for future
intersectional anti-racist movements in the country.

"I was coming out of the metro station, when two drunk men began to harass me by calling me *chernaya* ("black" in Russian). I pulled up my sleeve and said: 'Look, you idiots, I am whiter than you.' They continued to insult me, so I took out my pocketknife, inviting them to fight me. Cowards as [racists] often are, they retreated. I picked up my sports bag from the ground and proceeded to the minibus," Salihat, a Chechen woman in her mid-thirties, told me over tea at a small atelier, where three Muslim women made clothes for their clients and where Salihat and I met in the summer of 2019. She was a strong-built martial artist and a mother of four, with fierce light-brown eyes and an open smile. On the day of the altercation with the

MERIDIANS · feminism, race, transnationalism   20:2 October 2021
DOI: 10.1215/15366936-9547943 © 2021 Smith College

two men, she was identified as a Muslim by her hijab and pejoratively called "black."[1] In her attempt to resist stigmatization, underscored by the slur, and to claim belonging in the gentrified landscapes of Saint Petersburg, Salihat gestured to her "phenotypical whiteness": "Look [at my skin color], I am whiter than you!" With that, she unintentionally replicated the erroneous understanding of race as skin color and exhibited her subconscious investments in the racial hierarchies that have resurfaced in Russia after the collapse of the Soviet Union. On the day of our gathering at the atelier, nobody among Salihat's sisters in Islam seemed to question such investments, rejoicing instead in her bravery and defiance of the assailants.

This article draws on my ethnographic fieldwork with a community of working-class devout Muslim women, whom I befriended in Saint Petersburg between 2015 and 2017. I examine their daily experiences of and responses to racialization by foregrounding fragile solidarities and possibilities for anti-racist movements in Russia. To understand how my interlocutors such as Salihat navigated racist encounters, I trace how anti-Muslim racism in Russia is entwined with a particular iteration of global anti-blackness, operating in proximity to the hierarchical systems of gender, class, and citizenship. To underscore this particularity, I situate the ever-shifting meanings of "blackness" (*chernaya/chernyi*) in relation to Muslims within tsarist and Soviet histories, as they linger in the messy socioeconomic and political landscapes of today's Russia. In my analysis, I follow Alana Lentin's (2020: 22) definition of *race* as an evolving "technology for the management of human difference," rooted in the material realities of late capitalism, ongoing nation-building, and colonial legacies. Premised on racially enshrined inequalities, this technology of power, Lentin argues, informs discourses, practices, and infrastructures around white supremacy.

In what follows, I will first sketch out the histories of racial formations in tsarist and Soviet Russia and the articulations of "blackness" (and "whiteness") as they pertain to Muslims within the contexts of the post-Soviet vertigo. Then, I will discuss my interlocutors' experiences of and responses to particular iterations of anti-Muslim racism and, in conclusion, reflect on the burgeoning possibilities of anti-racist movements in urban Russia.

Historical Entanglements

In today's Russia, "race" (*rasa*) is rarely used as a legal category and, in the public discourse, it is firmly associated with the oppression of Black and

African Americans and their continuous struggle for liberation in the United States. However, racial logics have always shaped ideas and the material realities in Russia, functioning through categories such as ethnicity (*etnichnost'*) or citizenship (*grazhdanstvo*), among others. For instance, during the tsarist times, one's position within the social hierarchy was expressed in terms of religion, social estate (*soslovie*), and later ethnicity (*narodnost'*) tied to kinship. In the Union of Soviet Socialist Republics (USSR), one's class and nationality (*nazional'nost*) became the fundamental identities, rendering race and its operations difficult to detect. Given these particularities, David Rainbow (2019) proposes to examine the plural, fluid, and often incoherent "ideologies of race" in order to understand how and why—rather than if—race mattered in the tsarist empire and the Soviet Union in relation to global systems of racialization.

Up until the 1917 revolution, subjects of the vast and diverse Russian empire were differentiated and classified primarily with reference to their religious belonging. For example, ignited by global anti-Semitic tropes and Jewish involvement in revolutionary movements in Russia, the racialization of Jews as a distinct religious minority resulted in frequent anti-Jewish violence (*pogroms*), residency restrictions called the Pale of Settlement, and professional quotas, despite the occasional conversion of Jews to Orthodox Christianity (Avrutin, forthcoming). Along with religion, social estate was another conduit through which racial logics circulated in the Russian empire. Consider how ethnically Slavic peasants and the urban proletariat were collectively called *chern'* ("blacks") or *temnye lyudi* ("dark," meaning "uneducated," people). Fueled by fears of peasants and workers as an unruly social force, these designations justified physical violence against them, their exclusion from the "civilized humanity" of the upper classes, and their subjugation under the regimes of serfdom and later wage labor. Mostly poor and culturally distinct, Muslim subjects of the Russian empire were also caught in the processes of continuous racialization, as the government sought to convert and conscript them, while also supporting their religious institutions and competing for patronage toward them with other colonial powers (Crews 2006; Tuna 2015). Thus, Russian government officials associated Muslim pilgrims to Mecca with poverty, illiteracy, and potential political disorder, as they traveled long distances from the Caucasus and Central Asia through the Ottoman lands. Upon return, Muslim pilgrims, unlike their Christian Orthodox counterparts, were subjected to increased scrutiny as possible carriers of infectious diseases such as cholera (Kane 2015). These examples aptly illustrate how "ideologies of race" took particular shapes in tsarist Russia and operated primarily through the prism of religion and social positioning, while drawing on the globally circulating discourses about colonial subjects, fears of political instability, and imperial rivalries.

The Russian Revolution of 1917 ushered in a new society that sought to cultivate workers and peasants as creators of their collective destiny. As a result, class became the central category to which gender, religion, and ethnicity were yoked.[2] The Soviet state claimed to embrace anti-racism by promoting "friendship of peoples" (*druzhba narodov*) through intermarriages and migration within its vast territories (Graber 2020). Internationally, anti-racism took the form of anti-imperialism and internationalist solidarity of workers as the driving force of human emancipation (Guillory 2020). This rhetoric inspired Black radicals in the United States, plagued by systemic racism and anti-black violence (Roman 2012). Yet the Soviet project was far from being "racially innocent" (Todorova 2017).[3] Explicit racial logics animated state policies that sought to uplift ethno-religious minorities from their perceived "backwardness" and bring them into the fold of socialist modernity. Throughout the Soviet era, minority populations were treated as comrades and brothers, but also as internal others and enemies of the nation (e.g., see Tlostanova 2014 on Circassians). The latter notions fueled the violent suppression and deportations of Chechens, Ingush, and Crimean Tatars, among other peoples in the 1940s. These "red racisms," as sociologist Ian Law (2012) characterized Soviet racial logics, became especially apparent in relation to the Roma. They were caught in conflicting representations as nomadic and free-spirited rebels in literature and on theater stages and as cheats and liars, harassing pedestrians for money, in the streets of late- and post-Soviet Russia (Lemon 2000). Despite the ambivalent Soviet attempts to cultivate the written Romani language and support Romani intellectuals, the Roma were racialized as "nonwhite" for their sartorial choices, accents, and behaviors (Lemon 2019).

Despite the proclamations of common citizenship and shared destiny, Soviet citizens from the Caucasus and Central Asia were also racialized in large urban centers. Racial epithets such as *chernye* ("blacks") and *ponaehali* ("arriving in large numbers and unwanted") surfaced on the streets of Moscow and Leningrad as early as the 1950s (Sahadeo 2019). Emanating from the wealthiest Soviet cities, these slurs signaled simmering anxieties about intensified migration from the peripheries and illuminated how ordinary people made sense of the declining economic opportunities and food shortages, starting in the 1970s. In one of many interviews, Sahadeo's Muslim interlocutor recalls how in the early 1980s he was racially insulted at a store where he and his fellow citizens waited in line for over an hour to purchase meat. Racial tensions only intensified with the worsening socioeconomic situation and the violent disintegration of the USSR in the 1990s.

The Soviet collapse was accompanied by dramatic socioeconomic dislocations, separatist conflicts, and migratory waves from and into the newly established Russian Federation. Many people often experienced striking deterioration in their material status in ethnic terms, expressed in growing resentment toward the emergent oligarchic class collectively labeled as "Jews" and in animosity toward those categorized as "black." In the Russian context, "blackness" became a floating signifier cavalierly applied to diverse populations but especially to those perceived as Muslim. Today, the slur is specifically deployed to exclude and oppress Muslim migrant workers from Tajikistan, Uzbekistan, and Azerbaijan, and Muslim citizens of Russia from the North Caucasus. The entwinement of "black" with "Muslim" became more pronounced as a result of the Chechen wars that broke out in the 1990s and rapidly gained ethno-religious overtones, pushing the "Muslim question" within Russia to the forefront of political life (Zakharov 2015). Racially charged political discourses about Muslims circulated on national television and through VCR tapes, showing bearded guerrilla fighters engage in collective prayers and spectacular executions of Russian soldiers, now increasingly seen as "ethnic Slavs" and "Orthodox Christians." In the context of military violence, apartment bombings across Russian towns, and the tragic 2004 school siege in Beslan, "Caucasian" (*kavkazets*) became firmly associated with "religious fanatic," "barbarian," "terrorist," and "black."[4]

"Black" (Muslims), "White" (Russians)

Applied particularly to Muslims from Central Asia and the North Caucasus, the slur "black" seeks to underscore their low socioeconomic status and cultural difference, serving as a tool of exclusion and oppression.[5] For example, the racialization of Muslim migrant workers as "black" takes place as a result of their engagement in low-paying and physically demanding jobs of infrastructural development, janitorial services, petty trade, and transportation (Laruelle and Yudina 2018).[6] Their subjugation within the global capitalist system propped up by racial hierarchies leads to their harassment at the hands of law enforcement, immigration services, and medical systems, and on the labor and housing markets. There, landlords reluctantly rent to whom they call "people with non-Slavic appearances" (*lyudi ne slavyanskoy vneshnosti*) in fear of unwanted police attention and the assumed inability of racialized tenants to pay rent on time. The stigmatization of Muslim migrant workers became especially apparent in a 2012 migrant worker manual, where they were portrayed as cartoon characters—brushes, brooms, and rollers—greeted at the airport by human-presenting doctors, educators, and the police. In the manual, the Saint Petersburg government instructed migrants about appropriate attire and proper behavior, mandatory medical examinations, and lawful immigration status. This example illustrates how anti-immigrant, anti-Muslim, and anti-black sentiments come to define "the human" vis-à-vis the "nonhuman" or, as in this case, inanimate but indispensable work tools (for more on thingification and anti-blackness, see Jackson 2020). Such depiction refuses to recognize the social existence of migrant workers outside of the degrading manual labor they perform in Russia. While reflecting globally circulating racisms that sustain racial capitalism, the racialization of migrant workers also stems from tsarist and Soviet colonial legacies in Central Asia, whose peoples were often cast as "lacking," in need of "improvement," and responsible for their own "underdevelopment" (e.g., Cameron 2018).

The racialization of North Caucasian Muslims as "black" invokes more forcefully anxieties about their cultural difference, divorced from the widely shared understandings of "modernity" and "civilization" in Russia. Their caricatured "proneness to criminality," "unruly masculinities," and "clan-based socialities" render them bad or even terrifying Muslims, who continuously fail in comparison with "domesticated," "economically contributing" and "emancipated" Muslims, such as Tatars and Bashkirs (Mamdani 2002; Rana 2011).[7] Much like the racialization of the Roma analyzed by Alaina Lemon, North Caucasians are othered as a result of their sartorial choices, distinct accents, and ways of traversing urban landscapes. Consider, for example, how Timoti, a famous Russian hip-hop artist of Jewish-Tatar background, depicts Muslims from the North Caucasus in his 2015 song "Lada Sedan Baklajan." In the video, a young Caucasian man—"non-local" and "without registration"—cruises the streets of a Russian city in a low-cost Russian car, Lada Sedan. He antagonizes the police and sexually harasses women in tight tops, tiny shorts, and high heels. With his "brothers," he hustles by running a shady business at a neighborhood tearoom with "carpets on the walls" and tries to entice a young Caucasian woman to go on a date with him. The man is shown breaking traffic rules, engaging in street fights, and performing a traditional Chechen dance atop a police car. His gold teeth, scruffy looks, and emphatic gestures, compounded by leopard print car seat covers and religious paraphernalia hanging from the front mirror of his car, solidify an impression of him as the "other," as "non-white." Grotesque and caricatured in Timoti's video, these wayward ways of being in and moving through the city make eyes roll, lips purse, and slurs spew forth. Such presence often results in heavy policing near mosques, open markets, and immigration centers, where police officers check paperwork and surveil Muslims.

Othering Muslims takes place in a variety of ways on a micro level. Think of the racialization of noise associated with Muslim street vendors, or of sight, continuously drawn to hijabs and collective prayers outside mosques, or of contaminating touch, when Central Asian janitors pick up cigarette butts in the streets. Racialization of Muslims also occurs on a macro level, drawing from the global war on terror and the ongoing counterinsurgency in the Caucasus. As a result, Chechens, Ingush, and Avars constitute a large number of prison inmates, labeled as "radical Islamists" and often locked away on fabricated terrorism charges after exhibiting disobedience of the corrupt political elites. This was how the Chechen husband of my interlocutor spent years in prison, where she drove for hours to visit him and to contest the verdict. This was also how the Ingush owner of an apartment, where my other interlocutor and her family resided, was arrested for "political activity," leaving his unemployed wife and child with cerebral palsy without income.

Who in Russia comes to depend on the transnational and local circulations of anti-Muslim racism in relation to migrant workers and Caucasians, both labeled as "black"? How is "blackness," ascribed to these populations, continuously reproduced vis-à-vis the ever shifting "whiteness"? A structural position of advantage and privilege, "whiteness" in Russia coagulates around Slavic ethnic nationalism, Orthodox Christianity, and compulsive heterosexuality with clearly defined gender roles. In this regard, ponder the evocative representations of the Russian president Vladimir Putin, where he engages in religious rituals, tests out nationally produced and globally exported weapons, and rides horses bare-chested (Sperling 2014). These performative actions consolidate an impression of "whiteness" as a superior aesthetic, which is confidently "European" (read: "modern" and "civilized"), but also uniquely "Russian" (read: "authentic" and "missionary"). Such impressions are translated into real material and symbolic advantages for those perceived as "white" within the hierarchical systems that produce difference.[8]

With that, "whiteness" is not an ontological given or a property of certain bodies, although white nationalists see it as such. Rather, it is continuously reproduced as an effect of racialization. In her analysis of whiteness, Sara Ahmed (2007) invites us to consider what it *does* rather than what it *is*. To that end, she pays close attention to how "whiteness" creates attachments, orients bodies in specific directions, and becomes world-making. In today's Russia, along with the sense of pride and superiority, "whiteness" translates much resentment and anxiety. These feelings are mobilized in "Russia for [ethnic] Russians," a far-right slogan that has fueled attacks on vulnerable populations, deemed "non-white." These sentiments are garnered, when every November 4 ultranationalists participate in the so-called Russian Marches. On National Unity Day in 2020, the Far Right engaged in church services, paraded with the old imperial flag, and demanded the construction of a monument in honor of Russian soldiers killed in the Chechen wars (Arnold 2020; see also Fomina 2018). Defying coronavirus-related restrictions and the official ban on the event, the participants marched under the "Russian Lives Matter" banner, with some of them commemorating an infamous neo-Nazi, Maxim "Tesak" Martsinkevich, who was imprisoned for inciting hatred against Muslim migrant workers, the homeless, and Afro-Russians and who died under mysterious circumstances in his prison cell in September 2020.

Aggrieved "whiteness" also speaks when believers demand a legislative, material, and symbolic intercession from the state to protect Russia's Christian Orthodox identity, valorized by the mythology around Holy Rus. The course titled the Foundations of Religious Culture and Secular Ethics, introduced in 2010 into the school curriculum, the 2013 law protecting religious feelings, and the 2013 "gay propaganda" law are among many examples of how "whiteness becomes worldly," producing and maintaining infrastructures around itself (Ahmed 2007: 150). While the laws and changes in the school curriculum also seek to protect non-Christians— their feelings and religious traditions are said to matter too—the dominance of a white Christian culture is apparent in the disproportionately large financial resources, visibility, and autonomy afforded to the Russian Orthodox Church in comparison with other religious institutions.

The cyclical socioeconomic crises of the 1990s and the mid-2000s have challenged the privileged position of ethnically Slavic and Christian Russians, many of whom found themselves un(der)employed and politically disempowered, while being on the receiving end of shrinking welfare entitlements. Class resentment, lived through race, transpires in the opening scenes of the 2007 documentary *From Russia with Hate*, where a group of neo-Nazis (*skinhedy*) express disdain for the "poor people, streaming into Russia" after the collapse of "our ancient empire." "Poor people" is a shorthand for migrant workers who allegedly "steal jobs," ethnic and religious minorities who "replace Slavs," and the homeless who are "morally unfit." This example demonstrates how "whiteness" becomes a "modality in which class is lived, the medium through which class relations are experienced, the form in which it is appropriated and fought through" (Hall [1980] 2018: 216). In the context of ongoing socioeconomic dislocations and Slavic ethnic nationalism in Russia, "whiteness" becomes a symbolic wage, paid to the economically aggrieved for their demotion and exposure to precarity (see Roediger 2007). This entwinement of class and racialization became especially apparent when during the 2015–16 financial crisis, some of my "white" acquaintances attributed their loss of socioeconomic stability and respectability to the influx of migrants from Russia's peripheries and abroad. Racialized as "nonwhite" vis-à-vis long-time Saint Petersburg residents, those migrants were blamed for initiating a "race to the bottom" with their willingness to take up jobs for lower pay and less security.

Much like "blackness," "whiteness" in Russia is reproduced on a micro level through glares, slurs, and infliction of physical pain onto those seen as out of place. It is also produced on a macro level, drawing from globally circulating discourses of white supremacy and Russian exceptionalism. The latter is fueled by the country's anxieties about its place in the world after the dissolution of the Soviet Union and is reflected in the contradictory geopolitical projects that portray Russia as both a "white nation" and simultaneously as a "Eurasian empire" (see Zakharov 2015). As a result, pan-Orthodox and pan-Slavic military brotherhoods operate alongside the Eurasia movement, striving to protect the world from the "pernicious influences" of liberalism, feminism, and LGBTQ+ rights (e.g., consider the allure of "Gayropa" or "gay Europe" for white nationalists in Russia). These projects often masquerade as anti-racist, so Russia takes up arms to protect the Ukraine from neofascism, to safeguard a "multipolar illiberal world order" by intervening in Syria, and to undermine the United States—"the true source of global terrorism," to paraphrase Alexander Dugin, the "father" of the Eurasia movement. Domestically, these agendas entwine with the rehabilitation of the former royal family now canonized as Christian saints, alarming nostalgia for the Stalinist era, and authoritarian political tendencies more broadly (Laruelle and Karnysheva 2020; Robinson 2019). These policies are supported by many Russians and diverse groups abroad, from American converts to Orthodoxy and the global Far Right such as Richard B. Spencer, to populist anti-imperialists worldwide (Riccardi-Swartz 2020). Such oscillation between Russia as a "white nation" and a "multiethnic and multireligious Eurasian empire" reflects anxieties about its own peripheral "whiteness," which has been challenged historically by its Western partners and enemies. Russia's representations in the West as a specter of Judeo-Bolshevism, an Asiatic Horde, and a bulwark of illiberal authoritarianism have questioned its "whiteness" and belonging to the "modern," "civilized" world.

It is within these messy entanglements and legacies that my interlocutors—working-class devout Muslim women—composed and oriented their lives in Saint Petersburg, seeking to understand and respond to specific iterations of global anti-Muslim racism.

Living Anti-Muslim Racism

It was eight in the evening in October 2015 when Shahnaz and I rushed through the poorly lit alleyway toward the metro station after an informal women's gathering at the atelier. The women came out that evening to socialize over tea and homemade food, pray together, and listen to Shahnaz's lecture about fate and predestination in Islam. The meeting ran late, and we were in a hurry to get home. Unlike me, Shahnaz had a long ride to her dormitory, located on the outskirts of Saint Petersburg. As we passed through the main doors of the metro station, we saw a police checkpoint, made up of a metal detector and an interrogation room, where questions were asked, documents checked, and suspicious backpacks searched. Shahnaz hesitated, slowed down her pace, and followed my lead, speaking in a low voice to herself: "It will be alright, I am with the white person (*belyi chelovek*)." On the escalator, she cheerfully picked up where she had left off in our conversation, but I could not focus on her story. I thought about the

metal detector, her anxiety about a potential encounter with a police offi-
cer, and my designation as a "white person," despite the ongoing racialization of Jews throughout Russian history. As we got off the escalator, we
kissed each other goodbye and went in different directions to catch our
trains. I asked her to text me when she made it home.

Muslims like Shahnaz move daily through Saint Petersburg, where anti-
Muslim racism is enveloping, atmospheric, weather-like (Sharpe 2016).
Earlier in the 2000s, it manifested itself in violent and often lethal attacks on
migrant workers and antifascists.[9] In one such altercation, a student from
my university was murdered by a far-right group for his pro-immigration
activism. On the day Shahnaz and I rode the metro together, racism was viscerally felt in the imposing presence of the policeman by the metal detector,
in unpleasant stares from random metro passengers, and in the unease
about going home late. I could sense how Shahnaz, a migrant from Azerbaijan, was viewed as a stranger, "recognized as out of place, as the one who
does not belong, whose proximity is registered as crime or threat" (Ahmed
2017: 33).

My interlocutors experienced anti-Muslim racism in multiple contexts
and with different intensities. Sometimes their bodies became its material
repositories, as it happened to Aunt Zulfiya, a former nurse from Turkme-
nistan who became a janitor upon her emigration to Russia. When I visited
her family in their rented apartment on the outskirts of Saint Petersburg,
she showed me her calloused hands deformed by arthritis—one reason
why she had to leave her custodial work. For others, racism manifested
itself most apparently "along the road," when fellow metro travelers would
switch seats or step out of the wagon at the sight of a hijab (West Ohueri
2016: 179). It could be experienced as a sudden jolt in the stomach, when a
son requested that his veiled mother not attend his high school graduation,
or as a daunting feeling, when my interlocutors had to cross international
borders, reapply for work permits, or obtain registration for their commu-
nally run Islamic cultural center.

For the women, anti-Muslim racism had an acutely felt texture, inten-
tionality, and temporality. In a tiny kitchen that also served as a bedroom
for her daughter and son-in-law, Aunt Zulfiya worried about the diminish-
ing family budget, recurring migraines that complicated her caretaking
tasks, and her hijab compounded by what she perceived to be her "phenotypical darkness." "I look like a Gypsy (tsiganka)," she once told me over
lunch, "so when I was pregnant, I ate a lot of apples. Look at my daughter,

she turned out to be like a ruddy apple [fair-skinned] herself." Aunt Zul-fiya's anxieties mounted when in October 2015 the Islamic State of Iraq and Syria downed a Saint Petersburg–bound airplane, taking 224 civilian lives in retaliation for Russia's involvement in the Syrian civil war. Placed on top of the fridge, her small TV kept on playing news reports, making her gauge how the tragedy might impact her family and the broader Muslim commu-nity to which she belonged. As she worried about a potential spike in anti-Muslim racism, she continued to cook meals for her large family, her daughter patiently taught Quranic recitations to students over Skype, and Aunt Zulfiya's young grandchildren chirped over the Prophetic report their mother asked them to memorize.

In Russia, where there is no open conversation about or a robust move-ment against racisms, my interlocutors responded to racialization by adopting microstrategies of resisting, subverting, and navigating its uneven terrain. The most notable to me was the cultivation of a particular kind of subjectivity that projected endurance and self-reliance and coun-teracted racist stereotypes about Muslim women as submissive, lazy, and "in need of saving" (Abu-Lughod 2002). This stoic feminine aesthetic was often tethered to the experiences of childbearing, wage labor, and social reproduction more broadly. For example, during fieldwork I spent much time with the pregnant Arina, who continued to work at a pet shop, lift heavy bags with dry food and cat litter, and stand at the counter for hours until her due date. When her contractions began, she walked herself to the hospital, refused epidural anesthesia, and went through labor "with dig-nity" (*s dostoinstvom*). On a crisp and sunny day in the spring of 2016, I vis-ited her and her newborn daughter in their small apartment in a working-class neighborhood of Saint Petersburg, after her husband had left for his three-day work shift. As Arina changed the baby from her nap, she spoke to me from behind a suspended cloth curtain that divided the only room in the apartment into two parts:

> I was lucky to share the maternity ward with an Uzbek woman, who did not make a sound while in labor. She took the pain of childbirth with restraint and dignity. I was deeply impressed with the way she held her-self and followed her example. We bonded over the experience.

This resilient femininity, expressed in my interlocutors' ability to sup-port themselves, their loved ones, and a widening circle of others in need, shaped a counter-aesthetic to the popular Russian discourse, where Mus-lim women were caricatured as either dangerous religious fanatics or gullible followers of their husbands.[10] In some ways, this subjectivity resonated with the folkloric representations of peasant and working-class Russian women as capable of "stopping a galloping horse, entering a burning house, and enduring famine and cold." These ideas echo in songs by the Tajik performer Manizha Sangin, who represented Russia at the Eurovision competition in 2021. In her song "Russian Women," she sings: "Every Russian woman needs to know, you are strong enough to pass against the wall."

As my interlocutors shouldered a disproportionate amount of wage and emotional labor, especially during the socioeconomic crisis that marked the beginning of my fieldwork, they cultivated intimacy and spirituality among their Muslim sisters. The atelier I referred to above often served as a site of the women's joy, pleasure, and hospitality. There, they gathered for religious exhortations, friendly conversations over tea with sweets, and for an occasional manicure session and henna body art. There, the atelier's owners—a mother and her two daughters—produced affordable, elegant, and high-quality clothes for working-class Muslim women to celebrate their beauty and endurance. "Everybody in Russia is used to seeing Muslims as poor and backward," Madinat, the atelier owner, told me once as she knitted a purse. "They can't fathom that we [Muslims] also go to theaters." These different paths to creating and maintaining physical and emotional wellness were their way to pursue joy as a political project in the midst of economic hardships and anti-Muslim racism in Russia (Williams 2018).

In the spaces of the atelier, apartment kitchens, and cafés, the women nurtured durable solidarities with non-Muslim women, who also became targets of racism and misogyny. Thus, Sona, a young artist of Armenian descent, was a fixture of the vibrant atelier life. A long-term college friend of Madinat's daughter, she spent days and sometimes nights there, drawing, sharing meals, and attending religious gatherings, while Madinat occasionally made clothes for her. Sona affectionately called their friendship "Black solidarity" (*Chernaya solidarnost*), referring to the shared experiences of othering and to the bond the women forged as a result. Their unconditional support for each other was a lifeline that sustained them emotionally, when Madinat and her daughters struggled to weather the economic crisis and Sona strove to find her path in this inhospitable world.

The webs of solidarity drew my interlocutors deeper into collaborative relationships with human and animal rights organizations, informal feminist collectives, and mutual aid projects that involved Muslims and non-Muslims in difficult life situations. In September 2019, Natalia, a prominent figure in the Muslim community, sent me a WhatsApp message, where, in excitement, she told me about her prospective lecture on Islam and feminism on the platform of *Fem Talks*, a Moscow-based educational project that holds regular seminars, translates feminist texts into Russian, and records podcasts for the broader public. One project founder consistently turns to the issue of racism in Russia in her own writing.[11] These fledgling collaborations in the context of emergent discussions about racism serve as a safety net, where women from all walks of life forge solidarities, create opportunities for participation, and imagine possibilities for anti-racist politics in Russia.

Conclusion

Anti-Muslim racism takes specific forms in today's Russia, drawing on globally circulating negative sentiments toward and violence against Muslims. It is tied to anti-black racism and anti-poor discrimination and is embedded in the local histories of colonization and othering that complicate our understanding of race, comparative colonialisms, and possible trajectories for decolonization. As a tool of control and exclusion, anti-Muslim racism in Russia operates simultaneously on multiple levels, from state-sponsored globally traveling discourses to interpersonal relations, as well as in various spaces, from public transportation and streets to the intimacy of apartment kitchens and ateliers. Stories told by working-class Muslim women in Saint Petersburg also reveal how anti-Muslim racism is a gendered phenomenon, impacting women's bodies, subjectivities, ways of moving through space, and ways of relating to others. The cumulative impact of racist encounters and the pervasive effects of racist atmospheres have elicited responses from the women, who resisted, learned to navigate, and occasionally reproduced racist hierarchies. These responses take place in the context of racial capitalism, neoconservative policies, and repressive authoritarianism in a Russia that has recently lashed out with a vengeance at anti-government protesters.

Today, artists, academics, and progressive political forces attempt to reflect on the forms and long-term effects of racisms in Russia. For example, the Russian Socialist Movement (RSD) offers a leftist critique of racism, sexism, and homophobia despite incurring government attacks on its members. In his 2017 film *Closeness* (*Tesnota*), the young film producer

Kantemir Balagov, who hails from the North Caucasus, depicts the complexities of life in the region in the wake of the Chechen wars. Despite racist attacks against her, Manizha mobilizes powerful feminist messages in her songs, just as domestic violence has been decriminalized in Russia. While these attempts assemble, multiply, and magnify, anti-Muslim racism is being challenged in the streets, in families, and in people's minds.

Tatiana Rabinovich explores how marginalized groups practice solidarity and provide care in times of crisis. Her book-in-progress, titled "Embracing Precarity: Women, Islam, and Solidarity in Russia," examines the intersections of care labor, mutual aid, and spirituality in the post- socialist context. Tatiana is a postdoctoral scholar in interdisciplinary studies at North Carolina State University.

Notes

1 Scholars and activists often capitalize "Black" to emphasize a shared history and personhood among people who claim this identity category. However, in the Russian context it seems more appropriate to use the lower-case *b* in "black" to account for how this signifier is thrust upon diverse populations for the purpose of exclusion. Therefore, I write "black" throughout the paper, except for instances when "Black" connotes a shared sense of community and solidarity.

2 All religions were militantly done away with, while ethnicity was relegated to "national cultures," which were fostered and controlled. Gender and sexuality were also pronounced to be no longer an obstacle in women's lives. This materialized in concrete measures, such as the legalization of abortion, and in the pronouncements of complete equality among Soviet workers and peasants (e.g., "even a kitchen maid could rule the state," to quote Vladimir Lenin). To complicate these assertions, see Klots 2018.

3 The project was not gender-neutral either. For a discussion of masculine comradeship in the early Soviet Union, see Borenstein (2001). On the state-sponsored construction of gender in the USSR at different historical periods, see Zdravomyslova and Temkina (2003).

4 Consider how in the US context the term *Caucasian* is synonymous with "white," whereas in Russia it connotes non-whiteness. On the troubling history of the term, rooted in the fascination of Western scholars with the shape and size of skulls of the peoples from the North Caucasus, see Nell Irvin Painter (2010).

5 We should account for the expansiveness of "blackness," as it is indiscriminately thrust upon various peoples in Russia, often transpiring through different words. In relation to Muslims, "blackness" is also highly contextual. For instance, Slavic converts to Islam might not be racialized as "black," while being stigmatized and othered. Thus, we might consider "blackness" as an incoherent continuum.

6   Recently, there have been attempts to "rehabilitate" low-paying manual jobs through the "whiteness" of Russian citizenship and Slavic ethnicity. Consider, for example, a job flyer at a construction site in Moscow stating: "Work: a close-knit team of Slavs will accept within its ranks workers—citizens of Russia and Belarus—of the following kinds: welder, stucco worker, house painter, tile layer, and unskilled worker."

7   During my fieldwork, I noticed how some Muslims attempted to ascend to "whiteness" through consumption practices and forms of capital, legible to and valued by "white" middle-class Russians. For example, designer clothes, trips abroad, and certain kinds of work and leisure were promoted in Muslim magazines, by halal businesses, and during empowerment seminars held by the prominent Muslim televangelist and imam Shamil Alyautdinov.

8   Some businesses openly or surreptitiously express desire for and hire employees with "Slavic appearance" and with Russian citizenship. For women, such hiring requirements are often compounded by age limits (e.g., "under thirty-five") and body type ("slim").

9   For more, see www.sova-center.ru/racism-xenophobia/publications/2020/01/d41959/.

10 Here I refer to the hyper-sensationalized images of a "black widow" (*shahidka* in Russian) or a gullible convert to Islam, epitomized by Varvara Karaulova. In 2015, Varvara left Russia to join her recruiter-cum-husband to participate in jihad in Syria. Intercepted at the Turkish-Syrian border by the Russian security services, she was returned to Russia, tried in court, and sentenced to three years in a penal colony. Varvara was released last year but will remain under the oversight of the federal security services until 2029.

11 See she-expert.org/istoriya/ty-dolzhna-byt-luchshe-chem-oni-kak-rabotaet-rasizm-v-rossii.

References

Abu-Lughod, Lila. 2002. "Do Muslim Women Really Need Saving?" *American Anthropologist* 104, no. 3: 783–90.

Ahmed, Sara. 2007. "A Phenomenology of Whiteness." *Feminist Theory* 8, no. 2: 149–68.

Ahmed, Sara. 2017. *Living a Feminist Life*. Durham, NC: Duke University Press.

Arnold, Richard. 2020. "Russian Extreme Nationalists Rally across Country in Midst of Pandemic." *Eurasia Daily Monitor* 17, no. 167. jamestown.org/program/russian-extreme-nationalists-rally-across-country-in-midst-of-pandemic/.

Avrutin, Eugene. Forthcoming. *Racism in Modern Russia*. New York: Bloomsbury.

Borenstein, Eliot. 2001. *Men without Women: Masculinity and Revolutions in Russian Fiction, 1917–1929*. Durham, NC: Duke University Press.

Cameron, Sarah. 2018. *The Hungry Steppe: Famine, Violence, and the Making of Soviet Kazakhstan*. Ithaca, NY: Cornell University Press.

Crews, Robert. 2006. *For Prophet and Tsar: Islam and Empire in Russia and Central Asia*. Cambridge, MA: Harvard University Press.

Fomina, Victoria. 2018. "Between Heroism and Sainthood: New Martyr Evgenii Rodionov as a Moral Model in Contemporary Russia." *History and Anthropology* 29, no. 1: 101–20.

Graber, Kathryn. 2020. *Mixed Messages: Mediating Native Belonging in Asian Russia.* Ithaca, NY: Cornell University Press.

Guillory, Sean. 2020. "Despite Its Complicated Past, Soviet Antiracism was Ahead of the Historical Curve." *Moscow Times,* June 15. www.themoscowtimes.com/2020 /06/15/despite-its-complicated-history-soviet-antiracism-was-ahead-of-the -historical-curve-a70569.

Hall, Stuart. (1980) 2018. "Race, Articulation, and Societies Structured in Dominance." In *Essential Essays: Foundations of Cultural Studies,* vol. 1, edited by David Morley, 172–221. Durham, NC: Duke University Press.

Jackson, Zakiyyah Iman. 2020. *Becoming Human: Matter and Meaning in an Antiblack World.* New York: New York University Press.

Kane, Eileen. 2015. *Empire and the Pilgrimage to Mecca.* Ithaca, NY: Cornell University Press.

Klots, Alissa. 2018. "The Kitchen Maid as Revolutionary Symbol: Paid Domestic Labour and the Emancipation of Soviet Women, 1917–1941." In *The Palgrave Handbook on Women and Gender in Twentieth-Century Russia and the Soviet Union,* edited by Melanie Ilic, 83–100. London: Palgrave Macmillan.

Laruelle, Marlene, and Margarita Karnysheva. 2020. *Rediscovering Russia's White Movement: Politics, Culture, and Memory Today.* New York: Bloomsbury.

Laruelle, Marlene, and Natalia Yudina. 2018. "Islamophobia in Russia: Trends and Societal Context." In *Religion and Violence in Russia: Context, Manifestations, and Policy,* edited by Olga Oliker, 43–64. Washington, DC: Center for Strategic and International Studies.

Law, Ian. 2012. *Red Racisms: Racism in Communist and Post-Communist Contexts.* London: Palgrave Macmillan.

Lemon, Alaina. 2000. *Between Two Fires: Gypsy Performance and Romani Memory from Pushkin to Post-socialism.* Durham, NC: Duke University Press.

Lemon, Alaina. 2019. "The Matter of Race." In *Ideologies of Race: Imperial Russia and the Soviet Union in Global Context,* edited by David Rainbow, 59–76. Montreal: McGill-Queen's University Press.

Lentin, Alana. 2020. *Why Race Still Matters.* Cambridge: Polity Press.

Mamdani, Mahmood. 2002. "Good Muslim, Bad Muslim: A Political Perspective on Culture and Terrorism." *American Anthropologist* 104, no. 3: 766–75.

Painter, Nell I. 2010. *The History of White People.* New York: W. W. Norton.

Rainbow, David. 2019. "Introduction: Race as Ideology; An Approach." In *Ideologies of Race: Imperial Russia and the Soviet Union in Global Context,* edited by David Rainbow, 3–26. Montreal: McGill-Queen's University Press.

Rana, Junaid. 2011. *Terrifying Muslims: Race and Labor in the South Asian Diaspora.* Durham, NC: Duke University Press.

Riccardi-Swartz, Sarah. 2020. "Putin's American Comrades and Our Post-truth Moment." *Sightings,* December 10. divinity.uchicago.edu/sightings/articles /putins-american-comrades-and-our-post-truth-moment.

Robinson, Paul. 2019. *Russian Conservativism.* Ithaca, NY: Cornell University Press.

Roediger, David. 2007. *The Wages of Whiteness: Race and the Making of the American Working Class.* London: Verso.

Roman, Meredith. 2012. *Opposing Jim Crow: African Americans and the Soviet Indictment of U.S. Racism, 1928–1937.* Lincoln: University of Nebraska Press.

Sahadeo, Jeff. 2019. *Voices from the Soviet Edge: Southern Migrants in Leningrad and Moscow.* Ithaca, NY: Cornell University Press.

Sharpe, Christina. 2016. *In the Wake: On Blackness and Being.* Durham, NC: Duke University Press.

Sperling, Valerie. 2014. *Sex, Politics, Putin: Political Legitimacy in Russia.* Oxford: Oxford University Press.

Tlostanova, Madina. 2014. "How 'Caucasians' Became 'Black': Imperial Difference and the Symbolization of Race." *Lichnost, Kultura, Obshestvo* 16, nos. 3–4: 96–115.

Todorova, Miglena S. 2017. "Race and Women of Color in Socialist/Postsocialist Transnational Feminisms in Central and Southeastern Europe." *Meridians: Feminism, Race, Transnationalism* 16, no. 1: 114–41.

Tuna, Mustafa. 2015. *Imperial Russia's Muslims: Islam, Empire, and European Modernity, 1788–1914.* Cambridge: Cambridge University Press.

West Ohueri, Chelsi. 2016. "Mapping Race and Belonging in the Margins of Europe: Albanian, Romani, and Egyptian Sentiments." PhD diss., University of Texas at Austin.

Williams, Bianca C. 2018. *The Pursuit of Happiness: Black Women, Diasporic Dreams, and the Politics of Emotional Transnationalism.* Durham, NC: Duke University Press.

Zakharov, Nikolay. 2015. *Race and Racism in Russia.* London: Palgrave Macmillan.

Zdravomyslova, Elena, and Anna Temkina. 2003. "Gosudarstvennoe konstruirovanie gendera v sovetskom obshestve." *Journal of Social Policy Studies* 1, nos. 3–4: 299–321. ecsocman.hse.ru/data/072/627/1219/zdravomyslova_temkina_gosudar stvennoe_konstruirovanie.PDF.

Evelyn Alsultany

How Hate Crime Laws Perpetuate Anti-Muslim Racism

Abstract: This essay focuses on two cases in which Muslim youth were murdered yet law enforcement refused to classify the murders as hate crimes. It
examines the 2015 murders of Deah Barakat, Yusor Abu-Salha, and Razan
Abu-Salha in Chapel Hill, North Carolina and the 2017 murder of Nabra
Hassanen in Reston, Virginia. This author argues that the denial of these
cases as hate crimes contributes to the diminishment of anti-Muslim racism
and should be understood as a form of racial gaslighting—a systematic
denial of the persistence and severity of racism. In conversation with those
advocating for rethinking the criminal justice system through prison abolition and restorative justice, it posits that seeking state recognition for hate
crimes cannot provide justice given that the state is responsible for constructing Muslims as a national security threat. It explores how anti-Muslim
racism is upheld through extremely narrow and problematic definitions of
racism and hate crimes, through an approach to hate crimes that prioritizes
punishment over civil rights, and through creating a dilemma for Muslim
communities who must seek recognition of anti-Muslim racism from the
same state that enacts surveillance and violence on them.

On February 10, 2015, in Chapel Hill, North Carolina, Craig Stephen Hicks,
a forty-six-year-old white car-parts salesman, murdered his neighbors,
three Muslim American students: Deah Barakat (age twenty-three), his
wife Yusor Abu-Salha (age twenty-one), and her sister Razan Abu-Salha
(age nineteen). He shot each of them in the head. The Federal Bureau of
Investigation (FBI) labeled the murders a parking dispute, not a hate crime,
thus sparking a debate over the meaning of the latter. Hicks turned himself

MERIDIANS · feminism, race, transnationalism   20:2 October 2021
DOI: 10.1215/15366936-9547954 © 2021 Smith College

in and was charged with three counts of first-degree murder. His wife Karen insisted that the murders were not motivated by hatred, stating that her husband's actions were driven by "the longstanding parking disputes that my husband had with the neighbors. . . . He often champions on his Facebook page for the rights of many individuals. Same-sex marriages, abortion, race, he just believes everyone is equal" (Campbell 2017). Hicks pled guilty to three counts of first-degree murder and in 2019, four years after killing Deah Barakat, Yusor Abu-Salha, and Razan Abu-Salha, he was sentenced to three terms of life in prison (Watts and Hanna 2019).

Two years later, on June 18, 2017, in Reston, Virginia, twenty-two-year-old Darwin Martinez Torres, a construction worker and undocumented immigrant from El Salvador, killed Nabra Hassanen (age seventeen) in an incident law enforcement classified as road rage. At around 3:40 a.m. on a Sunday during the holy month of Ramadan, a group of fifteen teenagers were walking and cycling from an IHOP restaurant back to the All Dulles Area Muslim Society (aka the ADAMS Center), where they were attending an overnight event. Some of the teens were on the sidewalk and others were on the road when Torres approached them in his car and got into an argument with them. He then got out of his car and chased them with a baseball bat. The teens ran away, but he captured Nabra Hassanen, hit her with the baseball bat, and then put her body in his car. After abducting her, he sexually assaulted her, murdered her, and left her body in a pond in Loudoun County where the police recovered it (Digangi 2017). Torres was officially charged with abduction with intent to defile, first-degree murder, and rape (Digangi 2017). He pled guilty to the murder of Nabra Hassanen and in 2019 was sentenced to eight life terms in prison (Kuruvilla 2019).

The police were clear in their statements that despite the fact that a group of Muslim teens were attacked and that Hassanen was wearing a hijab at the time, this was not to be classified as a hate crime. Fairfax County police spokesperson Julie Parker said at a press conference that there was no evidence that the crime was motivated by race or religion and added that there was no evidence that Torres used any racial slurs as he chased the group of teens (Al Jazeera 2017). Tawny Wright, another spokesperson with the Fairfax Police Department, said, "Everyone looks at this crime and thinks that because the victims were participating in activities at a mosque, they assume that's what it was. . . . It seems like a guy got enraged and just went after the victim who was closest to him" (Suerth 2017).

In both this case and the Chapel Hill case above, the Council on American-Islamic Relations (CAIR) and other civil rights groups challenged law enforcement's characterization of the incidents, and insisted the events be investigated and classified as hate crimes. In the Chapel Hill case in 2015, over 150 civil rights groups signed a letter to Attorney General Eric Holder urging a hate crime investigation. In the Reston case in 2017, CAIR issued a public statement: "As we grieve for Nabra's loss, we also urge law enforcement authorities to conduct a thorough investigation of a possible bias motive in this case, coming as it does at a time of rising Islamophobia and anti-Muslim hate attacks nationwide" (CAIR 2017).

Why would law enforcement be reluctant to label cases in which Muslim youths are murdered as hate crimes? And what are the effects when the criminal justice system refuses to apply this category to instances of anti-Muslim racism? I contend that the denial of a hate crime contributes to the diminishment and denial of anti-Muslim racism and, as such, should be understood as a form of racial gaslighting—that is, a systematic denial of the persistence and severity of racism. The religious studies scholar Juliane Hammer (2019), writing about the two murder cases, points to how the term *Islamophobia* itself contributes to understanding the murders as individual acts, focusing on individual culpability rather than on the larger problem of anti-Muslim hatred that inspires such attacks. Throughout this essay, I deliberately use the term *anti-Muslim racism* instead of Islamophobia to facilitate an analysis of systemic discrimination and to reject conceptualizing discrimination as located in the individual or as a phobia. I use the ethnic studies scholars Nadine Naber and Junaid Rana's (2019) definition of anti-Muslim racism: the "inter-personal, media, and state-based targeting of those who are Muslim and those perceived to be Muslim. The targeting often relies upon the assumption that 'Muslims' are enemies of, and pose a threat to, the US nation." Anti-Muslim racism accounts for the dialectic between individuals and institutions (Beydoun 2016) and the deep-rooted structures of white supremacy in US history that continue to shape and inform logics that legitimize exclusion today. Furthermore, it expands our understanding of racism to account for the ways in which racism is not only based in phenotype but in visual markers, and how race thinking can be transferable to conceptions of culture and nation (Naber 2008).

This essay contributes to a movement in ethnic studies to include Muslims in conversations about race and racialization in the United States. As a cultural studies scholar, I conduct a critical discourse analysis of these murder cases that are not defined as hate crimes as covered in news reporting, police press releases, and responses in op-eds, on Twitter, and by civil rights organizations. In conversation with Women of Color feminist scholars advocating for rethinking the criminal justice system through prison abolition and restorative justice, I argue that seeking state recognition for hate crimes cannot provide justice because the state is responsible for constructing Muslims as a national security threat. Angela Davis (2003), Ruth Gilmore (2007), Mimi Kim (2018), and others have underlined that prison and punishment are not the answer. They have called for rethinking the criminal justice system through prison abolition, restorative justice, and transformative justice. In the case of redressing Muslims who are murder victims, a meaningful approach would not only address the state's responsibility in constructing anti-Muslim racism through a range of policies, but it would also problematize a larger trend characteristic of a neoliberal era that involves investing in crime and punishment and divesting from civil rights.

Given that the criminal justice system is an important arm of the national security state that constructs Muslims as "terrorists" and is responsible for the widespread surveillance of Muslims in the United States, these details cannot be bracketed out of the conversation about hate crimes against Muslims and anti-Muslim racism. Furthermore, given its role, the criminal justice system as currently configured cannot offer a meaningful resolution to victims of hate crimes or their families. Muslims in the United States seek state recognition for hate crimes while the very same state subjects them to violence and surveillance. Muslim communities are under surveillance. Mosques and even student groups like the Muslim Student Association on college campuses are infiltrated (Hawley 2012). "Terrorism" is commonly understood as being caused by "Muslim extremists" without attention to the role of US interventionist policies (Mamdani 2004). The United States employs secret drone strikes, targeted assassinations, military occupations, and the militarization of policing domestically in fueling the terror-industrial complex (Rana 2016: 114). So, to what extent can law enforcement be seen as an ally to US Muslims? Racial profiling is mobilized to fuel a state-sponsored, ongoing "war on terror" and inspires vigilante hate crimes. Tinkering with hate crime laws for greater recognition will not achieve justice (Spade 2015: 47); it will not end hate crimes or the project of US empire that results in countless deaths. In this essay, I will explore the denial of hate crime classifications and therefore the denial of anti-Muslim racism along with the importance of holding the state accountable for violence against Muslim communities. But first, what are gaslighting and racial gaslighting?

Gaslighting is a term adopted by psychologists that refers to psychological manipulation, originating in the 1938 play *Gaslight*, which was later adapted into a film in 1944. The story centers around an abusive husband who intentionally drives his wife to question her sanity so that he can conceal his criminal activity from her. The specific term *gaslighting* refers to the husband's practice of dimming the gaslights in the house, only to deny doing so when his wife notices the change. He insists she is imagining things, making her question her own perception. Thus, *gaslighting* refers to manipulating someone and driving them to the point of questioning their own sanity by controlling their perception of reality.

Some journalists and bloggers have also used the term to describe the denial of racism effected when, for example, someone describes the Black Lives Matter movement as anti-white and/or anti-police or respond with All Lives Matter and Blue Lives Matter to deny the systematic dehumanization of Black life throughout US history. Referring to the country's long history of downplaying its roots in white supremacy, Rachel Bjerstedt (2016) writes, "White America has been gaslighting Black Americans since our country was founded." What I propose in this essay is using the concept of racial gaslighting to understand anti-Muslim racism—or, more accurately, denials of its existence. Understanding how denial operates reveals the normalization of racialized violence.

Refusing to designate murders of Muslim people in the United States as hate crimes diminishes and denies anti-Muslim racism and thus operates as a form of racial gaslighting, or the systematic denial of the persistence and severity of racism (and other forms of discrimination). This racial gaslighting itself enacts a form of anti-Muslim racism by upholding an extremely narrow and problematic definition of racism and thus what constitutes a hate crime, and by adopting an approach to hate crimes that prioritizes punishment over civil rights. However, the larger problem is that simply designating such violent acts as hate crimes does not solve the root causes of hate crimes and will not prevent them from occurring. A paradox is revealed when Muslim communities seek recognition of anti-Muslim racism from the state that enacts surveillance and violence on these communities, both locally and globally. If we bracket state violence from this conversation, then we will not find an effective solution to anti-Muslim racism. While it is appealing to accept that law enforcement will ensure that justice is served through life-term prison sentences for individuals who kill US Muslims, it is not possible for justice to be served given that the criminal justice system subjects Muslims to surveillance, deportation, bans, and bombs. In what follows, I begin by providing a brief overview of the development of hate crime laws in the United States and why they have failed to be applied to these two Muslim youth murder cases, thus gaslighting anti-Muslim violence. I then consider how law enforcement assures the public that a hate crime designation is not needed because justice will be served in the form of imprisonment, thus prioritizing punishment over civil rights. Finally, I examine Muslim community advocacy for hate crime recognition that highlights a dilemma: seeking state recognition for hate crimes comes at the expense of state accountability for anti-Muslim violence. Ultimately, I show how racial gaslighting operates in these murder cases and that seeking state recognition is not the answer. Rather, in order to end hate crimes against Muslims, the state must be held accountable for its role in producing anti-Muslim racism.

The Limits of Hate Crime Laws

Hate crime laws date back to the Civil Rights Act of 1968, which made it illegal to threaten or interfere with a person because of their race, color, religion, or national origin. A slew of hate crime legislation was passed in the 1990s and 2000s that required the attorney general to collect data on hate crimes annually, increased penalties for hate crimes, and expanded the identities acknowledged as targets of hate crimes. President George H. W. Bush signed the first federal anti–hate crime law, the Hate Crime Statistics Act (HCSA), on April 23, 1990, which mandated that the FBI collect and disseminate data on hate crimes. When the HCSA was introduced in the House of Representatives in 1985, there were four hearings to discuss which particular identities were vulnerable to hate crimes and the need for state action to protect historically marginalized groups (Lewis 2013: 32). The hearings were: Crimes against Religious Practices and Property (1985), Anti-Gay Violence (1986), Ethnically Motivated Violence against Arab-Americans (1986), and Racially Motivated Violence (1988) (Lewis 2013: 31). The hearings as a whole identified white supremacy as the central cause of hate crimes and the first piece of legislation passed to address hate crimes focused exclusively on data collection (Leung 2018). Since then, hate crime laws have expanded to include crimes based on gender, disability, gender identity, or sexual orientation and have also increased penalties for crimes motivated by race, religion, national origin, color, sex, sexual preference, disability, or age (US Department of Justice 2019). While federal hate crime laws have developed, not all states have hate crime laws and thus some hate crimes will not be prosecuted as such (Lopez 2017).

According to the FBI's website, "a hate crime is a traditional offense like murder, arson, or vandalism with an added element of bias." The bias can be "against a race, religion, disability, sexual orientation, ethnicity, gender, or gender identity" (FBI n.d.). The FBI also points out that "hate itself is not a crime" and that freedom of speech must be protected. Thus, a hate crime involves violence or the destruction of property and not hateful speech. In order for a crime to be classified as a hate crime, it needs to meet two specific criteria. First, the act needs to qualify as a crime. This might seem obvious, but the point of this criterion is to distinguish between illegal activity and hateful speech and actions that are protected by the Constitution. Hateful actions, such as yelling racial slurs or spreading racist flyers, are protected speech and not considered to be a crime. In other words, the hate crime designation is applied only to existing/established crimes—e.g., vandalism, arson, murder—and is not a distinct category in itself (Lopez 2017). It is worth noting that because a hate crime charge is used to enhance the penalty on an existing crime, many law enforcement officials do not see a hate crime designation as necessary in a murder case since murder usually involves the highest penalty.

Second, once a particular crime has been confirmed, then it can be elevated to a hate crime if evidence suggests that the motive was hateful. But what determines a hateful motive? Did the attacker yell slurs, or otherwise say anything explicitly anti-gay or racist during the act? Does the attacker have a history, perhaps on social media or in other writings, of discriminatory ideas? If an attacker did not say something anti-Muslim while committing an attack against Muslims or if their Facebook profile does not exhibit anti-Muslim sentiments, then the act would not be classified as a hate crime. Law enforcement ask a series of questions before defining a crime as such, about the perpetrator's motives, intent, and history.

While Muslims of all genders are susceptible to hate crimes, women who wear the hijab tend to more often be the target of hate crime violence whereas Muslim men are more susceptible to government surveillance and government-sanctioned violence (Naber 2008). Many Muslims in the United States claimed that the murders in Chapel Hill were surely a hate crime given that Yusor Abu-Salha and Razan Abu-Salha both wore the hijab and were visibly Muslim. Their parents emigrated from Palestine via Jordan, and Deah Barakat's family emigrated from Syria. However, insistence that this was a hate crime was countered with evidence to the contrary; most notably, those who objected to the label pointed out that Craig Hicks did not fit the profile of the standard "hater." His Facebook and other online posts revealed that he was an atheist, against all religion, whether Islam, Christianity, or Judaism. What complicated his profile were his Facebook posts; alongside rants against religion, he had also expressed support for issues rarely seen as related, from freedom of speech and freedom of religion to the right to bear arms and gay marriage rights. An op-ed in the *Los Angeles Times* described him as a "militant atheist" and reported that his Facebook page included attacks on religion in general and a statement posted in 2012 that declared: "I hate Islam just as much as Christianity, but they have the right to worship in this country just as much as any others do" (McGough 2015). His archived posts even included commentary on the "Ground Zero mosque" controversy, arguing that Muslims were entitled to the right to practice their faith and noting the importance of distinguishing between Muslims and "Muslim extremists."

Offline, Hicks was described as a "known bully" in his neighborhood (Campbell 2017). He had flashed his gun to his neighbors to warn them to keep the noise down and not to park in a particular spot that he claimed belonged to his wife. Given that North Carolina is an open carry state, it is legal to carry a weapon. Neighbors who lived in the same apartment complex had complained to each other about Hicks's aggression (Talbot 2015). However, on the day of the murder, none of the three victims' cars were parked in the disputed spot. Professor of sociology and psychiatry Jonathan Metzl (2015) writes that Hicks's masculinity—"an increasingly prevalent form of stand-your-ground masculinity"—provides insight into his actions, especially in light of him being a "self-appointed watchman" in the apartment complex, patrolling hallways and parking lots, monitoring noise levels, and checking whether cars showed the appropriate parking stickers. As Metzl (2015) points out, "These actions went hand-in-hand with a complex psychological relationship to guns marked by disproportionate gun ownership."

Nonetheless, in the eyes of many, Hicks's profile would not fit expectations regarding the kind of person likely to commit a hate crime—i.e., a white supremacist. It does not follow, however, that the killing of these three Muslim youths was therefore not a hate crime. Indeed, the varied ways in which Hicks defies popular expectations reveals the limits and problems with how racism is conceptualized—namely, as explicit, clear, individual, and aberrant. This rigid conception of hate crimes, and by default racism, individualizes racism and thus makes systemic racism invisible. The legal scholar and trans* activist Dean Spade (2015: 42) notes that "the law's adoption of this conception of racism . . . make[s] it ineffective at eradicating racism and help[s] it contribute to obscuring the actual operations of racism." The hate crimes scholar Clara Lewis has likewise shown that hate crime coverage in the news focuses only on the most extreme cases like murder, thus reinforcing the impression that such crimes are exceptional events, committed by extremists who subscribe to views not shared by the general public (2014: 7). Hate crimes, as a result, appear completely disconnected from the culture at large, and only enter public consciousness as anomalies that can be collectively decried and disavowed. Because they hear only about such extreme cases, Lewis says that audiences get to feel that justice has been served and, indeed, that they have participated in this process, without implicating themselves or disturbing the social order (2013: 6).

So, if hate crime designations (and the media coverage of them) portray racism as an individualized, extreme, and exceptional phenomenon, then what happens when something is denied even that label, excluded from that category, notwithstanding all its limitations? By not classifying these murders as hate crimes, racism becomes even further exceptionalized and rendered invisible. This classification conveys that even extreme individual violence doesn't constitute racism and in doing so exceptionalizes Muslims' frequent exposure to hate crimes. In this case, "parking dispute" reclassifies reality through an act of labeling, coding a crime as race-neutral when it is anything but.

In the case of Darwin Torres, the murder of Nabra Hassanen was not classified as a hate crime because he did not have a social media presence that could prove anti-Muslim attitudes. Reports indicate that Torres accused one of the teens of blocking the road—the teen was riding his bike on the road—and that an argument ensued. The details of what was said are unclear, but what is clear is that law enforcement said that no racial slurs were uttered (Massimo and Iacone 2017). At a press conference regarding the murder of Hassanen, Fairfax County police spokesperson

Julie Parker stated, "Nothing indicates that this was motivated by race or by religion. It appears the suspect became so enraged over this traffic argument that it escalated into deadly violence" (Barakat 2017). The police indicated that Hassanen's murder was the result of road rage: "[Torres's] anger over the encounter led to violence when he hit Nabra with a baseball bat. Torres then took Nabra with him in his car to a second location nearby in Loudoun County" (FCPD Media Relations Bureau 2017a). The press release also states, "If during the course of this ongoing criminal investigation, information or evidence later surfaces that would indicate this was hate-motivated, detectives would certainly ensure appropriate charges are filed" (FCPD Media Relations Bureau 2017a). The police were clear in their statements that, despite the fact that a group of Muslim teens were attacked and that Nabra wore a hijab, this was not classified as a hate crime. To add insult to injury, a memorial for Hassanen created in Dupont Circle in Washington, DC, was vandalized and set on fire. Authorities stated that was not a hate crime either (Brennan 2017).

The failure to designate Hassanen's murder a hate crime was challenged in the news media and in op-eds, particularly the logic that an act can only be considered a hate crime if racism is explicitly vocalized. Ibrahim Hooper of CAIR argued, "You can't just say, 'Oh, he didn't say anything against Islam, so no hate crime'" (Richer and Rankin 2017). Others commented that the impact of the murder on the Muslim community was what mattered, and the impact was that of a hate crime, despite law enforcement's classification. A *Huffington Post* article quoted lawyer Frederick M. Lawrence, who noted that whether the incident was motivated by hate or not, community members and Muslims across the nation deeply identified with it and would increasingly fear that they or their loved ones could be next (Blumberg 2017). Other commentators specified the chilling message the murder had for Muslim women in particular. Azmia Magane (2017) wrote, "To deny that Islamophobia and anti-Muslim violence is a real—and dangerous—occurrence is to try and deny, discredit, and silence the experiences of Muslims—particularly women—in the West, who face violence *because* we are Muslim." Cases in which a murder appears to be a hate crime but is not classified as such have increased in frequency among Muslims and other groups. They point to a complex set of factors. On the one hand, law enforcement seek certain criteria, namely an overt verbal expression of hatred based on race or religion, in designating hate crimes. As a result, in addition to such cases being treated as isolated or happenstance rather than as part of a larger systematic problem, the rigid definition and denial of racial hatred's varied manifestations actually further the denial of racism and thus its perpetuation (Jilwani 2006: 87). On the other hand, Muslim community members insist on a hate crime designation in an effort to foreground how profoundly such crimes impact the community and signal a social crisis. The designation thus becomes important both practically and symbolically in acknowledging the existence and persistence of anti-Muslim racism. Despite the contradictions and failures of hate crime laws, they do serve an important purpose.

Ethnic studies and queer studies scholars have launched important criticisms of hate crime laws. They point out that hate crime laws do not reduce or prevent the phenomena in question, nor do they account for the intersectionality of people's actual identities; but most importantly, hate crime laws expand criminalization and penalization, and disproportionately impact poor people and People of Color. Over the decades, the Hate Crimes Statistics Act has become known for misrepresenting the prevalence of hate crimes because many agencies do not report or under-report hate crimes (Leung 2018: 40). A 2016 investigation into the Chicago Police Department revealed that hate crimes often go unreported to the Civil Rights Unit "because detectives minimize the seriousness of such crimes, saying things like, 'a crime is a crime,' or 'so they got called a name'" (US Department of Justice 2017: 141). A report by the Bureau of Justice Statistics found that the majority of hate crimes (54 percent) went unreported to the police between 2011 and 2015 (Langton 2017). Furthermore, it revealed that violent hate crimes reported to the police (10 percent) were three times less likely to result in an arrest than violent non-hate crimes reported to police (28 percent) (Langton 2017). The discrepancy between hate crimes reported to civil rights groups and hate crimes documented by law enforcement reveals the institutional diminishment of the category in general.

Critics also state that hate crime laws are ineffective in reducing or preventing hate crimes (Bronski, Pellegrini, and Amico 2013). One example is the case of thirty-seven-year-old Khalid Jabara, who was shot and killed on August 12, 2016 by Stanley Vernon Majors, a sixty-two-year-old gay white man in Tulsa, Oklahoma. Jabara and his family, Orthodox Christians from Lebanon, were repeatedly harassed and called "Aye-rabs," "Mooslems," "dirty Arabs," and "filthy Lebanese" by their neighbor (Vicent 2017). Jabara's murder was considered a hate crime because there was clear evidence of Majors's explicit racial and religious slurs. The fact that the Jabara family is not actually Muslim made no difference, as Majors's belief that they were was well established. What is particularly troubling in this case is that even though Jabara's murder was classified as a hate crime, repeated calls to the police and a restraining order did not prevent the murder. In addition to the hate crime designation failing to protect Jabara, his death was not reported as a hate crime in official hate crime statistics, further revealing inaccuracies in hate crime data collection.

Given that these Muslim youth murder cases were defined as "not a hate crime," it appears that the solution to the problem would be changing the designation to one of "hate crime" and ensuring that they are statistically counted. On the surface, this would seemingly resolve the gaslighting of racial denial. However, a hate crime designation does not resolve the issue because hate crimes must be understood as linked to rather than separate from state violence. Thus, asking the state for recognition through a hate crime designation absolves the state of accountability for producing the conditions that fuel anti-Muslim violence.

The Problem with "Tough on Crime" Approaches

In the case of Nabra Hassanen's murder, officials used press conferences to insist that her killer would be prosecuted to the fullest extent of the law and severely penalized, regardless of whether the hate crime designation was applied. Lieutenant Colonel Tom Ryan, deputy chief of the Fairfax County Police Department, stated, "I can assure you that while justice will not bring Nabra Hassanen back, justice will be done as the suspect of this brutal attack is in custody and will be prosecuted to the fullest extent of the law" (Massimo and Iacone 2017). Justice in the form of punishment is thus offered as the solution. I am not seeking to downplay the significance of taking murder seriously—especially in light of a rampant lack of accountability when Black people are killed by police officers—but what is problematic is how this assurance often comes at the expense of recognizing the racialized nature of the crime. There is, in a sense, a bait and switch: the authorities refuse to designate something a hate crime but attempt instead to appease the family members and communities in question by assuring them that penalties will nonetheless be severe, thus reinforcing the legitimacy of the neoliberal tough-on-crime approach.

Lewis (2013: 23–24) argues that "rising public recognition of hate crimes during the late 1980s and 1990s coincided, not accidentally, with the overarching ascendance of both neoliberalism and crime control culture."

In the 1980s and 1990s, a "tough-on-crime" approach emerged that led to an obsession with crime and punishment that included the appearance of more cop shows and legal dramas like *Law and Order* and further development of the prison industrial complex. Lewis (2013: 39) writes:

> Neoliberal state policy and popular thought affected how hate crimes were understood. In this context, the condemnation of the individual hate crimes perpetrator took precedence over broader structural critiques . . . [and] the radicalism of civil rights lost ground to tough-on-crime sentiments and neo-liberal policies.

The "tough-on-crime" approach coincides with the rise of neoliberalism, privatization, and deregulation that led to a shrinking of the public sector, redirecting state policy away from social welfare and toward punishing crime (Meyer 2014: 117). During the Reagan administration in the 1980s, crime became understood as moral degeneracy and thus focus turned to punishing individual offenders rather than addressing the causes of crime (Meyer 2014: 118). This tough-on-crime approach, in turn, interacts in unexpected ways with the hate crime designation. While one might have expected the two to work in tandem, it is more often the case that one is used to downplay the other.

In other hate crimes against Muslims that are not designated as a hate crime (and are not deemed newsworthy enough to make headline news), a few common gaslighting utterances emerge. Law enforcement often say things like "all murders are hateful" (Roschke 2017) or that the hate crime classification is irrelevant since the perpetrator will be prosecuted to the fullest extent of the law. The logic here is that, while a hate crime charge could increase the penalty if the crime was vandalism, it would not necessarily increase the penalty in a meaningful way in the case of murder, since murder already presumably comes with a significant penalty. Thus, some argue that seeking a hate crime charge in the case of murder is futile, or redundant even, while others say that it still has important symbolic meaning.

The debate over whether or not Hassanen's murder should be classified as a hate crime soon came to center, ironically enough, around the status of the assailant as an undocumented immigrant. Daniel Greenfield (2017), writing for the right-wing *Frontpage Magazine*, stated that it was not Islamophobia that killed Hassanen, but "the left's own Illegalophilia." In other words, the problem was not racism but undocumented immigrants, and the Left was to blame for not seeing them as illegal and criminals. Greenfield (2017) insisted that "Nabra Hassanen was killed by the left's love for illegal aliens." Far-right media pundit Ann Coulter echoed this line of thinking when she tweeted, "When a 'Dreamer' murders a Muslim, does the media report it?" (Coulter 2017), not so subtly suggesting that the media (coded as left-leaning) would prefer not to discuss such a crime as it would undermine leftist arguments in support of immigration. Coulter's Twitter followers responded enthusiastically:

"An illegal alien dreamer . . . Pres. Trump must do away with DACA!!!"

"Obviously 'dreamed' to kill a young girl . . . such an asset to our community . . . wake-up America."

"Leftist ideology kills."

"Win/win situation."

"Somehow the rabid Leftists will blame Trump. But the fact is the victim would be alive if her assailant was in Mexico where he belongs."

Torres is in fact, El Salvadoran, yet commentators on the political Right seized upon the idea that he was Mexican, strengthening the association of Mexicans as criminals who make the United States dangerous. Anti-immigrant discourses, in this case regarding undocumented immigrants from Central America, are unleashed while a range of emotions from remorse to ambivalence to celebration is expressed in relation to the murdered Muslim youth.

In addition to the racist assumption that undocumented immigrants are murderers, Greenfield (2017) also assumes that Torres was in a gang, stating that Fairfax "has become a magnet for the El Salvadoran MS-13 gang. It's unknown whether Torres was an MS-13 member, but his behavior matches the extreme brutality and fearless savagery that the group, which has been lethally active in Fairfax, is known for." The police later stated that there was no evidence Torres was affiliated with a gang (FCPD Media Relations Bureau 2017b). Despite the police saying that the murder was not gang related, the prosecutors in the case planned to introduce evidence that he was part of MS-13 (Douglas Moran 2018). Torres was thus portrayed as already a criminal before committing a criminal act. In contrast, Torres's neighbors described him as "a quiet, a friendly, solicitous neighbor who gave people rides, helped women carry groceries up the stairs" (Trull and Smith 2017).

What is crucial to see here is the way in which the tough-on-crime approach facilitates the mobilization of *other* racist discourses, or what historian Natalia Molina refers to as the relational nature of race (Molina 2014), and pits different communities of color against one another. As Mona Eltahawy (2017) aptly put it,

> Racists in the United States will try to use the tragedy to turn people of color against each other. Already, my Twitter mentions are claiming that if Donald J. Trump had built a wall to keep Mexicans out as he promised during the campaign to become president, Nabra would be alive. That is as ludicrous as claiming that if Trump banned all Muslims from the U.S., it would save us from being murdered, as Nabra was.

Given his undocumented status, Torres was held at an Immigration and Customs Enforcement (ICE) detention center before his trial and sentence (Sinclair 2017). And thus, communities that are themselves often treated with suspicion by immigration authorities find themselves looking to those same authorities to inflict penalties when one of their members is murdered for reasons purportedly having nothing to do with racism.

The cultural double standard is clear when we consider how white perpetrators are consistently talked about as individual aberrations or victims of mental illness, whereas a Latinx person who commits murder might be portrayed as an "illegal alien" and gang affiliated, or a Muslim who perpetrates violence might be framed as a "terrorist" motivated by Islam. Metzl (2015) highlights the double standard in how crimes are classified when the victims are People of Color and when they are not. Writing about the murder of the three Muslim youths in North Carolina for MSNBC, he states:

> Yet regardless of whether the North Carolina shooting is categorized as [a hate crime], the immediate response to it illustrates a larger reality: when shooters are white, we as a society have an exceedingly difficult time ascribing political or racial motivations to their actions. This dynamic is often acutely seen in the aftermath of high-profile mass-shootings. Horrific crimes such as Newtown or Aurora would almost certainly be labeled as terrorism were they perpetuated by members of racial, ethnic, or religious minority groups. Our research shows, however, that when mass-killers are white, mainstream U.S. discourse goes to great length to define the crimes as isolated incidents that result from the actions of wayward individuals, or individually disturbed brains, rather than resulting from larger, communal etiologies.

Metzel points to an important component to racial gaslighting: giving whites the benefit of the doubt when they are the perpetrators of crimes. Hicks as a white male is given the benefit of the doubt partly because his profile does not fit the narrow parameters of how racism is defined by law. Thus, his actions are discounted from being part of a larger pattern of anti-Muslim racism and seen as an isolated incident rooted in a parking dispute. In contrast, Torres was cast not as an individual but as reflecting a larger problem with illegal immigration and gang activity, amplifying his racialized criminality. While both men will spend their lives in prison, Hicks received three life sentences for murdering three people; Torres received eight life sentences for sexually assaulting and murdering one person.

The gender and racial politics that shape anti-Muslim racism determine who is deemed worthy of public grieving and sympathy. Hate crimes against Muslims rarely make headline news. Muslim death is not considered newsworthy unless it is to celebrate the murder of an alleged terrorist. Twenty-eight-year-old Somali-Canadian Mustafa Mattan was shot dead in his apartment in Alberta, Canada the day before the Chapel Hill murders, but it did not make headline news (Huncar 2015). Before the case of Deah Barakat, Yusor Abu-Salha, and Razan Abu-Salha became headline news, Muslims commented on the jarring lack of coverage in the media and the double standard in coverage of people killed by Muslims (NBC News 2015; Latif 2015). Nadia Ali tweeted, "No national media coverage on the #chapelhillshooting of a muslim [sic] family!!" (BBC News 2015). Samira (2015) tweeted, "The fact that the only info I am getting about the #ChapelHillshooting is via twitter showcases how permeating Islamophobia is in media." And journalist Abdullah Azada Khenjani (2015) posted to Facebook, "Muslims are only newsworthy when behind a gun, not in front of it." As if necessary to make them worthy of news coverage and public sympathy, when the media started to report on the Chapel Hill murders, the victims were immediately framed through the trope of patriotic Americans. A CNN headline read, "Chapel Hill Muslim Shooting Victim Said She Felt Blessed to Be an American" (Botelho and Ellis 2015).

Audiences are not primed to have sympathy for Muslim men and certainly not Black Muslim men. However, there is a history of sympathetic feeling for Muslim women, usually because they are perceived as oppressed (Alsultany 2012). In this case, the vulnerability and promise of these young women made them worthy of public sympathy. In addition, casting Yusor

Abu-Salha as a patriotic American and highlighting her husband Deah Barakat's humanitarian work framed them as worthy of sympathy. Razan Abu-Salha at nineteen and Nabra Hassanen at seventeen were presented as innocent youths full of promise, ultimately making the US nation appear to care about Muslims amidst rampant anti-Muslim racism. What was not part of the news coverage is the paradox at the center of this chapter: on the one hand, the state makes Muslims vulnerable to hate crimes and other forms of violence. And on the other, the state avenges the death of the vulnerable and appears like the guarantor of justice.

Spade (2015: 47) cautions us to guard against simply tinkering "with systems to make them look more inclusive while leaving their most violent operations intact." He argues that hate crime laws do not prevent violence against marginalized groups, but rather mobilize resources for criminal punishment systems. Thus, "investment in such a system for solving safety issues actually stands to increase harm and violence" because marginalized groups—trans* people, Black people, Latinxs, Muslims—are frequent targets of criminal punishment (Spade 2015: 14–15). The government's approach to hate crimes perpetuates a disconnect between concern for crime and concern for civil rights, revealing that ultimately a hate crime designation is not about social justice and combating racism, homophobia, and transphobia, but rather it is about punishing individual civilian crime (not police crime), particularly extreme forms such as murder. So, it does not matter from the perspective of law enforcement whether these cases are labeled as hate crimes or not. According to law enforcement, what matters is that the case is being taken seriously because the perpetrator was arrested and is being charged with murder.

The Problem with Seeking State Recognition

Muslims want their experiences of victimization to be recognized by one arm of the state, the criminal justice system, yet must wrestle at the same time with the ways in which they are subjected to violence and surveillance by both the criminal justice system and by another arm, that of the national security state. When considering violence to which Muslims are subjected, we must think about a war on Afghanistan that has killed forty-three thousand Afghan civilians (Watson Institute 2020), a war on Iraq that had nothing to do with 9/11 and has killed over two hundred thousand Iraqi civilians (Iraq Body Count n.d.), Guantanamo Bay prison, Abu Ghraib prison, extraordinary rendition, the Patriot Act, Special Registration,

Countering Violent Extremism, and the "Muslim ban." Hate crimes are but one facet of the multidimensional violence that Arabs, Muslims, and those mistaken to be Arab or Muslim face today. And more importantly, hate crimes are deeply connected to and shaped by state policies. The "war on terror" and Patriot Act, for example, convey that Muslims are a threat and are un-American. The legal scholar Muneer I. Ahmad (2004: 1264) argues that individual hate crimes and governmental policies of racial profiling "mutually reinforce a shared racist ideology." He says that government practices of racial profiling through airport profiling, secret arrests, and race-based immigration policies (like the "Muslim ban") fortify the belief that all Arabs, South Asians, and Muslims are terrorist suspects and therefore legitimate targets of violence (Ahmad 2004).

Seeking state recognition is important for symbolic reasons; communities need to push back against gaslighting in order to have their experiences with discrimination recognized. But local and national conversations about hate crimes are rarely paired with discussion of other forms of violence to which Arabs and Muslims are subjected. Applying this concern to the case of Muslims leads to the following question: How can we think about requests for recognition by the state when the state sees Muslims through a lens of national security? Arab and Muslim Americans are vulnerable to many forms of violence, yet hate crime debates give the impression that this is the primary form of violence. What about state violence? What about how state violence inspires hate crimes? What about how Muslims are most often framed either as terrorist threats to national security or useful for national security purposes?

Given that discourses around national security frame Muslims as good only when they are patriotic (in the narrowest sense) and support the state, it is not that surprising that the mosque in Virginia—the ADAMS Center— asked the community not to insist on a hate crime designation regarding Nabra Hassanen and to entrust law enforcement with the process. The statement read: "We request the community to not speculate on the motives and jump to conclusions. We thank both Fairfax County Police and Loudoun County Sheriff's departments for their diligent efforts in investigating and charging the suspect with murder." The ADAMS Center values their reputation as "good Muslims" who are willing to work with law enforcement. As a result, their statement assumes that law enforcement can and will resolve anti-Muslim racism, or at least bring justice to this one particular murder.

In contrast a letter, sent to Attorney General Eric Holder, was organized by CAIR and signed by Arab, Jewish, Sikh, Asian American, Latinx, LGBTQ, and other civil rights groups urging a federal hate crime investigation in the case of the Chapel Hill murders (Botelho and Ellis 2015). The letter points to a larger context of Islamophobia to justify why these murders should be investigated as a hate crime. It reads:

> These killings come in the wake of a disturbing rise in especially threatening and vitriolic anti-Muslim rhetoric and activities. In recent weeks, after the release of the movie *American Sniper*, many tweeted hateful and deplorable messages demeaning to Muslims and Arabs. For example, one user tweeted that the film "makes me wanna go shoot some f**kin Arabs," while another stated that "American sniper made me appreciate soldiers 100x more and hate Muslims 1000000x more." On Saturday, January 17, 2015, outside a Muslim community event in Garland, Texas, hundreds of protesters shouted hateful messages and comments at attendees. Some of the protesters brandished guns, creating a threatening and hostile environment for families attending the event (Muslim Advocates et al. 2015).

The Council on American-Islamic Relations and other civil rights groups are at the forefront of criticizing government policies like the Patriot Act, Special Registration, Countering Violent Extremism, and the travel/Muslim ban. However, the subsequent tough-on-crime approach has meant that Muslim communities seeking recognition from the state for hate crimes, with a focus on a climate of increased anti-Muslim racism, have had to accept the trade-off of silence regarding other violent state practices. Anti-Muslim racism is carefully limited to an individual problem. In seeking recognition from the state, this letter embraces the definition of hate crimes and racism as an individual problem, but it insists that it is not an exceptional problem, so it diverges from the conventional understanding of hate crimes in that way. Thus, in both examples of Muslim advocacy organizations responding to the "not a hate crime" classification of these murders, racism and hate crimes are embraced as individualized in seeking state recognition.

The sociologist Erik Love (2017) has analyzed the ways in which Muslim community organizations respond to Islamophobia, and particularly whether or not they articulate Islamophobia as a form of racism, which he terms the "racial dilemma." Love says that many community organizations strategically avoid framing the problems they face as one with racism and instead stress that they are Americans with First Amendment rights to religious freedom. Love (2017: 23) writes, "The racial dilemma for these advocates is the choice of how to frame their efforts—whether they choose to represent themselves as marginalized communities of color struggling against racism, or position their communities as mainstream, regular Americans who just want to be treated equally." In examining these responses to the murders of Muslim youths, an added dilemma emerges around whether or not to implicate the state; all too often, it seems that the safer strategy is not to criticize the state when you are seeking its recognition. In other words, while CAIR usually critiques state violence, it ignored such violence in addressing this hate crime, and in contrast, the ADAMS Center's message is to trust law enforcement. As Spade (2014: 6) observes, "When advocates seek inclusion in institutions, they tend to lift up and valorize those institutions, which means ignoring and erasing the violent realities of those institutions." And as the critical policy studies scholar Nicole Nguyen (2019: 10) aptly writes, "Although these transactional agreements affirm Muslim cultural identities and facilitates their greater inclusion into U.S. society, they do not redistribute power or dismantle the institutions, discourses, and logics that criminalize Muslim communities."

Fueling Gaslighting

The decision not to apply the hate crime designation to these cases is part of a larger trend in US politics to divest from civil rights and invest instead in criminal punishment. A label that has civil rights significance is not used, but rather punishment of the violent perpetrator is affirmed as justice. The ultimate irony is that this conception of "hate"—racism equals hate, just not this kind of hate—exempts not only racist violence perpetrated by the individual, but also brackets state violence. Muslims are gaslighted but their violent individual perpetrators are prosecuted to the fullest extent of the law.

What does one gain or lose through a "hate crime" classification? What are the limits to calling it hate? A hate crime classification would afford recognition for the racialized violence they face. However, such recognition has a number of effects that perpetuate violence against Muslims. Most importantly, Muslim communities lose out on addressing the root causes of hate crimes and anti-Muslim racism by not connecting hate crimes to state violence. Ultimately, it is not possible to prevent future hate crimes if the state is not held accountable for its role in racializing Muslims. The irony is that racial gaslighting operates both when the hate crime label is and is not applied. When it is not applied, there is no recognition of racialized violence but criminal punishment is presented as justice from the state. When the hate crime label is applied, then the racialized violence is acknowledged as an individual problem that the state justly resolves, but it is divorced from the state's complicity. This dilemma highlights a larger problematic with the neoliberal trend of divesting from civil rights and investing in the criminal justice system. Both options strengthen the criminal justice system and further the poverty in understanding and adequately addressing racism, whether systemic or individual.

In thinking about how state violence becomes invisible, it is also important to consider how the state is exempted from the rubric of hate crimes despite the surveillance of Muslims, deportation of Latinxs, and murder of unarmed Black Americans by law enforcement. The American studies scholar Christina Hanhardt (2013: 163) points out that "hate crimes are distinguished from acts that are lawful and that sanctioned state violence is intentionally left out of the definition because including the state would downplay the status of hate crimes as a category for state-administered condemnation." Ahmad (2004) says that it is not entirely surprising that the state would charge perpetrators of hate crimes because it is in the state's interest to preserve its own monopoly on violence. Therefore, vigilante violence is punished because it is vigilante, not necessarily because it is racist. Furthermore, denouncing individual racism is a way for the state to perpetuate state-sponsored racism. Ahmad (2004: 1325) writes,

> By condemning the racism of others, and of private actors in particular, the government implicitly seizes the mantle of equality. As the arbiter of racism, it lays claim to being free of racism itself. If it were not, the government's very ability to adjudicate the racism of others would be thrown into question. Thus, the condemnation of the most extreme racist acts of others obscures and normalizes the government's own racism.

What can we learn about racial gaslighting when we think about a spectrum of denials? How might we think about denying Muslims a hate crime designation and denying Black Americans recognition of persistent systemic racism in the cases of police brutality as interrelated operations of racial gaslighting? Sherene Razack (2020) argues that racial terror is at the heart of settler colonialism given the history of slavery and violence against Indigenous people and People of Color; that the state continuously consolidates itself through racial violence. I would add that ensuring "justice is served" in cases of extralegal or vigilante violence only serves to further consolidate the state's power and monopoly on violence, especially racial violence. The system works by showcasing justice for Muslims in the form of a multiple life sentence in these cases (while denying them as hate crimes), and at the same time protecting police officers (as state actors) from any consequences for shooting unarmed Black Americans. The system also works by giving this form of justice to Muslims (death penalty for civilians who murder them) while continuing surveillance, drone strikes, and other forms of violence against Muslims domestically and globally. Denial of the persistence of racism and other forms of discrimination relies on cases in which "justice is served," in the law-and-order sense of the term. Such cases operate to project a seemingly just system in which the state prosecutes perpetrators of racial violence but deems irrelevant the designation of racial violence. In other words, the violence that is prosecuted is approached as "equal opportunity" violence and thus the persistence of racism is gaslighted.

Scholars of hate crime law such as James A. Tyner, Doug Meyer, and Dean Spade caution against too great of a focus on hate crime laws. Tyner (2016: 1063) writes:

> The post-racial project of neoliberalism renders racism as a manifestation of individual prejudicial behaviour; in so doing, post-racial conceptualizations of racial violence deflect attention from a more deeply entrenched white supremacy. . . . Consequently, an uncritical engagement with hate-crimes as actions of racist, bigoted persons may reify white supremacy through a silencing of more subtle but decriminalized forms of racism.

In other words, the focus on hate crime laws renders invisible other forms of violence, such as state violence, and creates the impression that the social order is otherwise equal and just (Tyner 2016: 1071–73). The state is absolved from any wrongdoing or responsibility.

Centering both the history and ongoing legacy of white supremacy in the United States and the project of US empire that provides justification for endless wars and murder in predominantly Muslim countries offers an important analytical opening to this problematic of hate crimes. Anti-

Muslim racism (and other forms of racism) is often conceptualized as whites inflicting racist harm, overlooking how all people and communities are implicated in the US system of white supremacy. Nabra Hassanen's killer was an undocumented El Salvadoran immigrant. Many African Americans and Latinx people supported the racial profiling of Arab, Muslim, and South Asian communities after 9/11 (Ahmad 2011). Arab and South Asian taxi drivers in New York supported and perpetuated racial profiling by not picking up African American passengers. Molina (2014) proposes the term *racial scripts* to think about how different groups are racialized (in similar and different ways) and thus are connected through the process of racialization. She writes that "we can see different racial projects operating at the same time, affecting different groups simultaneously" (Molina 2014: 21). Driving while Black and flying while Brown are similar racial projects. Police violence against Black communities and military violence against Arabs and Muslims are similar racial projects. While Arab Muslims at times receive crime and punishment acknowledgment, it comes with gaslighting of their experience with racialized violence. While Black people's racial experiences are also gaslighted they do not get the crime and punishment acknowledgment. And while Arab Muslims can be lulled into feeling that the state cares about them and seeks to protect them, the state is also responsible for unimaginable murder in their homelands, as in Iraq, Palestine, and Yemen. More importantly, recognizing the impacts of white supremacy on multiple communities and drawing such connections has created important opportunities to form coalitions and to broaden the analysis.

The criminal justice system is one arm of the larger national security state that subjects Muslims to surveillance, detention, deportation, torture, drone strikes, and death. In the name of national security, the US government issues policies that construct Muslims as a terrorist threat and destroy Muslim life and livelihood. Given that the criminal justice system in the United States is part of perpetuating the problem of anti-Muslim racism, incarcerating individual perpetrators of hate crimes like Craig Hicks and Darwin Torres cannot resolve the problem of anti-Muslim racism. In other words, while criminal punishment for perpetrators of hate crimes and the possibility of state recognition of hate crimes might appear to be gains, such an approach actually delimits what is possible as a transformative politic. Ensuring that justice is served in these cases by issuing life sentences to the perpetrators of murders considered to be "not a hate crime" further consolidates state power by projecting the state as just even in its advancement of war and racial violence.

The ethnic studies scholar Chandan Reddy points out that the 2009 Matthew Shepard and James Byrd Jr. Hate Crimes Prevention Act was attached to the National Defense Authorization Act of 2010, in which Barack Obama approved $690 billion for the Department of Defense. It included sending ten thousand more troops to Afghanistan and the continued use of unmanned drone strikes in countries, such as Pakistan and Yemen, with whom the United States is not at war. Reddy (2011: 13) thus proposes that we see hate crime laws as attached to sanctioned state violence abroad, that we see "freedom with violence." In other words, discussions about hate and discrimination are framed as the state protecting marginalized groups from attacks from individuals, not from attacks by the state or even attacks influenced by the state. To be clear, I am not stating that Muslims should stop seeking recognition from the state. Rather, I am asking what it would look like if conversations about hate crimes extended beyond recognition from the state to include in the same frame state violence, and how these forms of violence are interrelated. Racial gaslighting operates by distancing hate crime violence, that is, violence perpetrated by individuals, from state violence, and approaching the state as if it is an arbiter of safety and security, of protection and justice. Furthermore, moments of "justice" for one group create the illusion of a just system and provide fuel for gaslighting injustice experienced by other groups.

Evelyn Alsultany is associate professor of American studies and ethnicity at the University of Southern California. She is the author of *Arabs and Muslims in the Media: Race and Representation after 9/11* (2012) and coeditor of *Arab and Arab American Feminisms* (2011) and *Between the Middle East and the Americas* (2013).

Works Cited

ADAMS Center. n.d. "ADAMS Continues to Call for Justice to Be Served in Brutal and Heartless Murder of 17 Year Old Community Member." www.adamscenter.org /adams-deepest-thoughts-and-prayers-for-the-17-year-old-youth-sister-and -family/ (accessed January 31, 2018).

Ahmad, Muneer I. 2004. "A Rage Shared by Law: Post-September 11 Racial Violence as Crimes of Passion." *California Law Review* 92, no. 5: 1259–330. doi.org/10.15779/ Z389H84.

Ahmad, Muneer I. 2011. "Homeland Insecurities: Racial Violence the Day after 9/11." *Race/Ethnicity* 4, no. 3: 337–50.

Al Jazeera. 2017. "Police: Nabra Hassanen Killed in 'Road Rage Incident.'" June 20. www.aljazeera.com/news/2017/6/20/police-nabra-hassanen-killed-in-road-rage -incident. www.aljazeera.com.

Alsultany, Evelyn. 2012. *Arabs and Muslims in the Media: Race and Representation after 9/11*. New York: New York University Press.

Barakat, Matthew. 2017. "Police: Road Rage Led to Bat Attack, Muslim Teen's Death." *Associated Press*, June 19. www.apnews.com/article/f99c296095604ebaa59c76e 917354297.

BBC News. 2015. "How North Carolina Murders Sparked Global Outrage." February 11. www.bbc.com/news/blogs-trending-31421363.

Beydoun, Khaled A. 2016. "Islamophobia: Toward a Legal Definition and Frame- work." *Columbia Law Review Online* 116: 108. columbialawreview.org/content /islamophobia-toward-a-legal-definition-and-framework/.

Bjerstedt, Rachel. 2016. "Dear White America—Can We Please Stop Gaslighting Our Black Friends and Family?" *Medium*, November 17. medium.com /@rachellaughing/dear-white-america-can-we-please-stop-gaslighting-our -black-friends-and-family-7370c6a6a462.

Blumberg, Antonia. 2017. "Police Call Teen's Beating Death 'Road Rage.' That Doesn't Sit Well with Muslim Americans." *Huffington Post*, June 20. www .huffingtonpost.com/entry/nabra-hassanen-road-rage_us_594953eee4b05 eccf2b4728c.

Botelho, Greg, and Ralph Ellis. 2015. "Chapel Hill Muslim Shooting Victim Said She Felt Blessed to Be an American." *CNN*, February 13. www.cnn.com/2015/02/13/us /chapel-hill-shooting/.

Brennan, Christopher. 2017. "South Carolina Man Sets Fire to Memorial for Slain Vir- ginia Teen Nabra Hassanen." *New York Daily News*, June 21. hwww.nydailynews .com/news/national/man-sets-fire-memorial-slain-virginia-teen-nabra -hassanen-article-1.3266085.

Bronski, Michael, Ann Pellegrini, and Michael Amico. 2013. "Hate Crime Laws Don't Prevent Violence against LGBT People." *Nation*, October 2. www.thenation.com /article/archive/hate-crime-laws-dont-prevent-violence-against-lgbt-people/.

CAIR. 2017. "CAIR Offers Condolences on Murder of Virginia Muslim Teen, Urges Probe of Possible Bias Motive." Press release, June 19. www.cair.com/press -center/press-releases/14416-cair-offers-condolences-on-murder-of-virginia -muslim-teen-urges-probe-of-possible-bias-motive.html.

Campbell, Andy. 2017. "Craig Hicks Was Threat With 'Equal Opportunity Anger,' Neighbors Say." *Huffington Post*, February 13. www.huffpost.com/entry/craig-hicks -threatening-neighbors_n_6678098.

Coulter, Ann (@AnnCoulter). 2017. "When a 'Dreamer' murders a Muslim, does the media report it?" Twitter, June 18, 9:35 p.m. twitter.com/AnnCoulter/status /876614502892154880.

Davis, Angela Y. 2003. *Are Prisons Obsolete?* New York: Seven Stories Press.

Digangi, Diana. 2017. "Virginia Man Indicted for Rape, Murder of Muslim Teen near Mosque." *CBS 6*, October 16.

Douglas Moran, Catherine. 2018. "Darwin Martinez-Torres Pleads Guilty to Murder of Nabra Hassanen." *Reston Now*, November 28. www.restonnow.com/2018/11/28 /darwin-martinez-torres-pleads-guilty-to-murder-of-nabra-hassanen/.

Eltahawy, Mona. 2017. "Don't Tell Me Nabra Hassanen's Murder Wasn't a Hate Crime." *The Cut*, June 19. www.thecut.com/2017/06/nabra-hassanen-murder-hate -crime-mona-eltahawy.html.

FBI. N.d. "Hate Crimes." https://www.fbi.gov/investigate/civil-rights/hate-crimes.

FCPD Media Relations Bureau. 2017a. "Road Rage Incident Leads to Murder of Reston Teenager: Evidence in Case Does Not Point to Hate Crime." *Fairfax County Police Department News*, June 19. fcpdnews.wordpress.com/2017/06/19/road-rage -leads-to-murder-of-reston-teenager-evidence-in-case-does-not-point-to-hate -crime/.

FCPD Media Relations Bureau. 2017b. "Update: No Evidence of Gang Affiliation for Nabra Hassanen Murder Suspect." *Fairfax County Police Department News*, June 28. fcpdnews.wordpress.com/2017/06/28/update-no-evidence-of-gang-affiliation-for -nabra-hassanen-murder-suspect/.

Gilmore, Ruth Wilson. 2007. *Golden Gulag: Prisons, Surplus, Crisis, and Opposition in Globalizing California*. Berkeley: University of California Press.

Greenfield, Daniel. 2017. "Leftist Illegalophilia, Not Islamophobia, Killed a Muslim Teen." *Frontpage Magazine*, June 26. www.frontpagemag.com/fpm/267064/leftist -illegalophilia-not-islamophobia-killed-daniel-greenfield.

Hammer, Juliane. 2019. "Muslim Women, Anti-Muslim Hostility, and the State in the Age of Terror." In *Muslims and U.S. Politics Today: A Defining Moment*, edited by Mohammad Hassan Khalil, 104–23. Cambridge, MA: Harvard University Press.

Hanhardt, Christina B. 2013. *Safe Space: Gay Neighborhood History and the Politics of Violence*. Durham, NC: Duke University Press.

Hawley. 2012. "NYPD Monitored Muslim Students All over Northeast." *The Associated Press*, February 18. www.ap.org/ap-in-the-news/2012/nypd-monitored-muslim -students-all-over-northeast.

Huncar, Andrea. 2015. "Mustafa Mattan Shot Dead through Fort McMurray Apartment Door." *CBC News*, February 12. www.cbc.ca/news/canada/edmonton /mustafa-mattan-shot-dead-through-fort-mcmurray-apartment-door-1.2954439.

Iraq Body Count. N.d. "Iraq Body Count." www.iraqbodycount.org/.

Jilwani, Yasmin. 2006. *Discourses of Denial: Mediations of Race, Gender, and Violence*. Vancouver: University of British Columbia Press.

Khenjani, Abdullah Azada. 2015. "Muslims are only newsworthy when behind a gun, not in front of it." Facebook, February 11. www.facebook.com/abdullah.khenjani /posts/1037648879584422.

Kim, Mimi E. 2018. "From Carceral Feminism to Transformative Justice: Women-of-Color Feminism and Alternatives to Incarceration." *Journal of Ethnic and Cultural Diversity in Social Work* 27, no. 3: 219–33.

Kuruvilla, Carol. 2019. "Killer of Muslim Virginia Teen Nabra Hassanen Sentenced to Life in Prison." *Huffington Post*, April 1. www.huffpost.com/entry/nabra-hassanen -murder-darwin-martinez-torres_n_5ca2179ae4b00ba6328069b7.

Langton, Lynn. 2017. "Hate Crime Victimization, 2004–2015." Bureau of Justice Statistics, June 29. www.bjs.gov/index.cfm?ty=pbdetail&iid=5967.

Latif, Ali M. 2015. "Only Newsworthy When behind a Gun, Not in front of It: On Media Coverage of #ChapelHillShooting." *Ceasefire*, February 14. ceasefire magazine.co.uk/only-newsworthy-gun-front-it-media-coverage-chapelhill shooting/.

Leung, Maxwell. 2018. "Points of Departure: Re-examining the Discursive Formation of the Hate Crime Statistics Act of 1990." *Patterns of Prejudice* 52, no. 1: 39–57. doi. org/10.1080/0031322X.2018.1429357.

Lewis, Clara. 2013. *Tough on Hate? The Cultural Politics of Hate Crimes*. New Brunswick, NJ: Rutgers University Press.

Lopez, German. 2017. "Why It's So Hard to Prosecute a Hate Crime." *Vox*, May 23. www.vox.com/identities/2017/4/10/15183902/hate-crime-trump-law.

Love, Erik. 2017. *Islamophobia and Racism in America*. New York: New York University Press.

Magane, Azmia. 2017. "Don't Tell Me Nabra Hassanen, the Muslim Girl Who Was Kidnapped outside a Mosque and Murdered, Was a Victim of Road Rage." *Independent*, June 21. www.independent.co.uk/voices/nabra-hassanen-islamophobia -ramadan-murdered-hate-crime-road-rage-a7800126.html.

Mamdani, Mahmood. 2004. *Good Muslim, Bad Muslim: America, the Cold War, and the Roots of Terror*. New York: Pantheon Books.

Massimo, Rick, and Amanda Iacone. 2017. "Police: Road Rage Blamed for Killing of Va. Muslim Teen." *WTOP*, June 19. wtop.com/virginia/2017/06/fairfax-co-police -not-investigating-murder-muslim-teen-hate-crime/.

McGough, Michael. 2015. "Opinion: Not Every Hateful Crime Is a Hate Crime." *Los Angeles Times*, February 18. www.latimes.com/opinion/opinion-la/la-ol-hatecrime -muslims-obama-20150218-story.html.

Metzl, Jonathan. 2015. "NC Shooting: When a Parking Dispute Is Also a Crime of Hate." *MSNBC*, February 14. www.msnbc.com/melissa-harris-perry/nc-shooting -when-parking-dispute-also-crime-hate-msna533691.

Meyer, Doug. 2014. "Resisting Hate Crime Discourse: Queer and Intersectional Challenges to Neoliberal Hate Crime Laws." *Critical Criminology* 22, no. 1: 113–25. doi. org/10.1007/s10612-013-9228-x.

Molina, Natalia. 2014. *How Race Is Made in America: Immigration, Citizenship, and the Historical Power of Racial Scripts*. Berkeley: University of California Press.

Muslim Advocates et al. 2015. "Letter to Attorney General Eric Holder, Regarding Chapel Hill Murders." February 13. muslimadvocates.org/files/FINAL-letter-to -Holder-re-Chapel-Hill-Murders.pdf.

Naber, Nadine. 2008. "'Look, Mohammed the Terrorist Is Coming!': Cultural Racism, Nation-Based Racism, and the Intersectionality of Oppressions after 9/11." In *Race and Arab Americans before and after 9/11: From Invisible Citizens to Visible Subjects*, edited by Amaney Jamal and Nadine Naber, 276–304. Syracuse, NY: Syracuse University Press.

Naber, Nadine, and Junaid Rana. 2019. "The Twenty-First-Century Problem of Anti-Muslim Racism." *Jadaliyya*, June 25. www.jadaliyya.com/Details/39830.

NBC News. 2015. "Chapel Hill Shooting: Muslim Leaders Criticize Media Coverage." February 17. www.nbcnews.com/news/asian-america/chapel-hill-shooting-muslim-leaders-criticize-media-coverage-n307751.

Nguyen, Nicole. 2019. *Suspect Communities: Anti-Muslim Racism and the Domestic War on Terror*. Minneapolis: University of Minnesota Press.

Rana, Junaid. 2016. "The Racial Infrastructure of the Terror-Industrial Complex." *Social Text* 34, no. 4: 111–38.

Razack, Sherene H. 2020. "Settler Colonialism, Policing, and Racial Terror: The Police Shooting of Loreal Tsingine." *Feminist Legal Studies* 28, no. 1: 1–20. doi.org/10.1007/s10691-020-09426-2.

Reddy, Chandan. 2011. *Freedom with Violence: Race, Sexuality, and the US State*. Durham, NC: Duke University Press.

Richer, Alanna Durkin and Sarah Rankin. 2017. "Muslims Question Whether Girl's Killing Was Road Rage." *Associated Press*, June 20. https://apnews.com/article/us-news-ap-top-news-crime-virginia-hate-crimes-e85b57a08168406e865023d3148b0874.

Roschke, Ryan. 2017. "How Missouri's Hate Crime Legislation Is Failing Ally Lee Steinfeld." *Popsugar*, October 8. www.popsugar.com/news/Transgender-Teen-Ally-Lee-Steinfeld-Murder-Case-44090602.

Samira @SSamiraSR. 2015. "The fact that the only info I am getting about the #ChapelHillshooting is via twitter showcases how permeating Islamophobia is in media." Twitter, February 11, 1:08 a.m. twitter.com/SSamiraSR/status/565391967727910913.

Sinclair, Harriet. 2017. "Who Is Darwin Martinez-Torres? Suspect in Murder of Muslim Teen Is Held by ICE." *Newsweek*, June 20. www.newsweek.com/who-darwin-martinez-torres-suspect-murder-muslim-teen-held-ice-627711.

Spade, Dean. 2014. "On Normal Life: Dean Spade, Interviewed by Natalie Oswin." *Society and Space*, January 15. www.societyandspace.org/articles/on-normal-life.

Spade, Dean. 2015. *Normal Life: Administrative Violence, Critical Trans Politics, and the Limits of Law*. Durham, NC: Duke University Press.

Suerth, Jessica. 2017. "Nabra Hassanen's Murder Highlights the Challenges of Designating a Crime a Hate Crime." *CNN*, June 21. www.cnn.com/2017/06/21/us/nabra-hassanen-hate-crime-designation-challenge-trnd/index.html.

Talbot, Margaret. 2015. "The Story of a Hate Crime." *New Yorker*, June 22. www.newyorker.com/magazine/2015/06/22/the-story-of-a-hate-crime.

Trull, Armando, and Tamika Smith. 2017. "Update: Where Is the Investigation into Nabra Hassanen's Death?" *WAMU*, June 28. https://wamu.org/story/17/06/28/update-investigation-nabra-hassanens-death/.

Tyner, James A. 2016. "Hate-Crimes as Racial Violence: A Critique of the Exceptional." *Social and Cultural Geography* 17, no. 8: 1060–78. doi.org/10.1080/14649365.2016.1152392.

US Department of Justice. 2017. "Investigation of the Chicago Police Department." Washington, DC: United States Department of Justice, Civil Rights Division and United States Attorney's Office. www.justice.gov/opa/file/925846/download.

US Department of Justice. 2019. "Hate Crime Laws." March 7. www.justice.gov/crt /hate-crime-laws.

Vicent, Samantha. 2017. "November Trial Date Set for Tulsa Man Charged with Murder, Hate Crime." *Tulsa World*, March 22. www.tulsaworld.com/news/courts /november-trial-date-set-for-tulsa-man-charged-with-murder/article_bd16c3a2 -610a-5c76-8f14-6521d5fa4849.html.

Watson Institute. 2020. "Afghan Civilians." *Costs of War*, Watson Institute for International and Public Affairs, Brown University. January. watson.brown.edu /costsofwar/costs/human/civilians/afghan.

Watts, Amanda, and Jason Hanna. 2019. "North Carolina Man Sentenced to Life after Pleading Guilty to the 2015 Murders of Three Muslim College Students." CNN, June 12. www.cnn.com/2019/06/12/us/craig-hicks-chapel-kill-shootings-guilty -plea/index.html.

Zulfikar Ali Bhutto

Searching for the Next Intifada:
Exercises in Queer Muslim Futurism

Abstract: This article explores the possibilities of distinctly queer and Muslim futures rooted not only in Muslim diaspora communities but in the Muslim world itself. The Palestinian intifadas of 1987 and 2000 are the author's primary inspiration, whereas the future becomes a blank canvas onto which one can imagine the next global intifada, a giant popular uprising fought on many fronts. The author examines the work of artists Jassem Hindi, Layla tul Qadr, Saba Taj, and Hushidar Mortezaie, who look at the future in terms of parallel imaginative possibilities rather than in temporal terms. In addition to these artists, the writings of scholars and artists Jose Estaban Muñoz, Ronak Kapadia, Etel Adnan, and Hamed Sinno further emphasize the future-facing nature of both queerness and Islam, as well as the radical possibilities of telling queer Muslim stories in the future.

Introduction

How do we express resistance as it exists in the Muslim world through a queer understanding? What does the Arab, Pakistani, and Iranian mujahideen, fedayeen, fighter, and revolutionary leader look like when read as femme or even simply homo/trans-welcoming instead of homo/transphobic? As an artist, curator, and poet it felt like a necessity and a duty to create this: a leader with contour paired with conviction, eyeshadowed with a sense of egalitarianism and wearing heels to stamp out heteropatriarchy, but make it Muslim.

Four years ago this creature crept out of her crypt to deliver a vision to a

MERIDIANS · feminism, race, transnationalism   20:2 October 2021
DOI: 10.1215/15366936-9547969 © 2021 Smith College

weary crowd at San Francisco's Asian Art Museum, the very first performance in what was to become a queer Muslim futurist multimedia series.
Faluda Islam was a warrior drag queen. Branded comrade by some and
terrorist by others, she was part of a roving band of bearded Muslim queens
who roamed the world striking fear into American- and European-backed
rebel groups stalking the Middle East. She was killed in the Great Queer
Revolution but has been resurrected through Wi-Fi technology and comes
back to this earth and time to tell us of the future, remind us of the past,
and warn what we need to brace ourselves for. She is mostly a reluctant
zombie, a gruesome mournful living martyr, at other points haunting jinn
and in some forms invading alien, but in all senses an antihero—complex,
troubled, and more extra than terrestrial.

In my short life I have experienced political violence at close range. My
father was killed by police when I was six years old, my grandfather was
executed by a CIA-backed military regime in 1979, my uncle was poisoned
and killed by the same regime in 1984, and my aunt was killed in 2007.
Political rebellion and martyrdom followed my family long before I was
born and their presence continued throughout my lifetime. It inspired me
to break the chain of blood that forcibly connected one martyred relative to
the next.

Faluda Islam's incarnation as zombie is a reflection of the nightmarish
and repetitive cycles of martyrdom experienced by many populations in the
Muslim world. They become our living dead, spoken to like the fathers,
sons, daughters, and mothers we once knew. We call them *shaheed* or *sha-
heeda*, an Arabic word that is commonly understood to mean "martyr" but
literally translates to "witness," people who have witnessed the truth, the
sorrow, and the horrors of our unjust world. In *Necropolitics* Achille Mbembe
(2003: 38) writes specifically of the martyr as "laboring under the sign of the
future." He adds that the policies of the Israeli state toward the Palestinian
people result in the "creation of death-worlds, [and] vast populations are
subjected to conditions of life conferring upon them the status of the living
dead" (40). Faluda Islam emerged out of these constellations of political
violence, life, and death.

In my context, revolution came with the narrative of a heteronormative
family structure and while I wanted to have a place in this movement I
needed to make it my own. I wanted to be politically engaged but in a different way, responding to the world that I lived and grew up in. As a multimedia artist I began to manifest this different political vision, first with

Faluda Islam, and later with my project *Tomorrow We Inherit the Earth*, a fictitious archive of a revolution the world has yet to see with an accompanying video subseries, ABJD. Textile collages are combined with performance, poetry, and film, using Islam as a vehicle to propel the queer and futurist imaginary. Queerness, Islam, and futurism were a natural merging to me, but felt tense for the society around me. At the time I lived in the United States, and Western society sees queerness and Islam as somehow at odds with one another, as if Muslims could not be queer. Muslims are people and people are queer. If we are to take queerness as being a political stance—to be at odds with normative society—and if the West is normalized in our globalized cultural and political discourse, then yes, Islam is queer. Islam in this sense is future facing; as a faith it idealizes a world that does not yet exist.

Through my creative and curatorial work, it quickly became apparent that there were many artists who felt similarly. The artists whom I will discuss through the length of this essay, Laylatul Qadr, Saba Taj, Hushidar Mortezaie, and Jassem Hindi, play with dominant perceptions of Islam and queerness in various ways. Their work does not fit into strict binaries or rigid methodologies. They are all wildly different parts of an emerging tapestry that could form the flag of the next intifada through a nascent art movement called Queer Muslim Futurism.

In searching for the next intifada I seek to remind the reader of the Palestinian intifadas in 1987 and 2000, two popular uprisings led by the Palestinian people against the Zionist occupation (Nasrallah 2013: 56). Since its inception, this occupation has been stealing Palestinian land, committing genocide, and pursuing aggressive expansionist policies that sent hundreds of thousands of people into exile as refugees. The response to both intifadas was brutal; the Israeli Defense Force killed thousands and injured tens of thousands.

In this essay I propose that the intifada is global, it is continuous, it is happening now, it is going to happen, it is historical, and it is future facing. The term *intifada* in Arabic is loosely translated as an "uprising" but it can also mean to "shake off," to relieve yourself of the irritation of an oppressive structure. Queer Muslim Futurism seeks to connect all of the small intifadas from Kashmir to Bosnia, to the struggles of Black Americans in the United States, to postcolonial movements in Africa and Asia as far as Indonesia, and see them as one unified global fight on a variety of battlefronts.

Figure 1. Still from the video *Grace and Mercy 566* by Zulfikar Ali Bhutto. Image courtesy of the artist.

Palestine is the locus because the struggle of the Palestinian people has been a rallying cry for worldwide political solidarity, and nowhere is this more evident than among postcolonial Muslim nations. Palestine has been robbed of its sovereignty, and because of that the Palestinian people have required the help and kinship of other countries. Palestine relies—for better or for worse—on their sense of duty toward this land and its people. In order to look toward the future, we must see the intifadas and the movements of today as a continuation of a historical movement of solidarity between third world countries that can be tracked through a series of conferences, including the Bandung conference of 1955 and the Islamic summits of 1969 and 1974 held in Rabat and Lahore respectively. The question of solidarity with the Palestinian people was key in all these meetings.

The Islamic summit of 1974, which took place in Lahore, Pakistan, was called specifically because of the events of the October War of 1973 in which Israel formally occupied all the land of historic Palestine, as well as Syria's Golan Heights and Egypt's Sinai Peninsula. It was a rare moment of solidarity as leaders came from as far as Sudan and Morocco to Bangladesh and Indonesia. The inaugural address was given by then Pakistani prime minister and my grandfather, Zulfikar Ali Bhutto (1977: 82), who suggested in reference to Jerusalem that Palestinian "Muslims alone could be its loving and impartial custodians for the simple reason that Muslims alone believe in all three prophetic traditions rooted in Jerusalem. We gladly recognize that Jerusalem affects the cherished sensibilities of men and women of three world faiths." He also addressed the differences between anti-Zionism and anti-Semitism, an issue sweeping through the Western world today as Israel seeks to claim space in Western liberal and political "woke" circles:

> The root cause of the conflict is not an innate animosity between the Muslim and the Jew or even between the Arab and the Jew. As Muslims we entertain no hostility against any human community; when we say this, we do not exclude the Jewish people. To Jews as Jews we bear no malice; to Jews as Zionists, intoxicated with their militarism and reeking with technological arrogance we refuse to be hospitable. The pogroms inflicted on them during the centuries and the holocaust to which they were subjected under Nazism fill some of the darkest pages of human history. But redemption should have come from the Western world and not have been subjected on the Palestinian people (Bhutto 1977: 78).

In *Cruising Utopia: The Then and There of Queer Futurity* (2009), José Esteban Muñoz references a 1971 issue of the gay liberation periodical *Gay Flames*, which published a manifesto by a group called Third World Gay Revolution. While certainly not Muslim friendly—or any religion friendly—the manifesto calls for the "liberation of all humanity, free food, free shelter, free clothing, free transportation, free healthcare, free utilities, free education and free art for all," ideals that can be seen reflected in Islamic socialist movements (Muñoz 2009: 19). Some might object that the Muslim world would not have welcomed a gay socialist agenda; however, it is worth remembering that almost all anti-sodomy laws present in Asia and Africa exist because of European values that were reflected in colonial policy making. Had the Third World and Non-Aligned movements not been thwarted by Western interventionist agendas, I would like to imagine that we could be seeing a very different Muslim world today.

Imagination is key to the Queer Muslim Futurist agenda. While not every political artist is or should be an activist, it is their work that imagines possibility, the possibility of global solidarity that stands against capitalist and colonialist models of globalization and instead creates visions of a new world and planetary order. José Esteban Muñoz (2009: 1) reminds us that artists and their work can help us "glimpse the worlds proposed and promised by queerness in the realm of the aesthetic. The aesthetic, especially the queer aesthetic, frequently contains blueprints and schemata of a forward dawning futurity." Here Muñoz (2009: 1) specifically draws upon queerness as a utopian future ideal, defined as "an insistence on the potentiality or concrete possibility of another world." Similarly, Ronak K. Kapadia (2019: 165), in his book *Insurgent Aesthetics: Security and the Queer Life of the Forever War*, defines *futurism* as an emancipatory practice calling forth Walidah Imarisha and adrienne marie brown's idea of "visionary fiction."

I extend this framework to capture various literary, visual, musical, cinematic, performative, theatrical, and other modes of expressive cultures aligned with social justice movements that at once critique differential distributions of power, resources, and life chances in the present and conjure what German Marxist philosopher Ernst Bloch once called the "anticipatory illumination of art necessary to envision social life anew" (Kapadia 2019: 165–67).

Taj, Mortezai, Hindi, and Qadr are artists who actualize this queer futuristic potential of art, in a Muslim way. They all come from Muslim or Muslim-adjacent backgrounds and invest their creative energies into what can be described as "fucking shit up," or, in other words, creating a framework to imagine or write a different history all grounded in the reality of today and using the tremendous generosity of the future. They have all done their own research, deep investigative studies into the lives of political figures, writers, stories, and quotes from Islamic texts such as the Quran and the Hadith (sayings of the Prophet Muhammad ﷺ), pre-Islamic ritual and belief, and the writings of scholars and researchers who do not address futurism directly.

Below I highlight these four artists whose works, alongside my own, blend together as time becomes a traversable road going back and forth and modern scholars intertwine with ancient gods. Linear time, as Muñoz (2009: 25) states, is straight time. In this article, I reject it as it sets up the non-Western subject for failure. Inevitably, our works become collaborative and the visions made manifest in our creative works all come from histories of war, resistance, and continued resilience. Solidarity building remains central to this collective work.

Hindi and Hennessy's Future Friend/ships

In any solo project of futurism, its discourse was ultimately reused by architects and politicians and all those in places of power to destructive and corrupt ends. This includes the Italians in the 1900s and modern-day Dubai, which is futuristic, which means it shouldn't exist now. Futurism should be a collective effort in order for it to be a positive one.

Figure 2. Jassem Hindi in *Future Friend/ships*, Counter Pulse, San Francisco, 2016. Image courtesy of Robbie Sweeny.

This is what Jassem Hindi, a French Palestinian artist based in Norway, said to me when I met him in San Francisco, where he was working on *Future Friend/ships*, a collaborative project with Keith Hennessy. Presented at Counterpulse in 2016, the performance opened with a parade of photos of the ancestors of Arab futurism, figures from Edward Said to Donna Haraway, Octavia Butler, and the Palestinian Arab Futurist, Larissa Sansour. Later in the performance Hindi asks, after all has been taken away, "What is left for us to offer? Our storytelling capacities," a lament of the relentless destruction inflicted on the Arab people, who are forced time and time again to recover. There is not one apocalypse in this story but many.

Hindi and Hennessy's *Future Friend/ships* brings the audience into a post-utopian future. The two performers take on characters within this world, first greeting you with baklava sweets as you enter the theater. Two huge floral fabrics stitched together come down once the audience members have taken their seats: Hennessy and Hindi are wearing costumes made from the same flower-printed material as the background tapestry laid out behind them, obscuring their bodies and making them barely visible in the sea of printed flowers. As the piece progresses there is no narrative arc but a deeper descent into this world, heightened by spectacular lighting and sound elements. All spoken dialogue is delivered directly to the audience, as if both characters are the storytellers they speak of, movement scores accompany buzzing drone sounds and high-pitched poetry readings. Poetry and lyrics are the main driving force of the piece and are used as "political practice" (Hennessy and Hindi 2015).

Throughout the performance, the audience is not really given any clues as to where and when this takes place. Is it Syria, Yemen, Iraq, or maybe even in another reality entirely? Is this happening now, is this a prediction of what is to come? This kind of geographical and temporal ambiguity permits *Future Friend/ships* to avoid a narrative of victimization through playful movements that flow into more serious verse. It also brings to mind Muñoz's very idea of queer time, and I would extend this to say queer geography. The performance does not feel a need to explain itself linearly, as "queerness's time is a stepping out of the linearity of straight time. Straight time is a self naturalizing temporality. . . . Queerness's ecstatic and horizontal temporality is a path and a movement to a greater openness to the world" (Muñoz 2009: 25).

Two prominent cultural figures quoted and referenced in *Future Friend/ ships* are Lebanese band Mashrou' Leila, and their song "Marikh" ("Mars"), and Lebanese writer Etel Adnan and her poem from the book *Arab Apocalypse.* "Marikh" centers on the struggles of daily existence—the desire to be lifted to another planet to escape the cycles that we are forced into. The lead singer of the band, Hamed Sinno, was at one time known as the only openly queer Arab musician that actually lived in the Arab world; he has since moved to New York City. In recent years, the band has received both praise and backlash in the region.

Arab Apocalypse puts into poetic verse the absurdity of the political turmoil in the Arab world. Divided into Roman numerals, Adnan's poetry goes deep into Arab history, resurrecting popular figures such as the pre-Islamic Sumerian god king of Ururk, Gilgamesh, and the Prophet Muhammad's ﷺ son-in-law Imam Ali عليه السلام, husband to the Prophet's heir and daughter Hazrat Fatima عليه السلا (Adnan 1989: XLIV). Adnan uses language to beautifully render the disturbing. Hennessy and Hindi (2015) use one particular poem, XXXIX, partially quoted below:

> When roses grow only in cemeteries
> When they eat the Palestinian's liver before he is even dead
> When the sun itself has no other purpose than being a shroud
> The human tide moves on . . .

Why these lifts from the verses of Mashrou' Leila and Etel Adnan? Adnan wrote primarily in French, a colonial language, and spent much of her life in Sausalito, California. To some, she is not considered part of the world of Arab literature. To Hindi, Adnan and Mashrou' Leila occupy a "culture of rejects," important in certain cultural spaces and cited as irrelevant by others. Hindi merges them beautifully toward the end of the hour-long piece as he begins to squirm on the floor, moving slowly as Mashrou' Leila's song "Marikh" ("Mars") is played alongside the poem from Etel Adnan's book, *Arab Apocalypse*.

Hindi prefers to call himself an artist dealing in Arab Future Fiction, which serves as a more generous predecessor to Queer Muslim Futurism. Islam for Hindi is not especially relevant—for him it is a small weave in the very thick fabric of Arabness. To be Arab is to be Christian, Jewish, Muslim, Druz, Yazidi, atheist, and so on. For Hindi, the question is not, "How do we imagine a future?" but "How do we write history in the future?" Within his practice, Arabness is not a static identity but a generous and active one, spread throughout the world in a series of diasporas, from the Jewish diaspora in the eighth century BCE to the diasporas of Iraqis, Syrians, Palestinians, and Yemenis. He continues to collaborate with artists across the world and the diaspora to investigate, in his own words, "the resources inside a poem."

Why then does Hindi, alongside myself and others, bring in Islam at all? Why use a mainstream religion, not too different to Judaism and Christianity, as inspiration for envisioning a radically different queer world? I believe that there is a great deal to gain from understanding Islam through a futurist lens, hence its relevance to these artists. Islam, we highlight, has always looked to the future. Springing from the deserts of Makkah in modern-day Saudi Arabia in the seventh century CE, it was created out of a political need to disrupt the economic stranglehold of the Qureysh tribe that controlled nearly all trade in the region. Islam put into writing rights for women, including the right to own and inherit property even after marriage; set regulations for the kind and gentle treatment of animals; and more. Its fight for dominance in the region has aligned the faith with constant resistance.

I am particularly inspired that the beliefs of Shia Islam pose that every generation has its oppressors, and therefore, every generation must also continue to fight for justice. The Quran and Hadith, as well as Imams and scholars explore a tightly connected multiverse of alien prophets, mosques on other planets, and unseen dimensions on Earth. Stories of the day of judgment are filled with demons, dead kings, immortal prophets, and the Anti-christ, all battling in what can only be described as the final showdown.

It must also be emphasized that Islam has no race, country, or ethnicity. There are white European Muslims who have been Muslims for centuries, Arab Muslims, African Muslims, Black Muslims, Latinx Muslims, South Asian Muslims, East Asian Muslims, and the list goes on. There is no monolithic Islam; it has changed, evolved, and left itself open to difference. South Asian Sufism—a mystical practice of Islam—is revered by not only Muslims but also Hindus and Sikhs alike, and early Sufi Muslim saints embraced Hindu rituals that continue to this day, nearly one thousand years after the arrival of Islam on the subcontinent. Considering the global nature of Islam, Queer Muslim Futurism in many ways becomes a form of queer globalizations, a guerrilla movement on an international scale.

"Jihadageddon" by the Muslims

Of course I am well aware that there are problems with how Islam has been practiced. Societies that have embraced Islam have interpreted its teachings in ways that are patriarchal, misogynistic, and homophobic. Islam's quick turn from oppressed faith to global empire left in its wake scores of conquered and oppressed peoples alongside a vibrant and undeniably intellectual culture. This is the paradox that many Muslims contend with today. It is precisely this complexity that leaves so much fodder for Queer Muslim Futurists like Laylatul Qadr.

Qadr is Sheikh of punk rock band the Muslims that formed shortly after Donald Trump was elected to the US presidential office in 2016. The band mocks our dominant culture's perception of Muslims as an invading army of aliens, foreigners who are dangerous and aggressive; they subvert, bastardize, and haramize dominant perceptions of Muslims within the political contexts of punk. The core of this project is to challenge and offend us all. The Muslims' latest album, Gentrifried Chicken, is a nineteen-minute, soul-destroying critique of practices around Islam, religion more broadly, an Islamophobic white supremacist society, and the danger of white moderates.

Their music video for the song "Jihadageddon," from their first and self-titled album, features a woman—Qadr's partner, the artist Saba Taj—wearing a bright pink, floral burqa and wandering around a mall in North

Figure 3. Still from the music video for "Jihadageddon," released 2018. Image courtesy of Laylatul Qadr.

Carolina, occasionally window-shopping and banging her head to music with lyrics such as, "You see us walking by, you think we're going to blow." The song and video imagery expose the fears and doubts that inform Islamophobia in the United States while another song, "Confess," tells the imaginary story of the kidnap and torture of white supremacists, demanding reparation using insurgent strategies. This ethos is present in the band's aesthetics, something Muñoz (2009: 106) would call "the celebration of an aesthetics of amateurism" that is "reminiscent of punk rock's aesthetics." In *Devouring Becky*—an image used on the band's social media page—Qadr utilizes digital graphics and collage combining a Jaws-style shark attack with an almost lava-like post-apocalyptic ocean. In "Jihadageddon" we are guided through the everyday spaces of the Southern United States, from a shopping mall to a parking lot to a park, and ultimately everyone ends up at a punk rock venue/bar. We are guided, in aesthetic and visual terms, through the spaces of the future intifada as "the aesthetic fuels the political imagination" (Muñoz 2009: 106).

While the Muslims is a multi-ethnic and diverse group of people, Qadr, who started and leads the project, creates work that is informed by her experiences of coming out while Black and Muslim. She investigates what it means to have those identities intersect and to navigate different locations that have complex relationships with queerness—culturally, spiritually, and socially. In the United States, Islam and Black identity have not been so

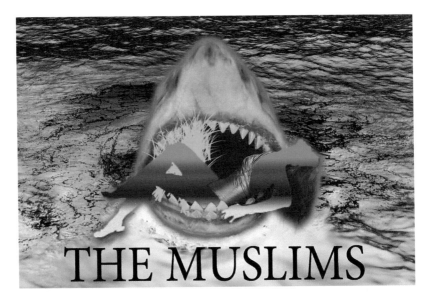

Figure 4. *Devouring Becky* by Laylatul Qadr. Digital collage. Image courtesy of Qadr and the Muslims, 2018.

separate; in the words of the curator and writer Yas Ahmed, "The first Muslims in this country were enslaved Black folks." In more recent history, the Nation of Islam, among other Muslim sects from the 1940s to the contemporary moment, presents Islam as a way out of the oppression of Black people and rejects Christianity because it has been used as a tool of colonialism and slavery. Bringing in Queer identity creates an incredibly potent mix of resistance to the status quo. Islam has been treated as an enemy by the government of the United States, similar to communism, homosexuality, and Black liberation.

Punk rock exploits and reveals social prejudices and anxieties. The zombie, the alien, and the monster are all welcome in punk's extensive embrace of rejects that includes queer Muslims. Punk's capacity to reappropriate and own these stereotypes, if only to throw them back in the oppressors' face, is exactly what makes it the music of protest that it is today and inshallah will be in the future. As Muñoz (2009: 105) insists, "Punk rock style may look apocalyptic, yet its temporality is nonetheless futuristic, letting young punks imagine a time and a place where their desires are not toxic." Punk has a do-it-yourself mentality, taking control over what isn't working and setting it right, deconstructing culture, and challenging long-held beliefs and ideas. It is a way out of rules, the very rules that oppress so many.

Prejudice has made Islam a religion of protest: to be a practicing Muslim in the United States is to challenge the status quo, and so is creating punk art. The future intifada needs to move toward a drum beat, and may that drum beat be the cacophony of Muslim punk bubbling under the surface of our *ummah* today. There are certainly other punk and death metal Muslim bands in existence today; that list includes bands such as the Kominas, Aurat Band, Bakht Arif's Urdu cover of the Cranberries' song *Zombie*, as well as the Muslim scholar and theorist Michael Muhammad Knight's book *Taqwacore* (2003), which fictitiously narrates a robust subgenre of punk that stems from the Islamic concept of *Taqwa*, our simultaneous love and fear of god (Crafts 2009). What makes the Muslims stand out is their explicitly queer stance. Qadr states:

> It could be argued, though, that Islam fits so perfectly within Punk . . . because again, it is a system and structure of rules to be bent—to be made right for the generation and people it speaks to. Like Yuletide to Christianity that created Christmas, I experience queering Islam as the correct bastardization that's so necessary to keep it true for the people that live and experience it today. And that's fucked up. It's rebellious and awfully sinful to do. It's punk.

Creatures from the Earth by Saba Taj

Saba Taj is another artist for whom cultural hybridity is central to artistic production. Taj conjures a queer femme creature, an evolved posthuman able to survive the toxicity of this world and emerge triumphantly in the next. In a personal conversation, Taj said, "In our histories, violence has been such a present component of change, an inevitable part of transformation." Taj would spend much of their childhood in North Carolina reading science fiction, where entire worlds were constructed, good and evil were interchangeable concepts, and humanity was not at the center. The apocalypses came in the form of zombie epidemics, fertility issues, and the evolution and destruction of humanity through hybrid forms. "It reminded me of Islamic stories you were told as a kid," Taj recalls.

Her series, *Creatures from the Earth*, illustrates a post-apocalyptic earth of amorphous creatures containing strands of different animals to survive and fight in a world so heavily polluted. This work is inspired by stories from the Quran, in particular "Dabbat al-ard" ("Beast of the Earth"), whose horrifyingly monstrous appearance signals the Day of Judgment (Quran 27:82), but more importantly for Taj, it has another purpose: "The way we have been dehumanized, how often that has been communicated through comparisons through animals, putting humans lower in a hierarchy of humanity." In "Monster, Terrorist, Fag," Jasbit Puar and Amit Rai (2002) state that the human monster has been created by a racialized society to set up a distinction between a normal, law-abiding citizen and a potentially threatening one. Through merging aesthetics, Taj's work both challenges and embraces these stereotypes, and it is aesthetics that help advance the revolutionary and futurist imagination.

A minoritarian aesthetics can be seen in Taj's work as motifs from popular culture are merged with images of animals and explicitly religious symbols through collage and painting to create a mythos that is both entirely new and hauntingly familiar. In his analysis of Palestinian Arab futurist artist Larissa Sansour's video series, *Nation Estate*, Kapadia (2019: 166) asserts that "minoritarian aesthetic forms can hold the potential to oppose the violent present while simultaneously proposing more hopeful and just futures." Taj's aesthetics depend on "a critical hermeneutic strategy through which racialized and dispossessed peoples, including Arabs, Muslims and South Asians in the diaspora, have created alternative world-making knowledge projects to render visible or sensuous all that has been absented by the abstractions of the forever war" (Kapadia 2019: 21). While Taj's series certainly does not elaborate on a peaceful future, it renders visible a world where there is strong resistance to oppression and where the resistance is proud, femme, and vibrant.

Another work of Taj's, *Interstellar Uber*, is a queer rendering of Buraq, a heavenly creature, described as tall and beautiful, half-human and half–winged donkey/mule. The Buraq takes the Prophet Muhammad from earth to heaven in a dream, making a stop in Jerusalem at a site that is today marked by the Dome of the Rock. The Buraq is only mentioned in the Hadith and only once in the Quran, yet its one gesture of carrying the Prophet Muhammad to meet his creator has become a significant part of Islamic folklore all over the world. The creature is referred to interchangeably as male and female. It is a symbol of the journey and its image is used as a charm to protect all those who travel, from bus drivers to seafarers. The Buraq's androgynous and protective nature has made it something of a symbol of the contemporary queer and Muslim movement that has

Figure 5. *Interstellar Uber* by Saba Taj, varying dimensions, 2017 at Elsewhere Residency. Image courtesy of Saba Taj.

emerged across the world. Abdullah Qureshi's film *Journey to the Charbagh* (2019) queerly renders a paradise on earth, using wrestling pits and historical sites in the city of Lahore, as well as Lollywood-inspired nightclub scenes to illustrate a hidden utopia. Within this film, the Buraq is played by two characters in glittering make-up and tunics who glide through the air, functioning as guides to the different levels of paradise that we as an audience are taken through.

In Taj's work, Buraq's modern queer rendering investigates the evolution of humanity into queer femme beings. Her Buraq has multiple blue eyes, traditionally used as a mark against evil eye, jealousy, and bad intentions in the Islamic world, yet for Taj, the meaning goes even deeper. They are the blue eyes of a white-dominated society, occasionally stabbed into blindness in *The Spoils of War*. They are also a mark of protection, exposing how unstable binaries of good and bad can be. Buraq's eyes direct the very gaze John Berger (1972) describes as active; they stand in for the Oriental gaze in Edward Said's *Orientalism* (1978). They are the eye of power that must be satisfied. These same eyes, however, can also be owned, controlled, and turned back around by the subject, who can and does usurp the gaze in order to stare back at power.

Figure 6. *Creatures from the Earth, The Spoils of War* by Saba Taj. Collage, spray paint, acrylic paint, glitter, ink, gold leaf, rhinestones, graphite on panel 18 x 24 in., 2016. Image courtesy of the artist.

Occupy Me by Hushidar Mortezaie

Hushidar Mortezaie, an Iranian artist based in California, similarly merges various figures from pre-Islamic tradition to the modern day, very specifically reclaiming narrative and history as he dreams of a genderless future creature. In his installation, *Occupy Me: Topping from the Bottom*, Mortezaie gives power back to the "bottom" or the so-called passive figure, the underdog and subaltern of history.

Mortezaie is inspired by his father's wide-eyed optimistic Marxism that began in the 1950s and preceded the revolution; this Marxism is unlike what he describes as the Mcmarxism of today, "a complete CliffsNotes deviation based on fads in the consumerist cool of academia." As the revolution continued, a vacuum was created and theocracy prevailed, resulting in the creation of the Islamic Republic of Iran. Left-wing activists were eventually sidelined and actively put down after Imam Ayatollah Khomeini's rise to power. His family's move to California sent him as a young adult to San Francisco and New York where he worked in the fashion industry wearing many hats, including those of buyer and designer. He fully engrossed himself in the club kid scene of the 1990s, and his work reflects the merging of these seemingly distant historical and political worlds.

"History is like fashion, it keeps repeating itself," Mortezaie said emphatically to me after speaking about his many projects, in which he merges the worlds of high fashion, performative masculinity, and conceptual art. History becomes an important lens through which to gaze into the future. His installation, *Occupy Me*, reflects the cycles of history and its ability to cocoon and gestate only to reemerge when the time is right.

The installation features three figures who became part of a new canon in queer Muslim, Arab, South Asian, and Iranian lineage. The first two figures are Mahmoud Asgari and Ayaz Marhoni, who—aged sixteen and eighteen—were publicly executed in the Iranian city of Mashhad in July 2005 (Rastegar 2013). To this day, there are debates as to whether they were hanged for engaging in consensual homosexual acts, but the pair nonetheless stand as a symbol of the injustices of the system that tried them. Mortezaie's third figure is Fereydoun Farrokhzad, an openly gay Iranian singer who was murdered—many suspect—due to his political writings infused with demands for acceptance. Mortezaie does not allow these figures to disappear. In fact, he does not even allow them to die. Asgari and Marhoni are brought back to life by an unnamed power. In this cocoon stage between life and death, they transform into Muslim gay beloveds Malik Ayaz and Mahmoud Ghazni, two soldier-poets who marched together from the Middle East to South Asia in the tenth century. Farrokhzad is reborn, phoenix-like, as the pre-Islamic androgynous deity Mithra of both Iranian Zoroastrianism and Vedic Hinduism, reminding us that these two cultures have always collided.

As installation pieces these figures turn eerily posthuman, risen from the dead in glamorous zombie gear; mannequins, stiff like the undead, waiting to be cajoled into action. They bring to mind Sarah Juliet Lauro and Karen Embry's (2008: 86) *A Zombie Manifesto*, which "proclaims the future possibility of the zombii, a conscious-less being that is a swarm organism and the only imaginable specter that could really be post-human." The zombie is the perfect revolutionary subject, concerned with a singular, unstoppable mission, undistractable, indestructible, without ego, and a recruiting force—to be bitten by a zombie is to become one, unless you are consumed entirely.

While the human is incarcerated in mortal flesh, the zombie represents a grotesque image that resists confinement—animating his body even beyond death. At the same time that the zombie emphasizes human

Figure 7. *Occupy Me: Topping from the Bottom*, Hushidar Mortezaie's installation at SOMArts Cultural Center for the exhibition *The Third Muslim: Queer and Trans* Muslim Narratives of Resistance and Resilience*. Image courtesy of Chani Bockwinkel.

Figure 8. *Occupy Me: Topping from the Bottom*, Hushidar Mortezaie's installation at SOMArts Cultural Center for the exhibition *The Third Muslim: Queer and Trans* Muslim Narratives of Resistance and Resilience*. Image courtesy of Chani Bockwinkel.

Figure 9. *Occupy Me: Topping from the Bottom*, Hushidar Mortezaie's installation at SOMArts Cultural Center for the exhibition *The Third Muslim: Queer and Trans* Muslim Narratives of Resistance and Resilience*. Image courtesy of Chani Bockwinkel.

embodiment, he also defies the very limits that he sets. The zombie, neither mortal nor conscious, is a boundary figure, a threat to stable subject and object positions, who creates a dilemma for power relations and risks destroying social dynamics that have remained largely unchanged in the current economic structure (Lauro and Embry 2008: 86).

There's a fierceness to Mortezaie's figures; they are stubborn and refuse confinement. They are masked yet confrontational, and bear the marks of the worlds and lives they once inhabited—a hanging noose in the case of Asgari and Marhoni, for instance. But Mortezaie does not want to satisfy the Western liberals' need to believe that their world is perfect. Behind these figures, we see symbols of Western capitalism, the destructive powers of the Ku Klux Klan, and the injustices of Zionism on the Palestinian people. This imagery suggests that things are not always as they seem, and that the oppressive systems around gender and sexuality present in the Muslim world are not always homegrown.

Queer Muslim Futurism

Queer Muslim Futurism complicates the rigid binaries that construct East and West and reaffirms that queer identity is neither static nor apolitical.

Violence is central to the stories it tells, but only because it is what we know. It is how we recognize change and more importantly, it is a way to destroy in order to create again, to make rubble and then rise from it.

In 2018 I cocurated, alongside my friend and colleague Yas Ahmed, *The Third Muslim: Queer and Trans* Muslim Narratives of Resistance and Resilience* at SOMArts Cultural Center in San Francisco. This exhibition highlighted the work of artists who identified as queer and Muslim and who strove for better self-representation at a time when Muslims were being spoken for in the American media. Included in that exhibition were Taj, Mortezaie, and Qadr. The exhibition received a great deal of press, but the emphasis was less on the art and more on the very fact that queer Muslims existed in the first place. Many were quick to make assumptions about the artists responding to anti-queerness from our own Muslim families and lineages when it was Western societies that we sought to confront.

Later that year Taj, Mortezaie, Qadr, and I collaborated on a takeover of the STUD bar, a historic San Francisco queer bar that closed in the summer of 2020. The event was called Queer Muslim Futures and was commissioned by the San Francisco Arts Commission's Sanctuary City Series. The event consisted of a mash-up of videos, performances, and an after-party hosted by Discostan, a Los Angeles–based nightclub—and an intergalactic nation in its own right—run by Arshia Fatima Haq.

Futurism is a way to complicate the narrative of what it means to be queer and Muslim, to move away from essentializing tropes and create new worlds through the incredible imagination embedded in the Muslim consciousness. We take inspiration from the futurists who have come before us, namely Afrofuturism and South Asian, Desi, and Arab futurisms.

While I call Queer Muslim Futurism a genre, it is hard to tell at this stage how it will evolve; it is an expanding and fluid idea with artists from multiple cultural backgrounds situated within the homeland, as well as in the diaspora. We are grasping for different worlds and imagining what could be possible. It is a becoming genre with emergent figures like Hindi, Qadr, Taj, Mortezaie, and Faluda Islam (myself).

The next intifada is on the rise and it is inherently queer. As we progress further into our unknowable future, Palestinians continue to resist Zionist oppression and queers and feminists continue to become an undeniable and unavoidable presence in all grassroots movements. In the 2019 *thawra* of Lebanon, a huge popular uprising against corruption and inequality in the country, queer folks showed up in huge numbers, making their presence known with spray-painted banners saying, "The Queers Are Here!" In Palestine, organizations such as alQaws (2014) fight to "disrup[t] sexual and gender-based oppression, and challeng[e] regulation of our sexualities and bodies, whether patriarchal, capitalist, or colonial" and work "to transform Palestinian society's perspectives on gender and sexual diversity, homosexuality and LGBT issues, and to struggle for broader social justice."

Queer Muslims face a plethora of obstacles and one of them is the racist vision of Muslims, and Arabs more broadly, as inherently homophobic. Israeli state propaganda and its pinkwashing mission are partially to blame. According to the Boycott, Divest, Sanction movement's website (BDS n.d.), pinkwashing is defined as "an Israeli government propaganda strategy that cynically exploits LGBTQIA+ rights to project a progressive image while concealing Israel's occupation and apartheid policies oppressing Palestinians." The Israeli government has made it a point to not only host popular gay pride festivals in its major cities but also to fund LGBTQ film festivals in Tel Aviv while continuing to oppress and kill Palestinians regardless of gender or sexual orientation (BDS n.d.).

Pinkwashing's broader violent implication is that it validates war and oppression in a way palpable to American and European societies. Muslim cultures in the imagination of the West do not protect their gendered and sexual minorities and are therefore regressive and savage. War becomes a global civilizing mission, as has been exemplified by George W. Bush's invasions of Afghanistan and Iraq. In 2001 Laura Bush framed the war on terror as a war for "the rights and dignity of women" and continued, "Civilized people throughout the world are speaking out in horror, not only because our hearts break for the women and children in Afghanistan but also because, in Afghanistan, we see the world the terrorists would like to impose on the rest of us" (Bush 2001). In Bush's framing, all the straight men are the terrorists and the rest are meek, to be pitied, and in need of saving. Similarly, queer Muslims are in need of saving from their heterosexual, inherently oppressive kinfolk. Save the queers, kill the rest.

I also do not wish to romanticize the Muslim world's relationship to queer and trans identity; there is violence that occurs against queer and trans bodies and many are deeply marginalized. Draconian colonial European laws such as Britain's Section 377 still exist, and cultural mores around sexual conduct dictate how police and governments treat LGBTQ people (Human Dignity Trust 2021). The physical and psychological toll of such oppressive actions can make life unlivable. As queer and trans folks in the Middle East and South Asia continue to gain visibility, they are simultaneously attacked. We have our martyrs too.

In 2016, Xulhaz Mannan, a Bangladeshi queer activist and founder of the nation's only LGBT magazine, *Roobpaan*, was killed by extremists in his own home in Dhaka (Hammadi and Gani 2016). In 2017, after raising a gay pride flag at a Mashrou' Leila concert in Cairo, the Egyptian activist, feminist, and communist Sarah Hegazi was arrested along with seventy-five others for simply attending the concert. Hegazi had raised a rainbow flag in elation and was photographed doing so. While incarcerated she was tortured, electrocuted, and sexually assaulted. On June 13, 2020, she died by suicide (Sinno 2020). It would be too long a list to name the many more trans women brutalized in Muslim countries and other queer folks who have faced violence and harassment.

It is in our grief that many queer Muslims and Brown folk from Asia and Africa turn away from their people and countries of origin; we have been rejected, cast aside, and brutalized, and so we look for validation and comfort elsewhere. It is often the West that provides partial "refuge" for its own purposes, weaponizing queer and trans Muslim bodies and narratives as proof of the need for Western military intervention in Muslim countries.

The global intifada is still being fought and on countless fronts, our vision of a queer-welcoming world is one that we look toward, it is what we strive for. Muñoz did not believe queerness to be a current reality; it was a utopic vision that rises from the contemporary need for a different reality. Palestinian people alongside other occupied and oppressed peoples continue to resist despite the odds. Queer Muslim Futurism witnesses this and reflects it in the nonlinear time of queer futurity. Queer Muslim Futurism writes this resilience into history as a victor yet to be seen.

. . . .

Zulfikar Ali Bhutto (b. Damascus, 1990) is a visual artist, performer, and curator. Bhutto's work resurrects complex histories in the South Asian, Southwest Asian, and North African regions. In the process he unpacks the intersections of queerness, Islam, speculative fiction, futurity, and environmental degradation through a multimedia practice rooted in printmaking, textile work, and performance. Bhutto has performed, shown work, and curated exhibitions globally, as well as spoken extensively on the intersections of faith, radical thought, and futurity at Columbia University; the University of California, Berkeley; New York University; Stanford University; and the Indus Valley School of Art and Architecture. Bhutto is currently based in Karachi, Pakistan, and received an MFA from the San Francisco Art Institute in 2016.

Works Cited

Adnan, Etel. 1989. *The Arab Apocalypse.* Sausalito, CA: Post-Apollo Press.

alQaws. 2014. "Mission Statement." alqaws.org/about-us.

BDS. n.d. "Say No to Pinkwashing." bdsmovement.net/pinkwashing.

Berger, John. 1972. *Ways of Seeing.* London: Penguin.

Bhutto, Zulfikar Ali. 1977. *Third World: New Directions.* London: Quartet Books.

Bukhari, Muhammad ibn Ismail. 1994. *The Translation of the Meanings of Ṣahih Al-Bukhari: Arabic-English,* translated by Muhammad Muhsin Khan. Vol. 1. Medina: Islamic University.

Bush, Laura. 2001. "Laura Bush Radio Text Transcript." *Washington Post,* November 17. www.washingtonpost.com/wpsrv/nation/specials/attacked/transcripts/laurabushtext_111701.html.

Crafts, Lydia. 2009. "Taqwacore: The Real Muslim Punk Underground." NPR, July 25. www.npr.org/2009/07/25/107010536/taqwacore-the-real-muslim-punk-underground.

Hammadi, Saad, and Aisha Gani. 2016. "Founder of Bangladesh's First and Only LGBT Magazine Killed." *Guardian,* April 25. www.theguardian.com/world/2016/apr/25/editor-bangladesh-first-lgbt-magazine-killed-reports-say-roopbaan.

Hennessy, Keith, and Jassem Hindi. 2015. *Future Friend/ships.* Circo Zero Performance. circozero.org/friendships/.

Human Dignity Trust. 2021. "Pakistan." www.humandignitytrust.org/country-profile/pakistan/.

Kapadia, Ronak K. 2019. *Insurgent Aesthetics: Security and the Queer Life of the Forever War.* Durham, NC: Duke University Press.

Lauro, Sarah Juliet, and Karen Embry. 2008. "A Zombie Manifesto: The Nonhuman Condition in the Era of Advanced Capitalism." *boundary 2* 35, no. 1: 85–108.

Mbembe, Achille. 2003. "Necropolitics," translated by Libby Meintjes. *Public Culture* 15, no. 1: 11–40. muse.jhu.edu/article/39984.

Muñoz, José Esteban. 2009. *Cruising Utopia: The Then and There of Queer Futurity.* New York: New York University Press.

Nasrallah, Rami. 2013. "The First and Second Palestinian *intifadas.*" In *Routledge Handbook on the Israeli-Palestinian Conflict,* edited by David Newman and Joel Peters, 56–68. New York: Routledge.

Puar, Jasbir K., and Amit Rai. 2002. "Monster, Terrorist, Fag: The War on Terrorism and the Production of Docile Patriots." *Social Text* 20, no. 3: 117–48.

Rastegar, Mitra. 2013. "Emotional Attachments and Secular Imaginings: Western LGBTQ Activism on Iran." *GLQ: A Journal of Lesbian and Gay Studies* 19, no. 1: 1–29.

Said, Edward. 1978. *Orientalism.* New York: Pantheon Books.

Sinno, Hamed. 2020. "Hamed Sinno on Pride and Mourning in the Middle East." *Frieze,* June. www.frieze.com/article/hamed-sinno-pride-and-mourning-middle-east.

Wilkins, Brett. 2015. "Doctors' Group Says 1.3 Million Killed in U.S. 'War on Terror.'" *Digital Journal,* March 25. www.digitaljournal.com/news/world/study-1-3-million-killed-in-usa-war-on-terror/article/429180.

Taneem Husain

Queering Islam and Muslim Americanness:
Perversity, Recognition, and Failure in Usama
Alshaibi's *Profane*

Abstract: In the United States' current cultural and political climate, stereotypes of Muslims, such as the destructive terrorist and oppressed burqa-
clad woman, are ever-present. For Muslim Americans, breaking outside of
these stereotypes is fraught: merely contesting these stereotypes is insuffi-
cient for inclusion. Muslim Americans are often required to construct central aspects of their identities—particularly religion, gender, and
sexuality—so they become acceptable to mainstream American sensibilities, thus becoming "good" Muslims. This essay theorizes an alternative to
this good/bad binary by imagining a "queer" Muslimness through Usama
Alshaibi's 2011 film *Profane*. *Profane* centers on Muna, a Muslim Arab-
American professional dominatrix who attempts to reconcile her perverse
sexuality with her religious identity. In doing so, she unravels understandings of both her role as a dominatrix and her Muslim identity, questioning
the boundaries of these categories. Using queer of color critique and feminist theorizing on BDSM, this essay examines how Muna demands recognition of her Islamic sexuality and perverse Islam, navigating tensions as she
disidentifies with these categories. While her attempts at recognition inevitably fail, Muna continues to insist on Islamic sexuality/perverse Islam by
consuming the jinn that haunts her throughout the film. This essay demonstrates how Muna's refusal to succumb to tensions of essentialized
identity—particularly through linking religion and perverse sexuality—
works to refute the standard monolithic view of Muslim American identity.
Ultimately, in emphasizing how nonnormative and perverse religious practice helps build queer perspectives on identity, this paper expands queer
theory's burgeoning analyses on Muslim identity.

MERIDIANS · feminism, race, transnationalism   20:2 October 2021
DOI: 10.1215/15366936-9547980 © 2021 Smith College

In the United States' current cultural and political climate, stereotypes of Muslims are utterly familiar; they are ever present in mainstream media and politics. Muslim Americans often struggle to move past static images of destructive terrorists and oppressed women without a voice. Breaking outside of these stereotypes requires engaging with the binary between good and bad Muslim. Political scientist Mahmood Mamdani (2004: 15), who originated the terms "good Muslim" and "bad Muslim," places the outset of the binary at the September 11, 2001 terrorist attacks (9/11):

> "Bad Muslims" were clearly responsible for terrorism. . . . "Good Muslims" were anxious to clear their names and consciences of this horrible crime [9/11] and would undoubtedly support "us" in a war against "them." But this could not hide the central message of such discourse: unless proven to be "good," every Muslim was presumed to be "bad." All Muslims were now under the obligation to prove their credentials by joining in a war against "bad Muslims."

It is clear from both this quotation and from popular discourse that the bad Muslim is defined monolithically. The quotation also demonstrates that the good Muslim, too, is a monolith. In discussing the racialization of Muslims in the United States, Neil Gotanda (2011: 194) points out that "the disciplinary function of the 'good Muslim' corresponding to the 'model minority' is available for use against Muslims . . . who protest or disagree with American domestic or foreign policy." While supporting US policy is crucial in defining oneself as a good Muslim, the binary between good and bad Muslim is a neo-Orientalist ideology. As such, while it is "indebted to classical Orientalism," it also "engenders new tropes of othering" (Behdad and Williams 2010: 284). In this case, the good Muslim as disciplinary mechanism requires aligning Muslim American identity with dominant American understandings of gender and sexuality. This essay theorizes an alternative to this good/bad binary by fusing together scholarship on this binary with queer of color critique to imagine a "queer" Muslimness through Usama Alshaibi's 2011 film *Profane*.

Profane centers on Muna, a Muslim Arab American professional dominatrix who attempts to reconcile her perverse sexuality with her religious identity. In doing so, she unravels understandings of both her role as a dominatrix and her Muslim identity, questioning the boundaries of these categories. In defining and understanding *identity* here, I am pulling from José Esteban Muñoz's work in *Disidentifications: Queers of Color and the*

Performance of Politics (1999). Muñoz argues that minority subjects struggle with accepting or resisting identity as defined by the dominant sphere. Solely working within the dominant understandings of minority identities would mean "an easy or magical identification with dominant culture," while wholly resisting dominant notions of identity would mean existing "outside of ideology" (Muñoz 1999: 12). Instead, minority subjects can dis-identify, or "work with/resist the conditions of (im)possibility that domi-nant culture generates" (Muñoz 1999: 6). Rather than imagine oneself outside of an identity, minority subjects can attempt "to hold on to this object and invest it with new life" (Muñoz 1999: 12).

Using queer of color critique and feminist theorizing on BDSM, I exam-ine how Muna holds onto Muslim identity by demanding recognition of her Islamic sexuality and perverse Islam, navigating tensions as she deconstructs and connects these categories. While the film sets up Muna's sexuality as "profane," as in the sacred/profane dichotomy, I describe Muna's sexuality as "perverse" to call attention to how Muna disidentifies with Orientalist understandings of Brown, Muslim sexual perversity. On the white, Orientalist gaze, Jasbir Puar (2007: 87) writes: "As the space of 'illicit and dangerous sex,' the Orient is the site of carefully suppressed animalistic, perverse, homo- and hypersexual instincts." While Muna acquiesces to the stereotype of the hypersexual Muslim woman, this sexu-ality is not hidden, nor it is it for the white gaze. Yet her sexuality remains perverse in its nonnormativity. Embracing this nonnormativity, rather than hiding or suppressing it, marks Muna as "foregrounding and reclaiming the sexual perversities of the brown terrorist" (Puar 2007: 169). Thus, in describing her sexuality as "perverse" rather than "profane," I am reading Muna's sexuality through the line of queer of color critique that emphasizes nonnormative sexualities in order to both reclaim and disidentify with the identities aligned with those sexualities.

For Muna, recognition of her disidentification from Islam and perverse sexuality, and of her creation of Islamic sexuality and perverse Islam, seems central to her being able to live out these versions of religious and sexual identities. While Muna's attempts at recognition inevitably fail, she con-tinues to insist on Islamic sexuality / perverse Islam, encompassing inco-herence by consuming the jinn[1] that haunts her throughout the film. This essay demonstrates how Muna's refusal to succumb to tensions of essen-tialized identity—particularly through linking religion and perverse sexuality—works to refute the standard monolithic view of Muslim

American identity and instead build a queer Islam. Ultimately, in emphasizing how nonnormative and perverse religious practice helps build queer perspectives on identity and disidentification, this essay expands queer theory's burgeoning analyses on Islam and Muslim identity.

To convey how *Profane* builds and demands recognition of Islamic sexuality / perverse Islam, I will first discuss the understandings of religion and sexuality the film is resisting: those of the good Muslim. I will then describe the film, discern the standards of religion and sexuality it works within, and use the film to determine the parameters of Muna's Islamic sexuality / perverse Islam. Third, I will describe how Muna seeks recognition from her clients and friends and how this recognition fails. Finally, I will explain how, despite this failure and by consuming her jinn, Muna maintains her Islamic sexuality / perverse Islam and opens the potential for a queer Islam.

Gender, Sexuality, and the Good Muslim

Understanding how gender and sexuality play a role in constructing the good Muslim is perhaps best exemplified through popular representations, which convey the type of Muslims mainstream US culture is willing to accept.[2] Two examples of this are comedians Aziz Ansari and Kumail Nanjiani. Both men's trajectories toward fame convey how, as Roderick A. Ferguson (2004: 3) argues, "racist practice articulates itself generally as gender and sexual regulation, and . . . gender and sexual differences variegate racial formations." Both Ansari and Nanjiani gained fame by developing representations of Brown Muslim or "Muslim-ish"[3] men who are relatable partially because of love lives that fit into familiar romantic comedy tropes. Ansari created and stars in the Netflix television show *Master of None* (2015) and Nanjiani wrote and starred in the romantic comedy film *The Big Sick* (2017). Both the show and the film focus on the love lives of their protagonists, who are described in reviews as "likeable and relatable" (Goodman 2017) and "authentic and endearing" (Berkshire 2017). Nanjiani's film focuses on the tensions he experiences dating a white woman while "his family is actively searching for a Pakistani bride for him, for a traditional arranged marriage, and . . . for him, dating a white woman is asking to get disowned" (Yoshida 2017). The serialized plot in the second season of *Master of None* focuses on Ansari's character Dev playing "the lovelorn victim, the nice guy who finishes last" as he navigates a relationship with a white Italian woman (Heritage 2017).

As critiques of Ansari and Nanjiani point out, these "relatable" and "endearing" representations rely on demonizing Islam, ethnicized culture, and/or Brown women.[4] Critics argue that these representations often depend on the "lazy justification for marrying outside of your culture . . . by denigrating the options within your culture" (Freeman 2017). Further, it is these characters' "rejection of certain practices understood to be Islamic—such as arranged marriage, compulsory ritual prayer, and dietary restrictions" that marks the characters as "male protagonists making heroic choices" (Michael 2018: 65). In what is now a standard neo-Orientalist trope, becoming a Muslim-ish protagonist therefore requires distancing oneself from Islam. A part of this distancing involves an acceptable, secular gendered sexuality.

Muslim or Muslim-ish women have not gained the mainstream attention received by Ansari and Nanjiani, making it difficult to discern what gendered and sexual requirements exist for "good" Muslim women. Still, drawing connections between Muslims—often racialized as perpetually foreign[5]—and other diasporic subjects makes it clear that a Muslim woman attempting good Muslimness must be aware of dominant American post-feminist standards. This point is taken up by Gayatri Gopinath (2005) in her discussion of diasporic film. She notes that films depicting young South Asian diasporic women exploring sexuality are often "very self-consciously 'feminist' in [their] depiction of the women of the family as (hetero)sexually autonomous subjects" (115). Thus, diasporic film and literature often use sex—particularly for women—to convey the assimilatory and/or modern possibilities of first- and second-generation immigrants. Gopinath's example is the film *Bend It Like Beckham* (2002), in which British Indian Jess can convey her independence through a sexual relationship with her white soccer coach. Importantly, this version of sexuality must be agential enough to negate assumed oppression, but for good Muslim women sexuality must also be demure enough to refuse the "strand of Orientalist thought [that] has constructed our contemporary visions of Arab and Muslim societies as . . . completely decadent, immoral, and permissive" (Naber 2011: 81).

From a dominant neo-Orientalist perspective, then, a good Muslim woman must be willing to buck some of her Islamic and ethnic cultural expectations in favor of autonomous sexuality, which, as described above, is wholly postfeminist in its construction. This also means giving up or rejecting aspects of Islam. Quite obviously, the bad Muslim's religiosity is thought to be too much. In terms of sexuality, this means too fundamentalist and too sexually repressed. As Sunaina Maira (2009) points out, the good Muslim must be critical of Islam. Returning to comedic figures Ansari and Nanjiani, Jaclyn Michael (2018: 65) notes:

> A trend in the humor of New Brown America foregrounds the impiety of young, male protagonists who firmly believe that their parents' interpretation of Islam constricts the way of life they wish to lead. . . . In a post-9/11 American context, it is remarkable that these [parental] practices are also the very ones used to construct Muslims as backward, illiberal, and un-American. Seen in this light, the heroic impiety of New Brown America lends itself to supporting some of the negative and racist assumptions about Islam that undergird contemporary Islamophobic discourse.

Being "good" thus requires distancing oneself from Islam, and indeed, denigrating traditional understandings of Islam. As the requirement of postfeminist sexuality indicates, this is particularly true when it comes to noting "the oppression of women in Islam [and] the 'freedoms . . . in the West'" (Maira 2009: 635). The figure of the good Muslim encourages Muslims to either negate their religion or emphasize its potential differences from US values.

However, Orientalism does not just produce "a single binary of East-West" (Moussawi 2020: 8). Rather, through his theorizing on fractal Orientalism, Ghassan Moussawi (2020: 8) argues that "transnational discourses of national and sexual exceptionalism operate on multiple scales. They are multifaceted and circulate at global (not just in the West), regional, and local levels; they are informed by and in touch with one another." Accordingly, Muslim American women's sexual behavior matters not only to how they are viewed by mainstream American society. As Eithne Luibhéid (2005: xxvii) points out, "women are typically constructed as the repositories of cultural tradition, [and] their sexual behavior tends to become viewed—*by both migrant communities and dominant cultures*—as 'evidence' of the worth of the group, and policed accordingly" (my emphasis). Thus, Muslim women's sexuality is controlled by both dominant American standards—which I understand here as embedded in whiteness and postfeminism—and Islamic standards. Ultimately, as I will demonstrate in the next sections, I argue that Muna's religion and sexuality push past essentialized good and bad Muslimness because she fuses religion and sexuality in ways considered perverse by both mainstream American and

Islamic standards. "Islamic standards," however, vary wildly depending on one's ethnicity, school of thought, and piety. To further think about how *Profane* engages with both dominant American standards of sexuality and how it sets up Islamic standards, a more detailed film analysis is required.

Profane

Profane (Alshaibi 2011) centers on Muna, a Muslim Arab American dominatrix with a complicated past. Her family moves to the United States from Jordan after Muna is "caught with boys." Her family "thought [she] was possessed. There were exorcisms." In the film's narrative present, Muna continues to be haunted by a jinn, consistently hearing it speaking to her nonsensically. Despite or because of this, Muna maintains an active Islamic practice. Throughout the film, she prays and recites Quran. Still, the movie is centered on her crisis of faith, which stems from the jinn, traditional patriarchal understandings of Islam, and her work. Mary and Ali—the major supporting characters in the film—attempt to help alleviate this crisis. Mary, a white, non-Muslim friend and coworker, pushes back against Muna's Muslimness while also trying to understand it. Ali, a traditionally devout Muslim cab driver whom Muna and Mary befriend, acts as a spiritual guide for Muna. He learns to take part in Muna's drug- and sex-filled personal life in an attempt to guide her toward a more orthodox Islam.

While this summary might make the film seem simple, *Profane* is a tough film to describe for several reasons. First, as Alshaibi (2012) notes in his "Forced Artist Statement," the film works on "re-imagining time and space in a dizzying and chaotic experience for both the audience and the film's main character, Muna." This means the narrative is never straightforward. It is unclear when events are taking place within the time line of the narrative. Second, the film resists genre. It presents a fictional narrative of Muna's life. But it also depicts interiority through non-narrative scenes and presents interviews of Muna with an unseen interviewer.

Profane and Sexuality

The "dizzying and chaotic experience" is visible in the first three minutes of the film, which confusingly cut back and forth between different scenes, times, and points of view. Still, these shots demonstrate that Islam is an obvious theme of the film by using the hijab, an overused symbol for Islam particularly within Western society. Through clothing, these first minutes depict dominant American views of Islam and sexuality, the Islamic standards of sexuality the film is working with, and Muna's own views of Islam and sexuality.

As the film opens, Islam is depicted in a manner likely familiar to mainstream US audiences: oppressive and patriarchal. In the first shot where Muna is recognizable, her face is expressionless, the lack of emotion disconcerting. Black eyeliner is drawn on her face to mimic tears. Her hijab lies at the middle of her head, dark hair poking out of the scarf's opening. Muna's face demonstrates her discomfort. Through the sequence, the oppressive and patriarchal nature of Islam is much more forcefully depicted. A man's disembodied arm, for instance, points at and chastises a hijab-wearing Muna, her face fearful. This initial setup gives viewers a rather soul-sucking and Orientalist rendition of Islam.

Importantly, however, the idea of Islam being repressive and oppressive here is not just stereotype. It is the Islamic standard Muna grows up in, and the standard she continues to associate with orthodox Islam. This is demonstrated in the story of her upbringing I alluded to earlier. Muna is assumed to be possessed as a child because she is "caught with boys," though she notes that her activities were those of "a normal girl. I mean, I, yeah, I experimented with boys just like anyone else, but it wasn't really looked upon as something that people do over there."[6] Thus for Muna, sexual repression is a reality. This is further conveyed later in the film as Muna discusses her past escorting with the interviewer. In the interview, she says that while escorting, she "used to get a lot of Arab clients" who would seek her out because of their shared ethnicity. One of these clients asked if she was Muslim, and she said yes. Muna describes the client's response: "It made him really angry and he started calling me a slut and all this stuff and he didn't want to go through with it. It was really weird and kind of unsettling." The client's response complies with the assumed chasteness Muslim women must have, again presenting repression as an Islamic standard Muna lives within.

The opening scene of the film—Muna fearfully cowering to the disembodied arm—does present one solution to this repression, the one most familiar to mainstream American culture: the US savior. Because Islam is oppressive to women, it is necessary to save Muslim women. This scene depicts the savior as the arm suddenly ceases chastising and pointing and becomes soft. The arm touches Muna's shoulder, then tears her hijab off.

The arm, which previously stood for Islamic patriarchal control, is now a savior. This brings the representation of the hijab in *Profane* in line with standard neo-Orientalist depictions, in which "the veil is always constructed in terms of a binary between freedom and oppression, secularism and religion, modernity and tradition, and democracy and tyranny" (Behdad and Williams 2010: 294). This man unclothed a covered Muslim woman, bringing her into acceptable American secularism and therefore saving her.

This opening sequence defines the film's view of expectations of Muslims via two recognizable, neo-Orientalist options: cover or uncover. The film is thus engaging with and disrupting the binaried way gender and sexuality are often thought about in critical activist circles. As Nadine Naber (2011: 87) writes, "Attempts to develop feminist or queer critiques" of sexism and compulsory heterosexuality in Arab and Muslim communities are "often confined between two extremes: untenable silence, on the one hand, and the reification of Orientalist representations, on the other." In *Profane*, Orientalist representations of gender and sexuality are depicted and reckoned with, as is the potential silence Muna could enact—reflected by the lack of dialogue in the scenes described here. However, Muna is clearly uncomfortable with remaining silent and accepting patriarchal domination, whether it comes from orthodox Islam or the US savior. Throughout the sequence, fear is palpable on her face. She flinches at any sign of movement from the arm, looking around warily for off-screen movement. When the arm removes her hijab, Muna looks fearful, covering her head to protect herself, and potentially to replace her hijab. When the arm chastises her, she cowers timidly. The only moments where she appears serene in this opening sequence are when she is alone, which begins to convey to viewers the solitary nature of her perverse religious practices.

In addition to setting up both dominant American and Islamic standards of sexuality, the opening sequence also introduces viewers to Muna's sexualized perspective on Islam. Following the scenes with the disembodied arm, viewers see Muna praying in a fashion typical of most Muslims. At first, the shot is close-up, giving viewers a fairly standard view of a Muslim woman praying: Muna reverently whispering while wearing the hijab. When the shot goes wide, however, the camera shows that Muna is praying wearing only underwear and a bra. According to orthodox Islamic law, women's bodies should be fully covered when praying, save for their faces, hands, and feet. Here, Muna is clearly violating these orthodox Islamic standards, yet she prays anyway. I label her actions here perverse, and not just odd, because her nakedness inserts sexuality into a practice that is purportedly devoid of sexual energy. Within most understandings of orthodox Islam, sexuality is encouraged between a married couple; outside of marriage, modesty is generally advised. Muna's insistence on praying unclothed inserts sexuality where there should be none, marking her prayer as perverse. Importantly, too, Muna's nude or barely clothed prayer happens not just in this scene, but at multiple points in the film.

Even through this short example, it is clear Muna is fusing sexuality and religious practice, which may be enough to mark Muna as queerly antinormative when considering orthodox Islam. However, merging sexuality and religion is not inherently subversive. Indeed, the idea of fusing Islam and sexuality is fraught with Orientalist tropes. Pulling on Edward Said (1979), Mohja Kahf (1999: 8) argues that in the eighteenth and nineteenth centuries, Western images portrayed Muslim women through "irredeemable difference and exoticism; intense sexuality, excessive ornamentation and association with fetish objects; and finally, powerlessness in the form of imprisonment, enslavement, seclusion, silence, or invisibility." As current consistent tensions around the hijab indicate, this anxiety about Muslim women's bodies and sexualities has not lessened. Muslim women remain subject to concern, exoticism, and fetishism, particularly with regard to sexuality. This is in addition to the broader ever-present patriarchal control of all women's sexuality.

What marks Muna's sexuality as subversive, then, is how *Profane* does not ignore the tendency to fetishize sexual religiosity. Rather, the film acknowledges and pushes back against this Orientalist insistence on fetishizing Muslim women, particularly through Muna's interactions with a white male partner. In the only scene depicting Muna in a seemingly non-work-related sexual moment, she kisses a white male partner in bed. The man asks her to stop and notes that he wants to talk. He wants Muna to tell him about herself, particularly her "past, or you know, Muslim stuff." Muna responds incredulously, asking him what he's talking about, and says she wants to go back to having sex. While this white male partner wants to bring more of Muna's religion and race into their sexual encounter, Muna challenges him by refusing to give him information that might further fetishize their rendezvous.

This scene does convey Muna's resistance against Orientalist views of Muslim women's sexuality. However, it could quite easily be read as an example of postfeminist agency. Indeed, even the scenes of Muna praying in her underwear could be read through a postfeminist lens. Returning to the concept of the good Muslim, from a postfeminist perspective, perhaps a Muslim dominatrix would be read as appropriate. Muna has renounced religious and ethnic guidelines that discourage sex outside of marriage, instead embracing a "performed fierceness by reveling in female sexual power" (Nguyen 2013: 159–60). Such an understanding of agency aligns Muna with the postfeminist SlutWalks and SuicideGirls as read by Tram Nguyen (2013)—precisely the women dominant US culture would pit against burqa-ed "Bundles of Black" (Shaheen 2014: 28).

Where the film moves beyond a simple, neo-Orientalist binary between agency and oppression and toward a fully fleshed out Islamic sexuality / perverse Islam is in exploring submission and domination. While Muna works as a dominatrix, throughout the film she expresses interest in submission, as in submission to God. Here it is important to note that the word *Islam* is often translated as "submission." As Laith Saud (2013: 65) writes, "Islam means 'peace achieved through submission to God.'" The film pulls on this understanding of Islam as Muna notes that she wants to "put love in Allah." In one scene, the interviewer asks Muna why she no longer has sex for money. While Muna dominates her men clients, including pegging them, she no longer takes the penetrated position for her clients. She responds that "having sex with someone for money was like a form of submission and I just wanted to submit to God." While generally the "submission" in Islam is not thought of as innately sexual, Alshaibi connects religious and sexual submission through the two cultural spheres Muna moves between: BDSM and Islam.

Submission—sexual or otherwise—as has been thoroughly detailed by Amber Jamilla Musser (2014) and Ariane Cruz (2016), has been construed as antifeminist, particularly when performed by a woman of color. Submitting to another is often read as denying individual agency in favor of often problematic hierarchy. And yet, as Musser (2014: 3) describes, psychoanalytic, postmodern, and queer theorists have also argued that submission is consistently subversive. Following Musser (2014: 14), to combat these sometimes simplistic readings, I want to focus less on Muna's individual agency, instead viewing her "as a component of a larger structure." First, that structure involves Muna's religious identity. Muna identifies as Arab— a racial marker that has a long and complicated relationship to whiteness[7]—and Muslim, a religious identity that has been racialized in US society. As an active participant in BDSM, Muna demonstrates how BDSM can be a powerful tool in engaging with racialization and refuting "the whiteness of BDSM" (Martinez 2020: 3). Further, Muna's position as a dominatrix interested in sexualized religious submission deconstructs hegemonic understandings of BDSM. She performs both sides of a purportedly clear dichotomy. Rather than asserting either agency or oppression, desiring *both* submission and domination allows Muna to reject the purportedly clear agency of acting as a dominatrix.

Further, Muna imbues her sexual practices with Islam. Thus, it is important to consider how Muna performs submission. Though Muna is consistently performing sexual acts throughout the film, arguably the most important "sexual acts" are those with God, or with Islam. Not only do these acts convey Muna's interiority to the audience, but they echo beyond Muna's experience to the larger structure, forcing viewers to call into question both sexual and religious practices.

One example of Muna's questioning of sex and religion is the scene I describe above, where Muna prays in hijab and underwear. Pulling on Juana María Rodríguez (2014), I argue that this is an example of creating new understandings of religion and sexuality. Rodríguez (2014: 109) writes that "spirituality is performatively produced through gesture in ways that mirror how gender and sexuality are produced." Through this sexualized performance of religion, Muna produces a vision of religion that fuses sexuality and religion. Beyond this, though, is the idea that her sexual religiosity is being broadcast to the film's viewers. Viewers are introduced to her perverse religion through her gestures, broadening her perverse religion past the character and to the audience.

Directly following this prayer scene, Muna more explicitly melds religion and sexuality. She describes dreams where she "would see the Prophet [Muhammad] and he would make love to [her]." After this voice-over, she is depicted masturbating while reading the Quran. Using Rodríguez, I want to again read this performance of sexuality as a performance of religiosity, and vice versa. Rodríguez (2014: 132) writes, "To be possessed sexually, to be inhabited and mounted by another, is to give over corporeal control to another entity—human or divine—that demands surrender." Both Islam and sex signify surrender. Here, particularly because the film is thematized around BDSM, Muna uses masturbation as a kind of prayer; she is submitting to God through sex. This slippage between sex as submission and religious practice as submission is what demonstrates how Muna can "activate abjection as a resource for a reclamation of . . . world-making" (Rodríguez 2014: 21). This "world-making" is a different understanding of both Islam and Muslim American identity.

Muna's sexual deviance prevents her from being marked as either a "good" or "bad" Muslim. Regarding the "binary Orientalist categories that counterpose the presumedly oppressed and conservative *muhajjabat* versus the presumedly assertive and independent feminist," Muna is too dominant to be oppressed and too submissive to be independent (Hatem 2011: 28). She is too perverse to fulfill the ideal role of the Muslim woman according to the Islamic standards the film sets up. And she is too religious to fulfill the ideal of the diasporic Muslim woman according to mainstream American standards. Instead, she resists the Orientalist binary by insisting on a different version of both Islam and sexuality, what I call Islamic sexuality / perverse Islam.

Demanding Recognition

Muna's inability to be seen as good or bad, as traditionally Muslim or truly agential in a postfeminist sense, becomes clear as she seeks recognition for this Islamic sexuality / perverse Islam. As Anne McClintock (1993: 109) notes on the politics of sadomasochism, "S/M rituals may be called *rituals of recognition*. In these rituals of recognition, participants seek a witness—to trauma, pain, pleasure, or power." Throughout the film, Muna seeks recognition for her Islamic sexuality / perverse Islam. This happens first as she practices BDSM with her clients. In many scenes depicting Muna working, she wears a hijab. This is a direct example of Muna merging her sexuality with her religion and seeking recognition of her Islamic sexuality / perverse Islam from others—here, her clients. In these scenes, however, the participants do not provide Muna with recognition. Muna, instead, seems disconnected from her clients. As a ritual of recognition, rather than seeing recognition of her selfhood in her clients, Muna sees it in herself. Acting as a Muslim dominatrix allows Muna to bring together the two poles of her identity, without comment from her clients. In these scenes, Muna is in power as a sexually perverse Muslim woman.[8]

Beyond her clients, Muna most obviously seeks recognition from her friends in the film: Mary and Ali. Muna and Mary—Muna's white non-Muslim coworker—are often presented as two peas in a pod. They dominate clients together; attend parties together, arriving and leaving together; and drink and do drugs at each other's houses. Their characters are in many ways similar, particularly in that they revel in their rebellion, never presenting their life choices as problematic.

Muna's Islamic sexuality / perverse Islam, however, creates a barrier between her and Mary. Throughout the film, Mary demonstrates little understanding of Islam and does not ask about Muna's interest in cultivating her Islamic beliefs and practices. In one scene, for example, Muna prays while fully clothed and wearing hijab. Mary lies on the ground next to Muna, waving her hand in front of Muna's face. As Muna prostrates, Mary whispers in her ear, trying to distract Muna. Mary begins imitating Muna's prayer positions, mocking her, saying "Allah, please, Allah come fuck me." Muna chuckles but tells Mary to stop. Mary's behavior here demonstrates a refusal to comprehend what prayer and religion mean to Muna. While Mary is concerned about Muna's jinni—"I'm worried about you . . . 'Cause you're hearing things," Mary tells Muna at one point in the film—she refuses to see the religious connection in this possession. When Muna tells Mary she is hearing her jinn, Mary asserts that "it's not real. . . . I think there's something wrong with you."

Instead of working to recognize Muna's Islam, Mary asserts a rather typical mainstream white feminist response to Muna's religion. In one scene, for instance, Muna, Mary, and Ali leave a party in Ali's cab. On the ride home, they listen to a recitation of the Quran. Surah an-Nas, the last *surah* or chapter of the Quran, translated as "Mankind," plays. Ali translates for Mary:

> Say: I seek refuge in the lord of mankind,
> The king of mankind,
> The god of mankind,
> From the evil of the sneaking whisperer who whispers in the hearts of
>   mankind,
> From the jinn and from the mankind.

During Ali's translation, both Muna and Mary look contemplative. This *surah* speaks directly to the themes of the film: Can God save mankind from evil? What is evil? Is Muna's jinn evil? Suddenly, however, Mary responds brashly to Ali's translation: "Um, do *we* [meaning women] count when it says 'mankind'? I don't think so. But I do feel sorry you guys, all that 'whispereth in the hearts of mankind.' Sorry, Allah, no go." In this scene, Ali is providing desired information about Islam to both Muna and Mary. Mary's response, however, is aggressive. While she does point out the patriarchal implications of Islam, in doing so, she ignores the *surah*'s relevance, including its patriarchal subtext, to Muna's religion and her jinn. Instead, she provides a boringly white feminist reading of Ali's translation.

Through these instances, Muna seems to be reaching out for recognition from Mary. She wants Mary to see and comprehend her Islam. Muna prays with Mary, seeks out religious answers with Mary, and works in her hijab with Mary. Indeed, she attempts to include Mary in these religious practices as she does in most other aspects of her life. However, as these scenes also demonstrate, this attempt at recognition fails. Mary does not understand how and why Islam is important to Muna.

Similarly, Muna attempts to obtain recognition of her Islamic sexuality / perverse Islam from Ali. Ali slowly becomes a part of Muna's life by giving her rides in his cab and offering her desired information about Islam and the Quran. Throughout the film, Ali serves as Muna's only Muslim compatriot. When the two first meet, Mary and Muna ride in Ali's cab. Muna tells Mary she hears someone whispering to her and Mary asks the cabbie for help:

> **Ali:** Hello sister Muna. Are you Muslim?
> **Muna:** Yeah.
> **Ali:** Maybe you're hearing a *jinn*. He whispers to your soul all the time.

After this interaction, Ali gives Muna his business card, telling her she can call him to ask for a ride or to talk more about Islam. This interaction directly opposes Muna's discussion about her jinn with Mary. Unlike Mary, Ali believes Muna's possession. He is open to this aspect of her Islam.

Muna continues to struggle for recognition of her Islamic sexuality / perverse Islam by trying to bring Ali into her world. She does not shy away from discussing her perversities around Ali, laughing when Mary offers to give Ali a blow job as payment for a cab ride and inviting him into her house while Mary sits bound on the couch. Ali does seem to work to recognize Muna's Islam. He attends parties with Mary and Muna and accepts a lap dance from Mary. However, as with Mary, this recognition is never fully complete.

Just as Mary wants to recognize Muna as perverse without Islam, Ali wants to recognize Muna as Muslim without perversity. Throughout the film, while attempting to get to know Muna, he helps Muna without much commentary on the aspects of her lifestyle that fall outside of many orthodox Islamic practices, including her sexuality. However, this changes near the end of the film, when Ali brings an Imam, or religious leader, to "help with [Muna's] understanding of Islam." Here, Ali is no longer tolerant of Muna's deviance from orthodox Islamic dictates, trying to recognize her as an orthodox Muslim, rather than seeing her Islamic sexuality / perverse Islam.

In this part of the plotline, Muna and Ali joke about praying in the wrong direction while Ali drives Muna in his cab. Muna takes this opportunity to ask Ali for "help reading the Quran better." Ali mentions he has a good friend who is skilled at Quranic recitation, Imam Tariq. He offers to bring Imam Tariq to Muna's house, and she accepts his offer. Soon after this, Mary and Muna have a wild night together at Muna's apartment; they drink and do drugs, and Muna binds Mary with rope. Both fall asleep, Muna in her bed topless, and Mary still bound on the couch. In the morning, Ali knocks on Muna's door with Imam Tariq in tow. Muna ties a scarf around her naked breasts, chugs some alcohol, wakes Mary up, and answers the door. Mary sits on the couch, naked and still bound, her hands awkwardly positioned behind her head. Muna throws a blanket on top of her, and invites the men in. Imam Tariq addresses Muna: "So, brother Ali tells me you need some help with your understanding of Islam," which is not what Muna asked of Ali. The scene then cuts to a shot of Muna in a chador being choked by a bodiless man's arm, similar to the scenes at the beginning of the film. This signals how Muna feels in this scene: cut off by rigid, patriarchal interpretations of Islam—the Islamic standard the film works within. The film then cuts back to the narrative scene, where Ali moves to cover Mary more fully with the blanket. Mary thanks Ali: "Thank you, Mr. Ali," with a wink and a blown kiss. Muna chuckles, says "whatever," and uncovers Mary. Imam Tariq and Ali get up to leave. Muna insists that they stay, asking Ali and Imam Tariq, "Where are you going?! I need help reading the Quran!" However, when Ali tells Muna that he and Imam Tariq are "here to help," Muna responds angrily: "I don't need your help, or his. Now get out before I piss on you!" Ali and Imam Tariq hurry out, Ali apologizing deferentially to Imam Tariq.

Just as Mary finishes the film asserting a white feminist outlook on Muna's religiosity, Ali finishes the film asserting a traditional (in the film's view) Islamic outlook on Muna's sexuality. With the introduction of Imam Tariq, Ali pulls away from Muna's Islamic sexuality / perverse Islam. Siding with Imam Tariq's orthodox understanding of Islam, Ali instead attempts to change Muna's religious perspective. After this point, Ali leaves Muna's life; he is no longer figured in the film. Muna's attempt at recognition through Ali fails.

In wearing hijab while dominating her clients, performing Islam around Mary, and performing perversity around Ali, Muna is grasping for recognition—from herself and others—as a sexually perverse Muslim woman. While Muna gets no real acknowledgment from others, the insistence on including Islam within sexual acts and the insistence on including sexuality in Islamic acts work to imbue perverse sexuality with Islam. In "Queer Sociality and Other Sexual Fantasies," Rodríguez (2011: 338) writes:

> Through . . . real and imagined sexual encounters, queers enact the possibility of disentangling bodies and acts from preassigned meanings, of creating meaning and pleasure anew from the recycled scraps of dominant cultures. Through eroticization and pleasure, we are thus presented with the possibility of remarking and remaking the pain and refusal of social intelligibility that constitute our daily lives.

This is precisely what Muna does by blending BDSM and Islam. Muna takes aspects of both subcultures and ignores others. She makes her own religious and sexual practices with the aspects she chooses, and in doing so, Muna shapes her identity and practices as Muslim. While outside recognition fails, Muna's queer Islam becomes intelligible at least to herself.

Failure of Recognition

While both Mary and Ali try to find Muna's identity intelligible, their feelings toward her Islamic sexuality / perverse Islam are ambivalent at best. Despite this, Muna persists with her religious and sexual practices, continuing to aim for recognition from both herself and others. The intelligibility of these practices and her identity, however, start to break down in the last scene of Muna working, in which the film takes a strange turn to engage with and in some ways acquiesce to the Orientalist conception of "a culture of Arab Muslim sexual savagery that needs to be disciplined—and in the process, modernized—through U.S. military violence" (Naber 2011: 81).

In the scene, Muna works with a client coded as ex–US military. She stands facing the camera wearing a garter belt, panties, and a hijab. A bulky, tattooed white man sits behind her, rubbing his penis through his underwear. She faces away from him, posing. He looks from her to the camera and quickly back again. The film then cuts to a member of the US military shooting at a beige wall and continues to cut between shots of

Muna and her client and scenes of war: bombing of nondescript Middle Eastern–looking cities and children waving at US military. These scenes of war eventually overlay the shots of Muna and her client. The juxtaposition of Muna and her client and scenes of war conveys two things. First, it encourages viewers to see the client as a member or former member of the US military. The client's physique also indicates that he be read as a member of the US military. Second, the juxtaposition sets up the interactions between Muna and her client as aggressive and racially and religiously charged.

Once the film focuses back on the narrative scenes, Muna asks her client what he wants. The client responds, "I want you to rape me." Muna, now wearing a black strap-on, prepares to peg her client. Suddenly, the client brings up her hijab:

> **Client:** So, do you get a lot of requests to wear that kind of stuff?
> **Muna (*gesturing toward her hijab*):** You mean this?
> **Client:** Yeah.
> **Muna:** Sometimes. Sometimes I just like to wear it.
> **Client:** Yeah? What are you like Muslim or something?
> **Muna:** Yeah.
> **Client:** I met this Muslim girl once. She was covered head to toe. She had a hijab on. Every time I looked at her, I wanted to see what was underneath it.
> **Muna:** Was this a fantasy, or . . . ?
> **Client:** Shut up, I'm talking. This is my time. No, that's why I fucked her. I just wanted to see what was underneath, you know, 'cause I didn't know.
> **Muna:** Turn around and bend over.

In this scene, Muna's queer Muslimness breaks down. She, despite her best efforts, is still associated with a monolithic understanding of Islam. The client's "obsession with the veil masks the complexity and multiple meanings that attach to the Islamic notion of hijab," and Muna becomes just another woman in hijab (Behdad and Williams 2010: 293). Her agency in choosing to wear the hijab while working is also questioned. It is instead used to continue defining Islam as a monolith, as something that can be othered, exoticized, and fetishized. Muna's Islamic sexuality / perverse Islam becomes yet another territory that can be colonized by the American soldier.

This is a complicated scene, however, and it can be read in multiple ways. Muna holds the powerful sexually penetrative position. But at the same time, she is doing her client's bidding. Still, Muna remains in power as the penetrative subject. She, as a Muslim woman, is penetrating the American soldier. But the American soldier demands this. As the narrative continues, the film resolves this paradox by negating the potential of Muna's queer Islam.[9]

After Muna pegs this client, a disgusted look on her face as she works, the scene cuts to Muna in a green, forest-like setting. She smiles and looks at the camera. We hear the jinn speaking. This time, however, the jinn's whispers are not in the demonic masculine voice it had earlier: they are in Muna's voice, and viewers can now understand what she is saying: "You are me, so I'm bringing you back. It's up to me to bring you back." Suddenly, the film cuts back to the narrative: The shot is upside-down, the camera panning over Muna and Mary as they lie in bed, staring at their feet:

> **Muna:** I ate him.
> **Mary:** Who?
> **Muna:** My jinn.
> **Mary:** Really?
> **Muna:** Yes.
> **Mary:** What did he taste like?
> **Mary:** How do you feel?
> **Muna:** I feel good.

The camera then turns upright, signaling a major shift. Viewers then see Muna wrapping her Quran up in fabric—potentially an old hijab—and putting it in the closet. Both shots signify that Muna's Islamic sexuality / perverse Islam is liminal, and perhaps its boundary has been reached. Later, while working, Mary asks Muna what happened to Ali. She says she does not want to see him anymore, blaming the influence of Imam Tariq. Seemingly, then, in these last few minutes of the film's narrative, Muna's relationship with Islam is shut down. Muna's queer Islam fails.

However, Muna presents another option through her consumption of the jinn. The film ends with a documentary-style interview of Muna. The interviewer asks her if she still identifies as Muslim. She says no, she no longer identifies as Muslim.

Interviewer: What do you identify as?
Muna: That's private.
Interviewer: What happened with the *jinn*?
Muna: I am the *jinn*.

Through this dialogue and the shot of Muna putting her Quran into storage, one could determine that Muna has rejected Islam. However, importantly, she does not concede to this reading because she refuses to religiously identify to either the viewers or the interviewer. She thus prevents viewers from fully closing down her Islamic sexuality / perverse Islam. Additionally, while refusing to identify as Muslim, Muna takes ownership over her jinn—a decidedly Muslim figure. In doing so, I argue that Muna can hold onto a version of Islam that cannot be interrupted by traditionalists like Ali, nor interpreted by neo-Orientalist US understandings of "good" and "bad" Muslim. Rather, Muna both refuses identity and paradoxically also holds onto Islam, maintaining her Islamic sexuality / perverse Islam through the jinn.

Accordingly, while Muna fails to achieve recognition for her Islamic sexuality / perverse Islam, she is able to find another avenue through which she can hold onto her queer version of Islam. While she initially disidentifies with Islam and BDSM subcultures, she finds this lacking. She fails at constructing the version of Islam she needs through disidentification. Particularly because of the definitions of Islam she is working with—the dominant American viewpoint and orthodox Islam as represented by Ali—Muna seems to understand that her Islamic sexuality / perverse Islam will not be recognized.

In concluding this essay, then, I want to think about what Muna's failure to obtain recognition means in terms of her Islamic sexuality / perverse Islam. Following Jack Halberstam's (2011) "suggestion that we read failure as a queer refusal of mastery," Julietta Singh (2018: 21) argues that "in failing to master . . . we become vulnerable to other possibilities for living . . . , for *feeling* injustice and refusing it without the need to engage it through forms of conquest." While Muna's ability to define Islam or Muslim American identity is negated, she can refuse this injustice through her consumption of the jinn. Though her attempts at recognition fail, Muna's consumption of the jinn allows her to become open to "other possibilities for living."

Importantly, while jinn are often thought of as evil, demonic creatures[10]— as conveyed in the film through the concept of Muna's possession—their existence in Islam is much more complicated. While, as Amira El-Zein (2009: xi) notes, scholarly analyses of jinn in Islam are lacking, in her manuscript she details orthodox and folk understandings of jinn, writing that "jinn in Islam are not demons opposed to angels. They are a third category of beings different from both angels and demons." Like humans, jinn have free will and can "at anytime shift toward goodness or toward evil" (El-Zein 2009: xi). Thus, by consuming the jinn, Muna does not align herself with "good" or "evil." She rather aligns herself with incoherence. Jinn, as El-Zein (2009: 64) describes, are consistently thought about with a "lack of precision." They are "'intermediary' or 'imaginal' beings, above our terrestrial realm but below the celestial realm," yet they can move between these three worlds (El-Zein 2009: x). They exist in "a different time and space [and] . . . belong to what could be called 'an immaterial materiality'" (6). By consuming the jinn, then, Muna shifts from attempting recognition in this world to accepting her place in an incoherent, yet still Muslim realm. Thus, rather than accomplishing little to nothing, this failure coming from a racially minoritized and queer subject "is a failure that is more nearly a refusal or an escape" from the demands of the binary between good Muslim and bad Muslim (Muñoz 2009: 174). When read in a queer sense, her failure "is essentially about the rejection of a here and now and an insistence on potentiality or concrete possibility for another world" (Muñoz 2009: 1). While Muna's attempts at recognition for her Islamic sexuality / perverse Islam may fail in this world, by consuming the jinn, she holds on to queer Islam, even if it is through a different, immaterial world. By doing so, Muna creates a space for queer Islam.

....

Taneem Husain is associate professor of women's and gender studies at Keene State College. Her research and teaching centers on Islam in the United States, ethnic studies, queer theory, and literature and media studies.

Notes

1   In Islamic theology, jinn are "spiritual entities," who, like angels, "are considered dual dimensional, with the ability to live and operate in both manifest and invisible domains" (El-Zein 2009: 1). Unlike angels, jinn have "free will like humans. Both species are at liberty to group, to trust or to distrust the Word of God, and to religiously differ" (El-Zein 2009: 15). Thus, there are many myths surrounding jinn and their positive (e.g., genies) and negative (e.g., demonic possession) influences on human life.

2   In this essay, I discuss recent dominant understandings of Islam in popular culture. While a description of the longer history of Muslim Americans is

beyond the scope of this article, see GhaneaBassiri (2010) and Grewal (2013) for a thorough description of the history of Muslims in the United States and Alsultany (2012), McAlister (2005), and Shaheen (2014) for how Muslims have been depicted in US media over time.

3 I borrow this term from Tanzila Ahmed and Zahra Noorbaksh (2015–20), who use it on their podcast #GoodMuslimBadMuslim to describe people who may have grown up Muslim or are otherwise connected to the Muslim community, but no longer identify as Muslim.

4 For examples, see Freeman 2017, Michael 2018, and Niazi 2017.

5 While Muslims in the United States are ethnically diverse, they are often thought of in the cultural imaginary as perpetually foreign, and primarily Arab or South Asian.

6 Viewers can assume that "over there" refers to Jordan, where Muna says her family is from.

7 For more information on the relationship between Arab nationalities and whiteness in the United States, see Jamal and Naber 2008, Qutami 2020, and Bayoumi 2006.

8 Some might read Muna's donning of the hijab during sex acts as an extension of Orientalist fetishization of the hijab, potentially hearkening to "'hijab porn—pornographic films [where] the women only wear a niqab (as a means of defiling it)'" (Moors 2011: 132). However, until the last scene (which I discuss later in the essay), Muna's hijab is not remarked on by her clients. Therefore, her reasons behind wearing the hijab are ambivalent at best, and certainly seem like they have little to do with her clients' requests. I argue that this negates the potential aspect of fetishization in her hijab-wearing.

9 There are many other ways in which this scene can be read, considering US militarism, penetration, and war, and the torture and abuse that took place at Abu Ghraib prison during the Iraq War. Unfortunately, detailing the impact of these themes on this scene is beyond the scope of this essay.

10 See Khalifa and Hardie 2005; Lim, Hoek, and Blom 2014; and Islam and Campbell 2014 for examples.

References

Ahmed, Tanzila, and Zahra Noorbaksh. 2015–20. #GoodMuslimBadMuslim. Podcast audio. www.goodmuslimbadmuslim.com/.

Alshaibi, Usama, dir. 2011. *Profane*. Oaks, PA: MVD Visual. DVD.

Alshaibi, Usama. 2012. "Forced Artist Statement." artvamp.com/usama/artist-statement/.

Alsultany, Evelyn. 2012. *Arabs and Muslims in the Media: Race and Representation after 9/11*. New York: New York University Press.

Bayoumi, Mustafa. 2006. "Racing Religion." *CR: The New Centennial Review* 6, no. 2: 267–93.

Behdad, Ali, and Juliet Williams. 2010. "Neo-Orientalism." In *Globalizing American Studies*, edited by Brian T. Edwards and Dilip Parameshwar Gaonkar, 283–99. Chicago: University of Chicago Press.

Berkshire, Geoff. 2017. "Film Review: *The Big Sick*." *Variety*, January 20. variety.com /2017/film/reviews/the-big-sick-review-sundance-kumail-nanjiani-1201965554/.

Cruz, Ariane. 2016. *The Color of Kink: Black Women, BDSM, and Pornography*. New York: New York University Press.

El-Zein, Amira. 2009. *Islam, Arabs, and the Intelligent World of the Jinn*. Syracuse, NY: Syracuse University Press.

Ferguson, Roderick A. 2004. *Aberrations in Black: Toward a Queer of Color Critique*. Minneapolis: University of Minnesota Press.

Freeman, Hadley. 2017. "*The Big Sick* is Funny, Sweet, Original—So Why Did It Leave Me Furious?" *Guardian*, July 15. www.theguardian.com/global/2017/jul/15/the-big -sick-funny-sweet-original-leave-me-furious.

GhaneaBassiri, Kambiz. 2010. *A History of Islam in America*. Cambridge: Cambridge University Press.

Goodman, Tim. 2017. "*Master of None* Season 2: TV Review." *Hollywood Reporter*, May 12. www.hollywoodreporter.com/review/master-review-1003213.

Gopinath, Gayatri. 2005. *Impossible Desires: Queer Diasporas and South Asian Public Cultures*. Durham, NC: Duke University Press.

Gotanda, Neil. 2011. "The Racialization of Islam in American Law." *Annals of the American Academy of Political and Social Science* 637: 184–95.

Grewal, Zareena. 2013. *Islam Is a Foreign Country: American Muslims and the Global Crisis of Authority*. New York: New York University Press.

Halberstam, Jack. 2011. *The Queer Art of Failure*. Durham, NC: Duke University Press.

Hatem, Mervat F. 2011. "The Political and Cultural Representations of Arabs, Arab Americans, and Arab American Feminisms after September 11, 2001." In *Arab and Arab American Feminisms: Gender, Violence, and Belonging*, edited by Rabab Abdulhadi, Evelyn Alsultany, and Nadine Naber, 10–28. Syracuse, NY: Syracuse University Press.

Heritage, Stuart. 2017. "Smug, Toe-Curling, and Underwritten: The Many Flaws of *Master of None*." *Guardian*, May 24. www.theguardian.com/tv-and-radio /tvandradioblog/2017/may/24/master-of-none-aziz-ansari-sitcom-many-flaws.

Islam, F., and R. A. Campbell. 2014. "'Satan Has Afflicted Me!' Jinn-Possession and Mental Illness in the Qur'an." *Journal of Religion and Health* 53, no. 1: 229–43.

Jamal, Amaney, and Nadine Naber. 2008. *Race and Arab Americans before and after 9/11: From Invisible Citizens to Visible Subjects*. Syracuse, NY: Syracuse University Press.

Kahf, Mohja. 1999. *Western Representations of the Muslim Woman: From Termagant to Odalisque*. Austin: University of Texas Press.

Khalifa, Najat, and Tim Hardie. 2005. "Possession and Jinn." *Journal of the Royal Society of Medicine* 98, no. 8: 351–53.

Lim, Anastasia, Hans W. Hoek, and Jan Dirk Blom. 2015. "The Attribution of Psychotic Symptoms to Jinn in Islamic Patients." *Transcultural Psychiatry* 52, no. 1: 18–32.

Luibhéid, Eithne. 2005. "Introduction: Queering Migration and Citizenship." In *Queer Migrations: Sexuality, U.S. Citizenship, and Border Crossings*, edited by Eithne Luibhéid and Lionel Cantú Jr., ix–xlvi. Minneapolis: University of Minnesota Press.

Maira, Sunaina. 2009. "'Good' and 'Bad' Muslim Citizens: Feminists, Terrorists, and U.S. Orientalisms." *Feminist Studies* 35, no. 3: 631–56.

Mamdani, Mahmood. 2004. *Good Muslim, Bad Muslim: America, the Cold War, and the Roots of Terror*. New York: Three Leaves Press.

Martinez, Katherine. 2021. "Overwhelming Whiteness of BDSM: A Critical Discourse Analysis of Racialization in BDSM." *Sexualities* 24, nos. 5–6: 733–48.

McAlister, Melani. 2005. *Epic Encounters: Culture, Media, and U.S. Interests in the Middle East since 1945*. Berkeley: University of California Press.

McClintock, Anne. 1993. "Maid to Order: Commercial Fetishism and Gender Power." *Social Text* 37: 87–116.

Michael, Jaclyn. 2018. "Religion and Representation in the 'New Brown America' of Muslim Comedy." *Ecumenica* 11, no. 2: 62–67.

Moors, Annelies. 2011. "NiqaBitch and Princess Hijab: Niqab Activism, Satire, and Street Art." *Feminist Review* 98: 128–35.

Moussawi, Ghassan. 2020. *Disruptive Situations: Fractal Orientalism and Queer Strategies in Beirut*. Philadelphia: Temple University Press.

Muñoz, José Esteban. 1999. *Disidentifications: Queers of Color and the Performance of Politics*. Minneapolis: University of Minnesota Press.

Muñoz, José Esteban. 2009. *Cruising Utopia: The Then and There of Queer Futurity*. New York: New York University Press.

Musser, Amber Jamilla. 2014. *Sensational Flesh: Race, Power, and Masochism*. New York: New York University Press.

Naber, Nadine. 2011. "Decolonizing Culture: Beyond Orientalist and Anti-Orientalist Feminisms." In *Arab and Arab American Feminisms: Gender, Violence, and Belonging*, edited by Rabab Abdulhadi, Evelyn Alsultany, and Nadine Naber, 78–90. Syracuse, NY: Syracuse University Press.

Nguyen, Tram. 2013. "From SlutWalks to SuicideGirls: Feminist Resistance in the Third Wave and Postfeminist Era." *Women's Studies Quarterly* 21, nos. 3–4: 157–72.

Niazi, Amil. 2017. "*The Big Sick* Is Great, and It's Also Stereotypical toward Brown Women." *Vice*, July 7. www.vice.com/en_us/article/zmvmp3/the-big-sick-is-great -and-its-also-stereotypical-toward-brown-women.

Puar, Jasbir K. 2007. *Terrorist Assemblages: Homonationalism in Queer Times*. Durham, NC: Duke University Press.

Qutami, Loubna. 2020. "Censusless: Arab/Muslim Interpolation into Whiteness and the War on Terror." *Journal of Asian American Studies* 23, no. 2: 161–200.

Rodríguez, Juana María. 2011. "Queer Sociality and Other Sexual Fantasies." *GLQ: A Journal of Lesbian and Gay Studies* 17, nos. 2–3: 331–48.

Rodríguez, Juana María. 2014. *Sexual Futures, Queer Gestures, and Other Latina Longings*. New York: New York University Press.

Said, Edward W. 1979. *Orientalism*. New York: Vintage Books.

Saud, Laith. 2013. "Islamic Beliefs: The Development of Islamic Ideas." In *An Introduction to Islam in the Twenty-First Century*, edited by Aminah Beverly McCloud, Scott W. Hibbard, and Laith Saud, 51–80. Malden, MA: Blackwell Publishing.

Shaheen, Jack G. 2014. *Reel Bad Arabs: How Hollywood Vilifies a People.* Northampton, MA: Olive Branch Press.

Singh, Julietta. 2018. *Unthinking Mastery: Dehumanism and Decolonial Entanglements.* Durham, NC: Duke University Press.

Yoshida, Emily. 2017. "*The Big Sick* Is a Casually Revolutionary Joy." *Vulture*, June 21. www.vulture.com/2017/06/the-big-sick-movie-review.html.

Nadine Naber

Epilogue

In December 2019, in preparation for a TEDx talk (Naber 2019a), I reached
out to my longtime comrade, Palestinian feminist Nada Elia, for advice on
the content of my presentation. She asked me about my big idea. I hesitated
before I said, "Arab feminism is not an oxymoron." She screamed, "What?
We have been saying that since the nineties!" Indeed, Jo Kadi (1994) used
this phrase in the introduction to the first anthology on Arab American
feminisms. In the early 2000s, Amira Jarmakani (2011) used the concept of
"invisibility" to describe Arab American feminism, and Lara Deeb (2018)
has been addressing how scholars of the Middle East have been repeating a
litany to colleagues, the public, and other feminists for at least four decades that says, as she puts it, "Muslim women are not universally oppressed.
Muslim women have agency. They are not necessarily more oppressed than
other women. They are not solely defined by religion. Etc. Etc. We keep
repeating these basic facts because we feel a responsibility and pressure to
do so."

   The big idea I originally submitted to TEDx was "War is a feminist
issue," focusing on the current geopolitical realities that are concerning us
now, in Yemen, Afghanistan, Syria, Iraq, Palestine, Kashmir, and beyond.
Yet after months of back-and-forth, the event organizers, reminding me
that the primary audience would be white women, urged revisions that led
me to focus on challenging misconceptions about "the veil" and clarifying,
like the broken record many of us have become, that Arab—as well as
Muslim—feminisms exist.

MERIDIANS · feminism, race, transnationalism   20:2 October 2021
DOI: 10.1215/15366936-9547991 © 2021 Smith College

As the contributions to this special issue illustrate, the attempt to challenge misconceptions about "Arab and Muslim women" continues to entrap us. I often ask myself how much longer I can continue to put my body on the line for a feminist politics that begins and ends on the defense, challenging misconceptions, inserting and uplifting a counter-discourse.

On college campuses, many of us face ongoing targeting for raising critiques of US-led war and empire. While teaching on Zoom, a student told me he could only participate via chat rather than speaking out loud. He was scared his Islamophobic parents would overhear him discussing the anti-Muslim racism and sexism that underline the war on terror. That same week, I was forced to engage with university administrators after a Zionist organization contacted them in an effort to police my writing and my voice.

Despite how deeply we may yearn to disable the repeat button on this same old song and dance, and despite changes in the forms of warfare that drive anti-Muslim racism—from new forms of surveillance and unmanned aircraft technologies to immigration bans—one thing has not changed: even the newest and most improved forms of anti-Muslim racism are justified by recycled arguments about "Islamic sexual savagery." This is why I would argue that it is imperative to affirm, louder than ever before, the foundational arguments that anti-racist Middle East and Muslim feminists have been affirming for decades, despite how sick or how tired we may be. Indeed, the Biden administration has made it clear they will continue the war on terror (Sjursen 2021), a war that has relied heavily on racist arguments of Islamic sexual savagery as a justification for genocide, displacement, and the confiscation of land and resources. As feminists working to end anti-Muslim racism have contended, the repetitive blaming of gender violence in Middle Eastern and South Asian Muslim communities on culture and religion has the effect of turning attention away from the United States' own imperial and anti-immigrant violence and covering up how the US war on terror—including the Muslim ban—depends on the very gendered and sexualized violence that the Muslim ban seeks to protect "Americans" from (Naber 2019b). And now, more than ever before, we need to affirm our anti-imperialist/anti-racist feminism coalitionally and relationally through the solidarity framework of joint struggle—integrating, for instance, a feminist politics of prison abolition, anti-militarism and decolonization, immigrant justice, and beyond.

Indeed, liberal strands of feminist and LGBTQ activism often leave the problem of culture blaming, central to anti-Muslim racism, intact. Consider the outpouring of support for Muslims when the ban was first implemented. The most visible responses that had any sort of feminist or queer perspective reinforced the imperialist sensationalizing of "Muslim gender violence" and absolved the United States of practicing any violence against Muslims. A legal brief (amicus curiae) filed against the Muslim ban by a series of LGBTQ organizations in greater New York states that the Muslim ban will "inflict unique harm on LGBTQ people in the eight target countries by foreclosing escape from the venomous and often life threatening, anti-LGBTQ conditions that prevail there."[1] The lawsuit then explains the "venomous" conditions in these eight predominantly Muslim countries using repetition to make the point that across the board, Muslim-majority countries are plain evil, especially toward queers, as follows:

> Somalia: Thousands of LGBTQ individuals in Somalia keep their sexual orientation a "closely guarded secret," knowing that revealing that information could attract potential retribution from terrorist groups, armed gangs, or family members that results in honour killings and suicides. . . .

> Yemen: Homosexuality is taboo and is condemned under the country's strong Islamic beliefs.[2]

My point is not whether and to what extent violence against gender nonconforming people exists in these countries or whether these activists had good intentions. Instead, I want to point out how the brief's analytical framing poses a set of dangers of its own—especially since notions about "venomous homophobic culture and society" form the very basis of anti-Muslim racism and war. Put differently, you can't fight racism with racism!

Liberal interfaith responses, organized en masse to challenge the Muslim ban, presented similar problems. In this framing, since "religious discrimination" is the problem, then "religious tolerance" (rather than ending racism and war) is the solution. These approaches made it possible for the same organizations that rose up against the Muslim ban on the basis of religious discrimination to simultaneously condone the killing of Muslims and non-Muslims in places like Palestine and other Muslim-majority countries targeted by the US war machine.

As contributors to this special issue have shown, the work of undoing anti-Muslim racism beckons the work of undoing US-led militarism, occupation, imperialism, and colonialism—all of which sustain gendered

and sexualized racism. Attacks on Muslim women and gender nonconforming people are derivative and co-constituted by US empire building
(Naber 2014). In this sense, a key thread throughout all the essays is that
the condition for the continuation of anti-Muslim racism is US empire and
war. Given that the condition for the existence of the US nation-state is
slavery, empire building, colonialism, and war, the United States has
always been at war. The United States, since its founding, has been committed to the logics and practices of colonialism, slavery, and capitalism,
including accumulating land, resources, and labor and justifying these
structures through heteropatriarchy, classism, and racism. Just as the
United States justifies the colonialization of Native lands in the United
States through the racial idea of Native American savagery, the United
States justifies the domination of land, resources, and labor in Muslim-
majority countries through a racial logic of the misogynist Muslim savage
or terrorist. Indeed, the same anti-Muslim racist logic has been used to
justify US-led war, occupation, and colonization—from US policy in Palestine to US-led war in Iraq and Afghanistan and beyond. In this sense,
another key contribution of this special issue is to challenge the imperialist
notions of the "domestic" and "international" that legitimize US imperialism and empire. Put differently, racism against Muslims living in the
United States, including everyday acts like hate crimes, corporate and
social media images, and government policies like the Muslim ban, is not a
mere impact of war; it is constitutive of that very war, and of the US nation-
state itself.

It is more urgent than ever before that we stop analyzing the United
States' domestic forms of violence and US war abroad as separate issues.
Indeed, racism against Muslims in North America and imperial wars
waged on a global scale are moving parts of the same imperial present;
extensions of one another, not simply consequences. Perhaps what
emerges out of this special issue are what we can call anti-imperialist anti-
racist Muslim feminisms, a framework that holds the convergence of
global/war/occupation and the racism that takes on different forms transnationally, in different locations, to justify these global practices. The
implications of this special issue, then, is that if we really want to end anti-
Muslim racism, we are going to need to dismantle US-led war, militarism,
and empire building.

At the same time, contributors to this special issue remind us that we
need to do more than produce frameworks for ending, challenging, or

dismantling anti-Muslim racism and sexism. We are going to need to dream, create, and build alternatives, through feminist methodologies that insist on community-based accountability and coalitional strategies. Perhaps we can center these three feminist practices for ending anti-Muslim racism as we reflect on where we want this work to go from here: (1) center the people, (2) build the alternative you want to see now, and (3) resist gendered racism coalitionally and relationally.

Center the People

Sometimes, critiques of US empire can unintentionally reify the power of the empire by erasing the historical specificity of the people and regions targeted by the empire and the nuanced ways people live out their experiences with racism and the analysis, visions, and alternatives *they* are crafting. As Sherene Seikaly (2019) has committed to what she calls "casting the center of power to the shadows," we might do more to uplift what research themes like anti-racism, self-determination, dignity, liberation, or social justice mean to people disproportionately impacted by anti-Muslim racism, including immigrant and refugee women. In Chicago's southwest suburbs, working-class Arab immigrant women and refugees led a movement to remove an Islamophobic trustee from power. If we focused only on the Islamophobic representative, we might learn about how some local representatives are repeating the "anti-Muslim women" rhetoric that gained traction during the Trump era whereby elite white women portray themselves as more liberated and therefore superior to Arab and/or Muslim women. Yet we would lose sight of the kind of campaign Arab immigrant women led to push Sharon Brannigan out of office. In Palos Township, women activists *relied on a* "negative electoral strategy" focused not on supporting an electoral candidate through voting but on removing a candidate from office. The difference is crucial as voting and conventional electoral politics are exclusionary. Youth and undocumented people cannot vote, and other immigrants may feel alienated from electoral politics. Yet this popular organizing strategy centered the community's most vulnerable people and uplifted the voices and visions of immigrant and refugee women in holding elected officials accountable, as a result. At the same time, we need to challenge approaches that sentimentalize the "vulnerable Muslim woman or mother." Indeed, one trend among heteropatriarchal Arab or Muslim American social movements is to activate the "vulnerable Muslim woman" or "sentimentalize mothers and motherhood" to increase empathy. One need only think of the strategic positioning of "crying mothers" as protest speakers, addressing the killing of children at the hands of the US war machine. Yet as the Palos example illustrates, immigrant and refugee women and mothers are not only politically relevant when seen in connection to biological children; they are also political actors on their own terms. Do we really have to wait for a mother to suffer over biological children before we take her political analyses and actions seriously?

Centering people can also challenge how we think about family-based patriarchy. Oftentimes, prioritizing a focus on challenging the racist idea that "Muslims are hyper-violent toward women" produces a culture of fear or self-censorship whereby community members resist speaking up about gender violence within Muslim communities. This resistance assumes that speaking out about internal family-based patriarchy can reify anti-Muslim racism. Yet accountability to the diverse people impacted by anti-Muslim racism reveals that gender violence within communities is not a consequence of abstract religious or cultural values, as racist ideas would posit. Rather, internal-communal forms of sexism or patriarchal control are exacerbated by a community's experience with racism. A student on my campus who wears hijab was targeted by a man who asked her if she had a bomb in her bag. Campus police diminished the incident. As a result, her parents forbade her to attend events on campus or take night classes. Indeed, centering people's everyday experiences with anti-Muslim racism helps us understand the complex ways racism reinforces sexism within the domains of family and community (Razack 2008).

It also helps us understand how anti-Muslim racism directly impacts survivors of gender violence. It is well established that women of color often resist calling the police for help because they might arrest, deport, or even shoot them or their family members when they show up. As Nawal Ammar's preliminary study illustrates, Muslim women indicated that protecting their spouse is one reason why they may avoid calling the police (Ammar et al. 2014). And we have a lot to learn about how gender nonconforming people live and experience anti-Muslim racism. I have documented countless stories whereby LGBTQ Muslims have faced harmful experiences of racial profiling in the United States, from invasive pat-downs and harassment by the TSA (Transportation Security Administration) at US airports to separation from loved ones due to immigration policy. Indeed, anti-Muslim racism is compounded by US-grown homophobia and transphobia and targets gender nonconforming persons in distinct, exceptionally violent ways. Hana Masri's (2017: 37–38) research shows that racist concepts about queer Muslims as the ultimate victims reinforce rather than challenge their excludability:

> There lurks a paradoxical—and much more sinister—potential behind narratives that offer Western nations as liberated safe havens for queer refugees; when such stories are painted with a brush coated in stereotypes, not only do they affirm historically violent (and inaccurate) understandings of "backward" Arabs who have not progressed enough to embrace sexual openness and diverse gender expressions, they also put all Syrian refugees at risk by bolstering the very same narratives that justify their inherent excludability from allegedly more progressive nations.

In a piece called "Reflections of a Genderqueer Palestinian American Lesbian Mother," Huda Jadallah (founder of one of the first public networks for Arab lesbians in California in the 1980s) writes:

> Growing up I was always keenly aware of being marked as dangerous, "a terrorist." I never understood as a child that this was not simply a result of racial marking or being identified as Palestinian, but was also in part due to being marked as genderqueer. My gender non-conformity manifested itself in being stereotyped as violent and dangerous as opposed to submissive and oppressed as Arab women who conform to gender roles are often perceived. One specific site where I experience the intersection of race, gender, and sexuality is public restrooms . . . , I am often mistaken for an Arab man. The fear in women's eyes as they recoil away from me cannot be mistaken. The stereotype of Arab men as violent and hypersexualized is, I believe, a major aspect of why these women fear me. They fear being raped. They fear being hurt. They mistrust. The fear has been so intense at times that I have felt compelled to assure women of their safety, assure them that indeed I am a woman. But, of course, I cannot assure them that I am not Palestinian. And what of those who are transgender, those who do not have the luxury to assure others that they are indeed the "right sex in the right bathroom stall?" Do I betray them in my assurances? Do I betray myself as I seek to comfort those who are uncomfortable with my race, gender, and sexuality? (Jadallah 2011: 276)

The stories above remind us that neither the United States nor Israel are safe havens for LGBTQ People of Color, contrary to what imperialist feminism and pinkwashing (alQaws 2020; Naber et al. 2018) would like us to believe.

In addition to centering the people in our critique of heteropatriarchal anti-Muslim racism, we need to build the alternative we want to see now. As Black Abolitionist Feminism teaches us, resistance to structures like mass incarceration must entail both ending systemic violence and building the world we want beyond the structures of imprisonment, containment, and punishment (see Naber and Rojas, forthcoming). Abolitionist feminist analyses are growing today through practices whereby feminist of color organizers are building alternative (not system-based) neighborhoods, communities, health-care centers, schools, and social movement structures and practices.

In the 2020s, we find these discussions in the praxis of building feminist abolitionist futures through community accountability, transformative justice, harm reduction, and mutual aid. We might draw on the visions of Mariame Kaba's (2021) new book that inspires us to dream and foster social conditions that would lead prisons to become unfathomable. Feminists working to end anti-Muslim racism might draw on such visions as we work toward ending imperialism and war.

In a piece I coauthored with Clarissa Rojas (Naber and Rojas, forthcoming), we argue:

> We are positing that the potential for those same social conditions and practices that make prisons unfathomable also make war, empire and colonial occupation no longer relevant, or even imaginable. Indeed, undoing the work of carcerality in the broadest sense necessitates undoing the work the carceral "U.S." state does to stitch together structures that strengthen the "U.S." nation-state and its global heteropatriarchal racial capitalist and colonialist expansion.

We insist on the following actions:

> Animating socialities, relationalities, and intimacies that converge countercarceral, decolonial, and anti-imperialist ways of being in the world, beginning with, for example, a refusal to organize movements through imperial nation-based or 'domestic' vs. 'global' paradigm; crafting sensibilities that bring symbiotic balance to our relationships with each other and with the land; demanding an end to borders, accountability to Indigenous peoples, and defunding the police and the military.

The police, prisons, and detention do not keep us safe nor do they protect us; neither do the US nation-state and its imperialist wars and policing of the border.

There is a dire need for new visions of what we want and what kind of world we want to live in. It is clearer than ever that the systems that punish and criminalize through structures of racial profiling, surveillance, and war only secure the 1 percent. Are we ready to imagine a world without prisons, racism, or war, a social landscape no longer dominated by the concepts of the criminal or the terrorist? Angela Davis (n.d.) says that imagining a world without prisons means being able to talk about "the many ways in which punishment is linked to poverty, racism, sexism, homophobia, and other modes of dominance."

I would argue that heteropatriarchal anti-Muslim racism does not only operate through the logic of war but also through a specific logic of containment. Consider, for instance, the generalized surveillance of Muslims in the United States—which we might call an open-air prison or what I call internment of the psyche (Naber 2006). Surveillance strategies rely on racial profiling of Muslims and people perceived to be Muslim and contain communities through the production of fear, fear that one is being watched, fear that at any point, one may be picked up, locked up, detained, deported, tortured, or even killed, without evidence of any criminal activity.

Ruthie Gilmore (2007) says abolition is not just the absence of prisons but it's about building those institutions we need so that we don't need police or policing—which means we need a world where people's social and economic needs are met. She argues that abolition has nothing to do with making prisons or the criminal justice system better. I would add that decolonial feminist abolition does not seek to make surveillance and war better, or to ensure that "criminals" or alleged terrorists are treated well or humanely, or to claim that the military would be fine as long as women and queers were treated equally. Decolonial feminist abolition means starting from the root cause. For instance, rather than asking for Muslim Americans to be included or treated equally, we would be exploring the root cause of anti-Muslim racism, including the foundation of the US nation-state, built on ongoing structures of genocide, war, slavery, and colonial and imperial expansion. We might then ask what system we are calling for Muslim Americans to be included into, whether the US nation-state is recuperable, or if we should continue turning to the US state, founded upon empire and racism, for solutions. What would it mean to shift how we think about solving social problems, from ending state violence against immigrants and ending war from making demands upon the US nation-state, to imagining a world without it altogether?

While we may have to continue repeating our age-old litanies that "Muslim women are diverse," that "Arab feminism is not an oxymoron," my hope is that we will also continue to dream. A few years ago, while my aunt was in the process of dying from cancer, her family home of thirty years burst into flames in the Santa Rosa fires. Exactly two years later, just last month, my aunt's husband missed his brother's—my father's—funeral because he was stuck in another Santa Rosa fire. Given the disastrous state of the world, what are we truly going to do so that future generations can survive and thrive? Can we imagine a world where militarism and racism are unimaginable, or where gender violence is not even a possibility—even under the greatest kinds of pressure—even if we are fighting with each other over water? And what would conversations among Middle Eastern and Muslim diasporas look like so that we can challenge the widespread ideas in our communities that prisons and the current criminal justice system are the only solution for apparent violations of the law?

In closing, my hope is that the feminist struggle to end anti-Muslim racism grows as part of broader anti-imperialist, anti-racist feminist struggles, relationally and coalitionally. I believe we need to go beyond modes of solidarity forged on the basis of similarity (i.e., because the Israeli attack on Gaza and the militarized police attacks on Ferguson, Missouri, in the summer of 2014 look similar, Black folks and Palestinians should unite). Instead, I am calling for solidarity based on a theory and praxis of joint struggle. By joint struggle, I am referring to an analysis that articulates the conjoined nature of the structures of power each community is up against (i.e., because some Ferguson police officers were trained by Israeli soldiers, Black folks and Palestinians should unite). In other words, the structures that maintain US empire and the heteropatriarchal racism on which it rests (colonization of Native land, the prison industrial complex, militarism, war, border control) are interconnected and mutually constitutive. Given the histories through which feminists working to end anti-Muslim racism have been challenging the discourses and practices of war and racism, militarism, and forms of racial profiling that operate through the containment and policing structures of surveillance, perhaps the kinds of analyses we have seen in this special issue can help grow broader efforts to link social movements working to abolish the white supremacist systems of militarism and policing.

Such relational approaches can support efforts to grow transnational feminist solidarity based on the idea that one community's struggle is wrapped up in another's even if we experience state violence differently and to different degrees. We might recall how the discourse of the Muslim ban relied on the idea of "gendered and sexual 'backwardness' of 'Muslim' foreign nationals operationalizing imperialist feminism and pinkwashing" (Naber 2019b). We might also recall the white supremacist patriarchy that Black feminists have been critiquing all along, which uses the idea of "protecting white women" and their sexuality to justify the lynching of African Americans and contemporary state- and individual-led acts of anti-Black racism. Indeed, the Muslim ban's mobilization of the threat of Brown Muslim men violating white women in the United States legitimizes anti-Black racism. It allows hateful heterosexist white men in power to act as the protectors and saviors of white women. We also cannot forget that white settlers justified the colonization of the United States using similar arguments about brave white men protecting vulnerable white women from the "Native Americans' sexual savagery." It's no coincidence that the US military's name for Osama bin Laden was Geronimo—a Chicahua Apache leader who led resistance against white American settlers.

My hope is that the field of feminist anti-Muslim scholarship and activism will continue to grow through a framework of joint struggle, inspired by the idea that as long as US militarism, and the US nation-state as it has been structured all along, remain in place, we will remain entrapped within the logics of empire. Beyond offering critique and striving to end state violence, I also hope we will continue to dream, imagine, hope, and build alternative ways of being, including the relationships and communities that are structured and driven by a politics of radical love, healing, care, and dignity for all people and all forms of life.

· ·

Nadine Naber is a cultural anthropologist and an award-winning author, speaker, public scholar, and activist on women of color and transnational anti-imperialist feminisms and Arab and Muslim feminisms. She is a professor of gender and women's studies, global Asian studies, and anthropology at the University of Illinois, Chicago, and author and coeditor of five books. She has served on the boards of organizations like INCITE! and the Arab American Action Network, and she is the co-founder of Mamas Activating Movements for Abolition and Solidarity and founder of Liberate Your Research workshops at nadinenaber.com. Contact Nadine at: info@nadinenaber.com.

Notes

1   See page 2 of the amicus brief posted on the NQAPIA website. www.nqapia.org /wpp/wp-content/uploads/2018/03/SCOTUS-LGBT-Amicus-Brief-Muslim-Ban .pdf.

2   See pages 11 and 12 (Somalia) and 15 (Yemen) of the immigration equality amicus brief. cdn.ca9.uscourts.gov/datastore/general/2017/11/28/17-17168%20-%
     20Immigration%20Equality%20Amicus%20Brief.pdf. See Naber and Rojas,
     forthcoming.

Works Cited

alQaws. 2020. "Beyond Propaganda: Pinkwashing as Colonial Violence." alQaws for
     Sexual and Gender Diversity in Palestinian Society, October 18. www.alqaws.org
     /articles/Beyond-Propaganda-Pinkwashing-as-Colonial-Violence.

Ammar, Nawal, Amanda Couture-Carron, Shahid Alvi, and Jaclyn San Antonio. 2014.
     "Experiences of Muslim and Non-Muslim Battered Immigrant Women with the
     Police in the United States: A Closer Understanding of Commonalities and Differences. *Violence against Women* 19, no. 12: 1449–71.

Davis, Angela. n.d. "The Challenge of Prison Abolition: A Conversation with Dylan
     Rodriguez." *History Is a Weapon* (accessed April 22, 2021). www.historyisaweapon
     .com/defcon1/davisinterview.html.

Deeb, Lara. 2018. Keynote address at BRISMES Conference 2018, "New Approaches
     to Studying the Middle East," King's College London.

Gilmore, Ruth W. 2007. *Golden Gulag: Prisons, Surplus, Crisis, and Opposition in Globalizing
     California.* Berkeley: University of California Press.

Jadallah, Huda. 2011. "Reflections of a Genderqueer Palestinian American Lesbian
     Mother." In *Arab and Arab American Feminisms: Gender, Violence, and Belonging,* edited
     by Rabab Abdulhadi, Evelyn Alsultany, and Nadine Naber, 276–80. Syracuse, NY:
     Syracuse University Press.

Jarmakani, Amira. 2011. "Mobilizing the Politics of Invisiblity." In *Arab and Arab American Feminisms: Gender, Violence, and Belonging,* edited by Rabab Abdulhadi, Evelyn
     Alsultany, and Nadine Naber, 276–80. Syracuse, NY: Syracuse University Press.

Kaba, Mariame. 2021. *We Do This 'til We Free Us: Abolitionist Organizing and Transforming
     Justice.* Chicago: Haymarket Press.

Kadi, Joanna, ed. 1994. *Food for Our Grandmothers: Writings by Arab-American and Arab-
     Canadian Feminists.* Cambridge, MA: South End Press.

Masri, Hana. 2017. "A Liberated Life? Thoughts on the Paradoxical Binds of Queer
     Refuge." *Kohl* 3, no. 1: 36–40.

Naber, Nadine. 2006. "The Rules of Forced Engagement: Race, Gender, and the Culture of Fear among Arab Immigrants in San Francisco Post-9/11. *Cultural Dynamics*
     18, no. 3: 235–67.

Naber, Nadine. 2014. "Imperial Whiteness and the Diasporas of Empire." *American
     Quarterly* 66, no. 4: 1107–15.

Naber, Nadine. 2019a. "Arab Feminism Is Not an Oxymoron." TED video, 16:41.
     TEDx Oak Park Women. www.ted.com/talks/nadine_naber_arab_feminism_is_
     not_an_oxymoron.

Naber, Nadine. 2019b. "Here We Go Again: Saving Muslim Women and Queers in the
     Age of Trump." *Mada Masr,* April 18. www.madamasr.com/en/2019/04/18/feature
     /society/here-we-go-again-saving-muslim-women-and-queers-in-the-age-of
     -trump/.

Naber, Nadine, and Clarissa Rojas. Forthcoming. "Genocide and 'US' Domination ≠ Liberation, Only We Can Liberate Ourselves: Toward an Anti-imperialist Abolitionist Feminism." To be published in *Abolition Feminism*, edited by Alisa Bierria, Jakeya Caruthers, and Brooke Lober. Chicago, IL: Haymarket Press.

Naber, Nadine, Sa'ed Atshan, Nadia Awad, Maya Mikdashi, Sofian Merabet, Dorgham Abusalim, and Nada Elia. 2018. "On Palestinian Studies and Queer Theory." *Journal of Palestine Studies* 47, no. 3: 62–71.

Razack, Sherene. 2008. "The Muslims Are Coming: The 'Sharia Debate' in Canada." In *Casting Out: The Eviction of Muslims from Western Law and Politics*, 145–72. Toronto: University of Toronto Press.

Seikaly, Sherene. 2019. "Race, Religion, and Coloniality." Panelist at the conference "Feminist Approaches to Understanding Global Anti-Muslim Racism," University of California, Los Angeles, December 5.

Sjursen, Danny. 2021. "Joe Biden Is Following a Blueprint for Forever War." *In These Times*, March 2. inthesetimes.com/article/joe-biden-syria-bombing-saudi-arabia.

Malak Mattar

"When the World Sleeps"

This piece was created from a space of trying to find tranquility and peace through painting and sleeping. The theme is women sleeping, hoping to achieve peace through acceptance for our differences as human beings.

Malak Mattar (b. 1999) is an artist from the Gaza Strip, Palestine. Forced to stay inside during a blockade, she started painting with basic art supplies from her school. Mattar shared her work via social media and garnered interest from galleries worldwide. She aims to be an ambassador of her people through her art.

MERIDIANS · feminism, race, transnationalism   20:2 October 2021
DOI: 10.1215/15366936-9548002 © 2022 Smith College

2021 Paula J. Giddings Best Article Award

Winner

Robert J. Patterson for his article "Between Protest and Politics: Black Lives Matter Movement(s) for Black Lives," *Meridians* 19:2

Bio: **Robert J. Patterson** is professor of African American studies at Georgetown University. He is the author of *Destructive Desires: Rhythm and Blues Culture and the Politics of Racial Equality* (2019) and *Exodus Politics: Civil Rights and Leadership in African American Literature and Culture* (2013), coeditor of *The Psychic Hold of Slavery: Legacies in American Expressive Culture* (2016), and editor of *Black Cultural Production after Civil Rights* (2019). Currently, he is working on a book manuscript titled "Black Equity, Black Equality: Reparation and Black Communities."

Abstract: This article examines the official Black Lives Matter Movement (the Black Lives Matter Global Network) as a point of departure to argue that Black Lives Matter (BLM) in general expands our epistemological framework for thinking about black freedom movements, black freedom dreams, and black freedom strategies. By analyzing the movement's explicit refusal to be likened to civil rights movement organizations as a concurrent attack against intraracial sexism, heterosexism, and transphobia, the article insists that BLM deprivileges heteronormativity to show that black freedom dreams must include gender and sexual liberation. By considering BLM's rejection of capitalism as a broader critique of neoliberalism forceful role in maintaining black dispossession, the author posits that BLM desires to disrupt the state's tendency to use the black middle class to enact, enforce, and reinforce an economic order that relies upon race and racism to codify and cement black inequality. Finally, the author posits that the movement's tactics and goals provide a framework through which to enact short-term change, while pushing to dismantle the larger system of antiblack racism that is refracted through global capitalism.

Read the article: **doi.org/10.1215/15366936-8308476**

2021 Paula J. Giddings Best Article Award

Honorable Mention

Leigh-Anne Francis for her article "Playing the 'Lady Sambo': Poor Black Women's Legal Strategies in the Post-Civil War South's Civil Courts," *Meridians* 19:2

Bio: **Leigh-Anne Francis** is associate professor of African American studies; and women, gender, and sexuality studies at The College of New Jersey. She holds a PhD in U.S. and African American history, and MA in U.S. and world history, and a BFA in painting and illustration.

Abstract: In the post-Civil War South, Black women litigants made conscious tactical appeals to white male judges' racism, particularly the racist-sexist stereotypes at the heart of the white paternalism ethos, in order to win lawsuits against whites who defrauded them. African American women's arsenal of legal strategies include the "Lady Sambo," an intentional racialized gender performance of feigned ignorance. By performing the "Lady Sambo"—an ignorant, servile black woman in need of protection—some poor black women mobilized their expertise in white racism to defend their economic rights. In a white-dominated society predicated on the denial of black rights, freedom, and dignity, poor black women seeking justice in civil court cases had to employ resistance strategies that did not openly challenge white authority. In white paternalism, a cultural mainstay of the postbellum South, poor black women discerned and wrested an opportunity to covertly resist economic racism. Unable to attenuate or eradicate structural racism, black women treated racism as a weakness that, at times, made whites vulnerable to manipulation. As long as judges' legal decisions left the white male power structure intact, some black women were the potential beneficiaries of jurists' racial paternalism ethos. While whites imagined themselves as controlling paternalistic exchanges with blacks, black people engaged whites as conscious actors drawing on a keen understanding of white people's supremacist self-perceptions and projections onto blacks. When possible, black women exploited white racism to their advantage, and white judges' paternalism ethos occasioned such exploitation. In so doing, black women earned their legal victories by acting intentionally and with savvy.

Read the article: **doi.org/10.1215/15366936-8308363**

Keep up to date on new scholarship

Issue alerts are a great way to stay current on all the cutting-edge scholarship from your favorite Duke University Press journals. This free service delivers tables of contents directly to your inbox, informing you of the latest groundbreaking work as soon as it is published.

To sign up for issue alerts:

1. Visit **dukeu.press/register** and register for an account. You do not need to provide a customer number.

2. After registering, visit **dukeu.press/alerts**.

3. Go to "Latest Issue Alerts" and click on "Add Alerts."

4. Select as many publications as you would like from the pop-up window and click "Add Alerts."

read.dukeupress.edu/journals